THE WAR IN INDIA

THE WAR IN INDIA

By

VISCOUNT HENRY HARDINGE, VISCOUNT HUGH GOUGH,
SIR HARRY GEORGE WAKELYN SMITH

GYAN

ISBN : 978-81-212-1598-5(HB)

First Published, 1846

Published, 2018

Published by

Gyan Publishing House
5, Ansari Road
Daryaganj, New Delhi-110002
Phone: 011-47034999, 9811692060
www.gyanbooks.com
E-mail: books@gyanbooks.com

Printed at: G. Print Process, Delhi.

NORTHERN INDIA &c.

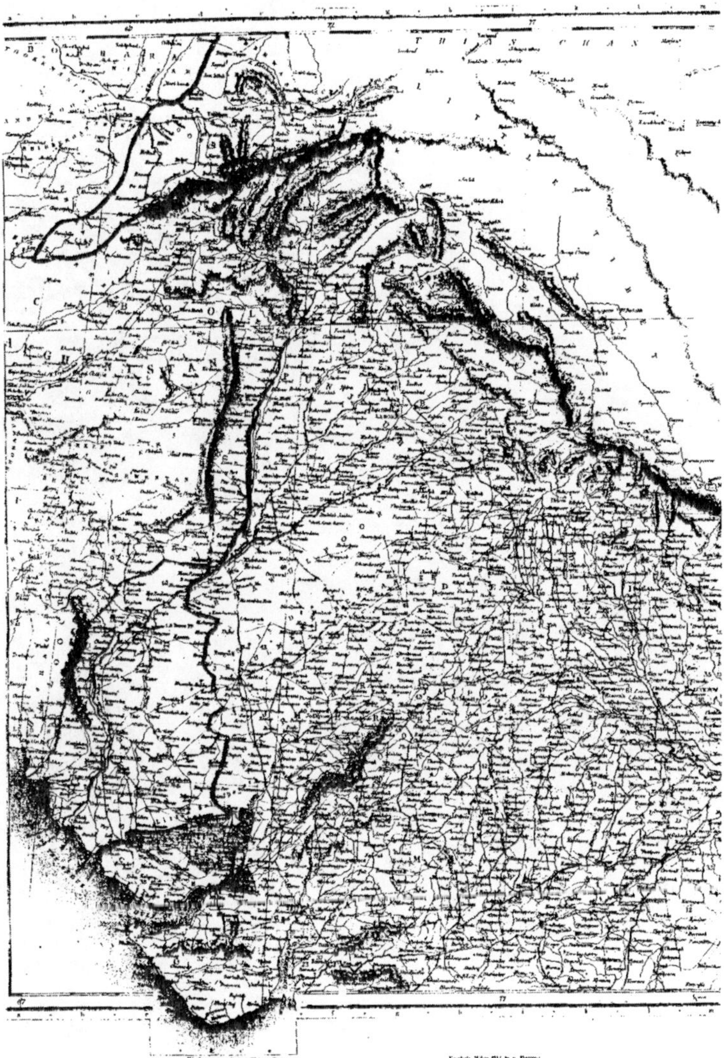

TABLE OF CONTENTS.

WAR WITH THE SIKHS.

Minute by the Governor-General of India.

June 16th, 1845.

As the time has now arrived when preparations will require to be made for the journey of the Governor-General to the Upper Provinces, I consider it most advisable to consult my colleagues before any steps are taken to carry that intention into effect.

Under ordinary circumstances I should have desired, on public grounds, to remain the next winter and summer at Calcutta, in order to have the advantage of the experience and advice of the Council, by which course the usual business of the Government can be transacted with more unity, regularity and general satisfaction than when the Governor-General is separated from his colleagues.

On the other hand, it is clearly my duty to place myself in that position, as regards the exercise of my functions, by which I can most advantageously apply my exertions for the service of the State.

In this, as in every other case, the real question for decision is, whether it is more for the public interests that I should this autumn proceed to the Upper Provinces, or remain at the usual seat of Government.

Between my colleagues and myself there has always existed a most anxious desire, and perfect unison of opinion, that no efforts or precautions should be spared to maintain a Sikh Government in the Punjaub as long as it may be possible.

To carry the pacific policy of the Government of India into effect, we have been content to suffer great inconvenience, considerable expense, and some risk, necessarily caused by the presence of a large disorganised Sikh force on the frontier, requiring, on our part, an army to be assembled for the protection of our frontier, and in close contact with that of the Sikhs; I need not enter into the consideration of the various questions of solicitude which are involved, in the proximity of a Sikh army, in a successful state of mutiny, so close upon our frontier.

We have never relinquished the hope that some amelioration may eventually take place, affording the prospect of the re-establishment of a Sikh Government, able to carry on its ordinary functions. We have never abandoned the expectation that, after anarchy and military violence have long prevailed, these disorders, having reached their maturity, might subside, worn out and exhausted by their own virulence; or that some man of superior capacity and master mind might appear amongst them, able to control this mutinous army, and to re-construct a strong Sikh Government.

I must confess that these hopes have not been strengthened by recent events; and now that we can, at this season, when all military operations are nearly suspended, deliberately review the political and military condition of the Punjaub, I can arrive at no other conclusion than that the state of our relations with that country has become more critical than it has been at any time since Rajah Heera Singh's death.

When the finances of the State shall be found to be insufficient to pay the troops, a state of things may arise at any moment requiring the instant decision of the highest authority on the spot.

The instructions which we may send from Calcutta may be very proper, and applicable to the state of things which may have happened on the frontier ten days before, when the report was made; and may, when the instructions are received, twenty days after the event, be totally inapplicable.

In ordinary transactions this is an inconvenience, but in the state of the Punjaub it is positively dangerous.

I have a firm conviction that the chances of preserving peace will be diminished by the powerless state in which the Government would be placed, by not being able to act with decision and promptitude, and that opportunities would be lost of effecting some good, and of preventing much mischief, if in the state of the Punjaub the responsible authority of the Government remains more than 1,000 miles off, at the other extremity of Bengal; it appears to me, therefore, to be expedient, as a means of averting risk, and of carrying our policy more securely into effect, that the Governor-General should, in the month of October next, proceed to the Upper Provinces, and that the authority should be entrusted to him with which the law enables the Council to invest him, when separated from his colleagues.

Having given my decided opinion that, under existing circumstances, it will be the duty of the Governor-General to proceed to the Upper Provinces in the autumn, I have to request the attention of my colleagues to this subject, at their earliest convenience.

H. Hardinge.

I concur, T. H. Maddock.
I concur, F. Millett.
I concur, Geo. Pollock.

As the separation of the Governor-General from the Council requires the sanction of a law, I presume it is proper that I should record my opinion upon the proposition.

I concur, C. H. Cameron.

The Governor-General to the Secret Committee.

On the River Ganges, off Monghyr, 30 *September,* 1845.

The forbearance of the Government of India has been carried to an extent beyond that which has been customary. Every military precaution has, however, been taken; advice and warnings have been repeatedly conveyed to the Lahore Government in the plainest language; even the risk of giving offence by such language has been incurred, rather than fail in the essential point of clearly defining the nature of our policy, and of having that policy well understood. I am convinced that our desire to see the Maha Rajah's government re-established on a basis of independence and strength, is well known to the most influential and leading chiefs. Their personal interests, endangered by the democratic revolution, so successfully accomplished by the Sikh army, may induce those chiefs to exert all their efforts to compel the British Government to interfere; but these attempts, and any danger resulting from them, will be attributable, not to our forbearance, but to their personal fears for life and property.

You may be assured that, whilst I shall omit no precautions, and be prepared for any event, I shall persevere in the direct course I have hitherto pursued, of endeavouring, by moderation, good faith, and friendly advice, to avert the necessity of British interference by force of arms in the affairs of the Punjaub.

The Governor-General to the Commander-in-Chief.

Agra, October 24, 1845.

I have the honour to inform your Excellency that, on or before the 12th of November arrangements will have been made, by which the commissariat department will be prepared to equip nearly two-thirds of the force at, and in advance of, Meerut, with the necessary means of marching at the shortest notice.

The extent to which it may be expedient to be prepared with

this description of equipment must always be dependent on contingent events, which fluctuate, in an unsettled Government like that of Lahore, in a manner which defies all ordinary calculations of probable results.

In the present state of our relations with the Lahore Government, your Excellency is aware that I do not anticipate the probability of any emergencies arising which can require the army, under your Excellency's orders, to take the field this autumn.

Nevertheless, having to deal with a mutinous Sikh army, which has usurped the functions of the Government, and whose caprice may, at any time, force on a rupture with our forces on the frontier, I have deemed it advisable to be prepared with the means of movement to the extent noted in the margin*; and as it is desirable that the arrangement should be made on the most economical scale, the whole will be hired at the halting rates.

If, as I expect, the tone of the Lahore Durbar should continue to be more friendly, as has been the case since Sirdar Jowahir Singh's death, I shall be anxious, according to events, gradually to diminish the scale of the present preparation, which, as before, is strictly of a defensive character.

No provision has been made for the baggage animals of the European officers, according to the decision of the Government of India last year. The number required would probably exceed 1,200 camels.

Lieutenant-Colonel Parsons, the Deputy Commissary-General, will be instructed to communicate with your Excellency on this subject, and will postpone his usual tour of inspection for one month.

* 7 Troops of Horse Artillery.
6 Companies Foot Artillery.
4 Light Field Batteries.
2 Regiments of Dragoons.
3 Regiments of Light Cavalry.
5 Regiments European Infantry.
13 Regiments Native Infantry.
6 Companies Sappers & Miners.
2 Regiments Irregular Cavalry.

The Despatch of the Governor-General of India to the Secret Committee of the East India Company.

Camp, Umbulla, December 2, 1845.

I left Delhi on the 19th ultimo, [November,] making the usual marches towards Kurnaul and Umballa, with the intention of meeting the Commander-in-Chief at the latter place, who was on his way to inspect the troops at Meerut, Delhi, and other districts.

On the 22nd November I received from Major Broadfoot the official despatch dated the 20th November*, detailing the sudden intention of the Sikh army to advance in force to the frontier, for the avowed purpose of invading the British territories.

The letter of the 20th was succeeded by a private communication of the following day*, stating the same facts, and inclosing news, letters, and papers of intelligence received from Lahore, which professed to give an account of the circumstances which have led to the present movement, and which would appear (if these papers are to be depended upon) to have originated with the Ranee and certain of the Sirdars, who felt the pressure of the demands of the army to be so urgent, and its present attitude and temper so perilous to their existence, that they desired to turn the thoughts of the troops to the objects which might divert their attention from making extortionate demands for higher pay, by employing their energies in hostile operations against the British Government.

The precautions already adopted to provide against the possibility of our forces being unprepared to meet any movement of the Sikh army this season, and the arrangements made by the Commander-in-Chief, on the receipt of Major Broadfoot's intelligence*, rendered it, in my opinion, unnecessary to allow these reports of invasion to make any change in my movements. I arrived on the 26th at Kurnaul, where the Commander-in-Chief met me, having proceeded from Umballa by dâk, returning to his camp the same evening; on the same day I was also joined by Major Broadfoot.

* The despatches here alluded to follow this of the Governor-General, see pp. 17 and 22.

I had the satisfaction of concurring in all the orders which his Excellency had given, to hold the troops in readiness to move at the shortest notice, and in the instructions which he had sent to the officers in command of the stations at Ferozepore and Loodiana. The force at the former post consists of one European regiment, seven regiments of native infantry, two regiments of native cavalry, and twenty-four field guns, exclusive of heavy ordnance. The force at Loodiana consists of one regiment of Europeans, five regiments of native infantry, one regiment of native cavalry, and two troops of horse artillery.

After a full and satisfactory consultation with his Excellency, and taking into consideration the improbability of the Sikh army crossing the Sutlej, I determined that no movement should be made towards the river by the forces from Umballa and Meerut, and I postponed, for further consideration with his Excellency, any change in the present distribution of the troops; eventually some alterations will be made, which, when they have been finally determined upon between me and the Commander-in-Chief, will be reported to you. At the present moment his Excellency coincides with me that no forward movement is required.

In the midst of much hesitation and irresolution, the enterprise ordered by the Sikh Government does not appear to have been formally abandoned; the intelligence received by Major Broadfoot*, on the day of his joining my camp showed that the three brigades of the Sikh force had actually left Lahore a few miles in advance, to be followed the next morning by three other brigades, including one of artillery. This was on the 24th ultimo. The intelligence received from that date has been communicated to me by Major Broadfoot each day, as it arrives.

It is said they intend, in reply to Major Broadfoot's remonstrance, to allege that the fact of our having collected so large a force, with all the munitions of war, on the frontier, is the cause of the concentration of their forces on the Sutlej; that they

* The despatches here alluded to follow this of the Governor-General, see p. 17.

intend to demand the reasons of our preparations; to insist on the surrender to the Lahore Government of the treasure which belonged to the late Rajah Soocheyt Singh; the restoration by the Rajah of Nabba of the village of Mowran, escheated by the Rajah, and the escheat confirmed by us; and henceforth the free passage of their troops into the Lahore possessions on this side the Sutlej.

I need only remark, on the first and most essential point, that the Sikh army did, in the beginning of last January, prepare to move to the Sutlej. The political agent remonstrated, and the troops were withdrawn: the reason then assigned for the movement being the same as that now intended to be brought forward, namely, the state of our military preparations on the frontier. The Governor-General in Council, in a despatch to Major Broadfoot of the 25th January, 1845*, entered into very full explanations, which were conveyed to the Lahore Vakeel.

The Government of India, through its political agent, has more than once complained of the inconvenience and expense of being obliged to retain so large a British force on the frontier, in consequence of the ungovernable misconduct of the Sikh army—a fact well known and never contradicted by the Lahore Government.

As regards the past, it is clear that no cause of complaint has been given by the Government of India. If it should be asserted that our military preparations this autumn have given offence, the assertion is equally unfounded, and is a mere pretext for hostile proceedings which have originated in the political weakness and the internal dissensions of the Lahore Government, and, above all, in their desire to be released, on any terms, from the terror which the ferocity of their own troops has inspired. The proof is to be found in the fact that, at the time these disorderly movements commenced, no additional British troops had reached our frontier stations. The additional regiment of native infantry, destined for the reinforcement of Ferozepore, had not

* This despatch follows next in this collection, p. 11.

arrived. At Loodiana, one of the two regiments of native cavalry had actually marched for Scinde before it was relieved, leaving that post, as it is at present, with one regiment, instead of the usual complement of two regiments of cavalry. At the other stations no alteration had been made, and the troops which had marched were peaceably engaged in completing the annual reliefs, according to custom at this season.

I have given these details to show the hollow pretences of such assertions, if they should be made.

I do not believe that this alleged grievance, or any of the other demands, will be made, or if made, that they will be pressed; but I need not say that they will and must be resisted.

Such is the state of affairs at the present moment, and, although my conviction is strong that the Sikh army will be deterred from acts of aggression, on account of the state of our military preparation, yet it is by no means impossible that we may be forced at any moment into war, and that operations, on a very extended scale, may be immediately necessary.

For this alternative I have made all preparations. Orders will be despatched to bring up, from stations in the rear of Meerut, the additional forces noted in the margin*, which, with the concurrence of the Commander-in-Chief, will be cantoned, with the exception of the European artillery, at or near Kimma, twenty-eight miles from Loodiana, and ten miles in advance of Sirhind. This intention will not be divulged at the present moment, pending events at Lahore; and no step will be taken calculated to excite alarm which in prudence can be dispensed with. The commissariat arrangements are nearly complete, on a scale adapted for defensive purposes, enabling the forces to march in any direction at the shortest notice.

My views and measures will be anxiously directed to avoid a recourse to arms, as long as it may be possible. On this point my determination is fixed. At the same time it is very apparent,

* Four companies of European artillery, from Cawnpore; one troop of European horse artillery, four regiments of native cavalry, five ditto native infantry.

from the general aspect of affairs, that the period is fast approaching when further changes will take place at Lahore, and that the weak government of the Regent will be subverted by the violence of the troops, instigated by the intrigues of the party favourable to Rajah Gholab Singh.

Up to the present hour, no act of open hostility has been committed.

I shall not consider the march of the Sikh troops in hostile array towards the banks of the Sutlej, as a cause justifying hostilities, if no actual violation of our frontier should occur. The same privilege which we take to adopt precautionary measures on our side must be conceded to them. Every forbearance shall be shown to a weak Government, struggling for assistance against its own soldiers in a state of successful mutiny.

I have no cause to doubt the loyalty of our admirable native army, but I have every reason to believe that endeavours have been systematically made, on a very extensive scale, to tamper with them; that promises of promotion and reward have been lavishly made; and that their religious prejudices have been forcibly appealed to.

Some chiefs of influence on this side, and with estates on both sides of the river, are anxious to come forward to prove themselves unconnected with the present movement against us, and to evince their adherence to our interests. The answer I have desired may be given to them is, that we do not anticipate that the Sikhs will proceed to unprovoked hostilities; but that, should such be the case, the parties who have estates on our side the Sutlej, and prove by their conduct their true adherence to the British Government, will be protected from any consequences to which such conduct might render them liable on account of their position in the Punjaub.

I have every reason to be satisfied with the ability, energy, and sound judgment displayed by Major Broadfoot in the course of these proceedings.

Letter referred to in the despatch of the Governor-General, dated December 2, 1845:—

The Secretary to the Government of India to the Governor-General's Agent.

Fort William, 25th January, 1845.

SIR,

I am directed to acknowledge the receipt of the copy of your letter of the 15th instant*, addressed to the Commander-in-Chief, on the subject of the alarms which prevailed at Lahore when you wrote, and the movement of troops towards the Sutlej, in consequence of certain rumours of orders alleged to have been issued by the Commander-in-Chief at Umballa.

2.—In the absence of information of the orders which may have been given by the Commander-in-Chief, and which probably his Excellency could not have avoided giving, the Governor-General in Council is disposed to attribute this manifestation of alarm in some measure to the successful intrigues of the party of Gholab Singh at Lahore, which party, by detaching a portion of the Sikh army towards the Sutlej, would weaken its efforts, then about to be directed in operations against that Rajah.

3.—Another cause which may have had some weight in the above movement, may be the anxiety of the Lahore Government to get rid of an army which is more formidable to its friends than its enemies, from the immediate vicinity of the seat of Government; and it may be convenient to ascribe this movement to the orders for military preparations issued at Umballa.

4.—Be this as it may, the Governor-General in Council desires me to refer you to the letter, Secret Department, of the 10th instant, addressed to the Commander-in-Chief, of which a copy was sent with my despatch of the same date, No. 17, and to beg you forthwith to state to the Durbar the exact truth, as follows:—

5.—That a barrack for a European regiment of infantry had for a length of time been ordered to be constructed at Ferozepore, of

* This letter is the next in this collection, p. 15.

which the foundations are already laid; that the Governor-General in Council, perceiving during the autumn the state of weakness in which the Government of the Maharajah had been for some time, under his Highness Wuzeer Rajah Heera Singh, had postponed to give orders for the completion of this building, in order that no question might arise, exciting any doubt or jealousy of our intention on the part of the Government of the Maharajah or of the Sikh army.

6.—That the British force stationed at Ferozepore has remained of the same strength as before, notwithstanding the recent violent proceedings of the Sikh army against its own Government, which conduct it is unnecessary now to comment upon, otherwise than to repeat that it is conduct utterly repugnant to British feeling and British policy; and that this army has become so notoriously beyond controul, that the Governor-General in Council, always anxious to preserve the tranquillity of the Sikh states under his protection, will, under existing circumstances, now proceed to complete the buildings at Ferozepore according to his original intention, and also to reinforce that post by an additional force of native infantry.

7.—You are requested to impress on the Vakeel, that the same forbearance has been shown since the death of the Wuzeer Rajah Heera Singh, in order to evince the friendly feeling of the Governor-General in Council towards the Maharajah, in proof of which you will advert to the sentiments expressed in the Governor-General in Council's letter to your address, and which you were desired to convey as from yourself to the Vakeel of the 15th instant, stating that if any attempts be made by violent proceedings to bring about any change, such as the army proclaiming Peshwa Singh as successor to his Highness the Maharajah, whom the British Government has recognised, that you would not feel yourself justified in recognising, without special orders, a chief whose power had been acquired by such means.

8.—You will observe to the Vakeel that, in despite of the friendly conduct of the Governor-General in Council, a portion of the Sikh army has been moved towards the Sutlej, on the pretext of rumours from the cantonments of Umballa; and you will say, that the Governor-General in Council advises the Maharajah's Government to disregard rumours and newspaper reports, over which the Governor-General in Council exercises no controul.

9.—You will impress upon the Durbar Vakeel that you possess the confidence of the Governor-General in Council, and that your instructions are to declare the truth plainly to His Highness's Government, reiterating the same sentiments as those conveyed by your predecessor, that the Governor-General in Council has a sincere desire to see a strong Government re-established at Lahore, such as that which existed at the time of our faithful ally, His Highness Maharajah Runjeet Singh.

10.—Having taken the opportunity which this movement of Sikh troops towards the Sutlej so suitably affords, of declaring our intentions as to the military arrangements about to be made at Ferozepore, you will state that the British Government does not desire to interfere in the internal affairs of the Punjaub; that the Governor-General in Council regrets the embarrassments under which the Sikh Government at present labours, and sincerely trusts that they may be overcome by firmness and prudence.

11.—In making these communications, you will modify them, if necessary, in reference to any events which have occurred in the interval which must unavoidably elapse before your receipt of them, taking care not to commit the Government of India to any line of action involving any principle of policy not in accordance with the spirit of your instructions.

12.—You will continue to do everything in your power to convince the Government of Lahore of the good faith of the Government of India, so as to enable the Sikh Government to direct the efforts of their army to the legitimate object of coercing its enemies; and, if the opportunity should occur, you will, without exciting any irritation, but in the most friendly terms, state that the Governor-General in Council has, in consideration of the difficult circumstances in which the Government of the Maharajah is placed, and for other obvious reasons, hitherto forborne to make the unruly and ungovernable condition of the Sikh army a subject of formal remonstrance to the Maharajah. The Governor-General in Council trusts that a returning sense of the duty which the army owes to the Maharajah may avert the necessity of his taking any such step, and that he may hear that which will be much more gratifying to him, that it has obediently marched against his Highness's enemies, and honourably fulfilled the true functions of an army, by supporting the just authority of its Sovereign and his Government.

13.—You will understand that this caution, although incidentally given, will be distinctly delivered. The state of this army, the Governor-General in Council observes, so close upon our frontier, may become an intolerable nuisance; and, although it would be a mockery to expect that the Lahore Government, in the state of anarchy and weakness in which it at present can scarcely be said to exist, can regulate the conduct of an army which exercises over that Government daily acts of coercion and tyranny; nevertheless, the Governor-General in Council deems it expedient that a notice, in the most guarded terms, should be given of the great inconvenience to which the British Government is exposed, and of which, if the Lahore Government was in a state of greater strength and responsibility, the Governor-General in Council would justly have cause to complain.

14.—You will observe, in the letter of the Governor-General in Council to the Commander-in-Chief, of the 10th January, that the reinforcements, European and native, to be posted at Ferozepore, were not to be moved up by the Commander-in-Chief, unless on a report of an emergency from yourself; and that, in that letter to the Commander-in-Chief, the Governor-General in Council would be satisfied if the reinforcements were posted towards the end of March and April—so short a time before the river would become unfordable as to be no longer a source of uneasiness to the Sikh Government, and at the same time placing our advanced post in that condition to be able to defend the post and the passage of the river, in which, under existing circumstances, it ought at all times to remain.

15.—I am directed to take this opportunity to send you a copy of papers, by which you will be apprised that two additional native regiments of infantry have been ordered up, making the additional four between Meerut and the Sutlej, one European regiment, two battalions of European artillery, seven regiments of native infantry, and one N. I. horse artillery.

16.—This movement of the Sikh army towards the Sutlej and its mutinous ungovernable state, will be your answer to any questions which may arise as to British reinforcements arriving on the Sutlej or its immediate neighbourhood.

I have, &c.,

F. Currie.

Letter referred to in the preceding Letter.

The Political Agent to the Commander-in-Chief.

Camp, Laskar-Khas-kee-Serai, January 15, 1845.

Sir,

I have the honour to enclose, for your Excellency's information, a translation of an extract from Lahore intelligence received last night.

2.—Coming immediately after the reports respecting European troops, which I had yesterday the honour of mentioning, this caused extreme excitement, and among other resolutions, one was to demand explanations from me. In order to enable me to meet these demands, if made, I beg that your Excellency will do me the favour of saying whether there has been any thing of the kind described as having occurred at Umballa, or whether the whole is not mere idle rumour.

3.—A second despatch, arrived this evening, brings further intelligence on this subject, and I regret that in consequence of these appearances of preparation, our position with respect to the Durbar is materially and unfavourably changed from what it was three days before, and that there is now more risk of collision than there has been yet, seeing that the Ranee, from circumstances not unlikely to deceive her, and others, suspects that we are in co-operation with her enemies, and had appealed to the troops at Lahore, communicating to them the report of the order for preparation at Umballa, ascribed to your Excellency, and the troops have offered to do whatever she will sanction against the English.

4.—But, though there is more risk of disturbance now than formerly, and though our intercourse with the Lahore state is, for the moment, embarrassed; yet I beg, with the utmost deference to your Excellency's better judgment, to state that I consider nothing as yet likely to occur, and indeed very little to be at present possible, which could lead me to do more than make the application usual in such cases for support from the officer commanding the division; and that I do not even now propose, as far as matters have yet gone, to call on him to do more than maintain his usual vigilance.

5.—The bulk of the Lahore army had been lately sent by this Government, in reliance on our good faith, against the Jummoo Rajahs, and towards Cashmere and the country beyond the Jhelum, which is disturbed; supposing the Durbar to collect every man in Lahore and its vicinity, including the garrison of Umritsir and other detachments, to countermand the march of the troops now proceeding to Jummoo, and allowing nothing for men on leave, or sick, or false musters, they can only collect of regular troops as follows:—

Infantry	12,200
Cavalry	1,200
Artillery	1,530
TOTAL	14,930

a number inferior, I believe, to that of the troops in the Sirhind division, and in a state of such utter disorder that their nominal leaders cannot get them to face the armed peasantry of Jessotas, nor do anything but plunder the people, insult and beat their officers, and return at will to their own homes. In addition to this, they have, however, the following undisciplined troops:—

Irregular infantry, 1,500; two battalions of Heera Singh's hill-men, who have joined the Sikhs for high pay, and have received muskets, and are now at drill:

Irregular horse, 4,750, including those at Umritsir, detached to the Sutlej, Jaghurdars, &c.

I think that the most probable source of disturbance will be, that the restriction to fourteen miles from Lahore of their troops detached towards the Sutlej will be withdrawn, and that this disorderly rabble will interrupt the dawks, and commit outrages on the south side of the river, as well as on the north; but it will be most likely in a way not easily distinguished from ordinary gang robberies and forays.

I have, &c.,
(Signed) G. BROADFOOT.

The Political Agent to the Commander-in-Chief.

Governor-General's Agency, November 20, 1845.

SIR,

Since I had the honour of waiting on your Excellency to-day, I have received Lahore letters of the 18th instant (morning).

During the night of the 17th the chiefs had agreed on, and the Durbar had ordered in writing, the following plan of operations:—

The army was to be divided into seven divisions, one to remain at Lahore, and the rest to proceed against Roopar and our hills, Loodiana, Hurrekee, Ferozepore, and Scinde, while one was to proceed to Peshawur; and a force under Rajah Gholab Singh was to be sent to Attock.

Each division was to be of 8,000 to 12,000 men against Ferozepore, under Sham Singh Attareewalla, whose estates adjoin the place against which it was to act. Against Hurrekee, is to go Rajah Lal Singh; against Loodiana, Sirdar Tej Singh, the new Commander-in-Chief; and against Roopar, a brother of Sena Singh Mujeeteea.

The force under Sham Singh is to be 4,000 horse and two brigades of infantry, with guns; under Rajah Lal Singh, 4,500 horse, and two infantry brigades; under Sirdar Tej Singh, four brigades of infantry (one of them irregulars, and one new levies), and 1,000 horse, &c.; but till the plans of the Durbar are in actual execution they cannot be considered fixed, and therefore I do not trouble your Excellency with further details.

With respect to the probability of their actual moving, I must say that my correspondents in Lahore seem to doubt it, though they are perplexed. The causes, however, which have so suddenly led the Durbar to such lengths may carry it further; and indeed it is difficult to see how they can stop now without a change of government—a thing not unlikely. Still, prudence requires that we should act as if they would not change their minds, and I therefore most respectfully venture to submit to your Excellency the following suggestions:—

First, that the carriage of the troops in this division should be drawn into the stations, both for security, and to enable the troops to move at the shortest notice; and that the European troops in the hills should be held in readiness to march; to move them is a work of time, and needs some preparation. I shall write to the sub-commissioner and the other local authorities without delay to collect coolies; but I shall be glad to hear from your Excellency the numbers required, and also on what roads supplies, &c., should be got ready.

With respect to further measures, I must of course speak with extreme diffidence; on the whole, I am inclined still to hold the opinions that I had the honour of expressing verbally; and I may now add, that the matter seems to have come to a pitch which makes some notice of it by our Government not easily avoidable; and this being the case, and as the Governor-General is so near, it may be desirable to await his arrival, or his decision as to the extent of what may be done, before making any movements, unless we hear of the Sikh army having actually crossed the Sutlej.

In all this, however, I speak with the utmost submission to your Excellency's better judgment; but I beg to add, that in whatever your Excellency may decide on, I shall esteem it an honour to give it whatever aid I can.——I have, &c.

(Signed) G. Broadfoot.

The Agent to the Governor-General to the Secretary to the Government of India.

Camp, Umballa, November 20, 1845.

I have the honour to forward, for the information of his Excellency the Governor-General, a copy of a demi-official letter to his Excellency the Commander-in-Chief, as affairs at Lahore assumed their present form.

Not to delay the messenger, I must reserve a fuller report till to-morrow; but I may add to what has been already communicated demi-officially, and what will be gathered from my letters, that no complaint of any kind has been made to me by the Durbar, and that the pretext of a grievance alleged has been dropped by the Durbar, and rejected by the troops. The truth is, all are in a false position, from the unlooked-for results of the cry against the English, to serve a party purpose, and all, moreover, are indifferent to war with us, from their firm persuasion that, if victorious, they will find new means of power and wealth, and, if beaten, that they will be, what most of them desire, the heads of a subsidiary, instead of an independent state.

This opinion has never received any countenance from me, but the very contrary; and the Durbar will by this time have received the perwannah which I addressed to the Vakeel, when the intrigues which had led to the present state of things assumed a serious form. It will be seen from the enclosed copy of it, that no warning could be plainer, and, as therein indicated, that it is only a repetition of former warnings.

Continued letters from my assistants, respecting the rumours on the frontier, showed that our posts there were vigilant; and I abstained, therefore, from communicating with the military authorities, in order to prevent the Durbar having the smallest ground to say that any menacing preparations or movements on our part had been taken up, for this ground has been already alleged in their consultations, as justifying their present movements; nay, even after I had yesterday received a communication on the subject from the Major-General commanding the division, I forebore to write to his Excellency the Commander-in-Chief, and even to-day I ventured to recommend to his Excellency that no steps should be taken for the present. Since then, however, authentic intelligence has reached me that the Durbar has openly adopted, and ordered in writing, a fixed plan of operations against the English, and I, accordingly, addressed to his Excellency the Commander-in-Chief the letter, of which a copy is annexed.

I now only suggest abstinence from movement on account of the vicinity of the Governor-General, who will probably think the matter now one which has gone too far to be left unnoticed, whether the troops actually move from Lahore or not.

That I presumed to suggest any delay whatever is owing to this: It appears to me that the frontier is too long to be defensible in all points by any force we can move; that our two posts on the frontier are strong enough to maintain themselves till relieved; and that to attempt reinforcements, therefore, in anticipation of those of the Sikhs would be useless as protecting the open country, and might impede any operations which the Governor-General may resolve on. Moreover, the delay recommended is only one of two or three days, till an answer to this letter can be received.

The Sikh sirdars on this side of the Sutlej have for many months past been called on to keep their troops in readiness to repel the invasion of their territories, and I have now directed them to prepare to repel the threatening aggression. I have, &c.

(Signed) G. BROADFOOT.

P.S.—It is right to add, that up to the last moment the regular troops were discussing the propriety of murdering Rajah Lal Singh and Sirdar Tej Singh, and sending for Rajah Gholab Singh to lead them. The two chiefs menaced look for escape to exciting enthusiasm against the English. This may delay or precipitate invasion.

The Commander-in-Chief to the Agent to the Governor-General.

Camp, Umballa, 20th November, 1845.

SIR,

I have the honour to acknowledge the receipt, this moment, of your letters of this date, conveying to me intelligence of the hostile attitude which has been assumed by the Lahore Durbar.

Under the circumstances, I have ordered the following preparations to be entered upon immediately, to meet whatever may take place:—

Her Majesty's 9th Lancers to move at once from Meerut to Umballa.

To be held in readiness to move from Meerut to Kurnaul on the shortest notice; two troops of horse artillery, her Majesty's 16th Lancers, the 3rd Regiment of Light Cavalry, her Majesty's 10th Foot, save one company, the corps of sappers and miners, all, save one, of the regiments of native infantry.

The 8th Regiment of Irregular Cavalry will likewise be held prepared to move from Hansee to Kurnaul, and the Simoor battalion from Deyrah to Saharumpore, where it will be centrically situated, and ready to be moved wherever it may be most required; the 4th Regiment of Irregular Cavalry will be brought up from Bareilly to Meerut.

I beg that you will instruct the civil authorities at Simla to place themselves in communication with the officers commanding European corps in those hills, and ascertain from them what number of coolies will be required to enable the regiments to move, in order that they may be collected at once. Supplies for the corps in the hills will be required to be laid in on the roads leading thence to Sirhind.

I shall direct the other corps of all arms in this division to draw their carriage into cantonments, in view to the troops being prepared to act on the shortest notice.

Previous to adopting any further measures at present, I would await a communication of the views of the Governor-General.—
I have, &c. (Signed) H. GOUGH.

The Agent to the Governor-General to the Secretary to Government.

Umballa, 21st November, 1845.

The Durbar of the forenoon of the 18th was protracted till two o'clock, but I have not the details of the afternoon Durbar.

Eleven A.M. was the hour found by the astrologers as auspicious for the march of the troops; not a chief stirred from his house. The officers and punchayets of the troops, regular and irregular, to the number of a couple of thousand, crowded to the Durbar and demanded the reason; the Ranee tried to soothe them, saying, that the fortunate hour being passed, the march could not be undertaken till the astrologers found another. The crowd demanded that this should be instantly done, and the court astrologer was ordered into their presence to find the proper time. He pored through his tables for two or three hours, while the Ranee sought to divert the attention of the military mob; at length he announced that the most favourable day was not till the 15th Mujsur (28th November). The military were furious, and declared that he was an impostor, and that they had to get from him two crores of rupees which he had made from the public money; the pundit implored mercy, and said the 7th Mujsur (20th) was also a good day; the military were still angry, and the poor pundit left amidst their menaces.

They proposed that the Ranee and her son should march, and intimated that till they made an example of some chief no march would take place.

The Ranee complained that whilst the troops were urging the march, they were still going home to their villages as fast as they got their pay; and Sirdar Sham Singh Attareewalla declared his belief that unless something was done to stop this, he would find himself on his way to Ferozepore with empty tents. The bait of money to be paid, and to accompany them was also offered, and at length the Durbar broke up at two P.M. Great consultations took place in the afternoon, but I know only one result, that the Ranee had to give to her lover his formal dismissal, and that he (Rajah Lal Singh) actually went into the camp of the Sawars he is to command, and pitched his tent.

What the Ranee says is quite true of the sepoys dispersing to their houses; the whole affair has so suddenly reached its present height, that many of the men themselves think it will come to nothing, and still more who had taken their departure do not believe it serious enough to go back. On the day after this scene took place, *i.e.*, the 19th, the usual stream of sepoys, natives of the protected states, who had got their pay, poured across the Sutlej, at Hurrekee, on the way to their homes. Every preparation, however, for war is making with probably more energy than if it had been a long-planned scheme, for every person of whatever party must show his sincerity by activity and virulent professions of hatred to the English.

Enclosure No. 1, in No. 10.

The Agent to the Governor-General to the Lahore Vakeel.

2nd December, 1845.

I wrote to you a letter on the 18th ultimo, requiring explanations as to the reported orders of the Lahore Durbar to its troops, to move towards the Sutlej with unfriendly intentions.

On the 20th instant, you answered from Loodiana, that you had forwarded a copy of my letter to the Durbar immediately on receiving it, and you stated that on receiving an answer you would forthwith communicate it.

For several days past I have been in hourly expectation of your answer, but none came.

This day, on your waiting on me, you informed me, that though you had some days ago received from the Durbar an acknowledgment of the receipt of your letter, you had received no answer to it, but that you had in the interval written repeatedly to the Durbar on the subject of it, and that you confidently expected an answer this day, or, at furthest, to-morrow morning.

I pointed out to you that, notwithstanding the notoriety of the events which had occurred at Lahore, and notwithstanding the inconvenience suffered by the detention, on the frontier, of the battalions about to leave it for Scinde and Bareilly, the Governor-General, in hopes of receiving without delay satisfactory explanations in answer to my letter, had continued the forbearance he has exercised so long, and to so great an extent; that no new troops had arrived on the frontier, and that the Governor-General had proceeded slowly on his journey in this direction, as intended, before the occurrence of the events of which explanation is now demanded; that I pointed out that, notwithstanding this forbearance, you had appeared, after so long an interval, without any answer to my demand for an explanation, and that I saw this with surprise and regret.

I have now to communicate to you the following orders from the Governor-General:—

His Excellency has directed me to say, that the rules of friendship between the two states, and indeed the customs of all nations, require that in answering a demand for explanations of events so grave as those which have occurred at Lahore, not a moment is to be lost, because delay cannot but operate to confirm the (MOST UNFRIENDLY) *worst* construction of such events, and is, moreover, an act of the highest discourtesy towards the Government demanding explanations. In this instance the requisition for explanation has been disregarded, and the apparently hostile movements have been continued.

Under these circumstances, the Governor-General feels it

impossible to permit you, who are the authorised representative of the Government which has offered to his Government so great a slight, to continue in his Excellency's camp, while this slight is persevered in; he has directed me not to admit you to any further interview with me, unless you come as the bearer of the answer of the Durbar to my remonstrance; and his Excellency further commands, that if this answer be not delivered before noon to-morrow, you will quit this camp.

To prevent, however, interruption to the business of this agency, as regards the Mahaja's estates on this side of the Sutlej, I request that you will leave with me a confidential Moonshee to communicate, during your absence, my orders, or those of the subordinate courts of the agency, to the managers of those estates; and you will warn the Kardars and residents in those estates to obey all orders coming from the ordinary courts through your Moonshee in the same way as if received from yourself.

(Signed) G. BROADFOOT.

Enclosure No. 2, in No. 10.

The Lahore Vakeel to the Governor-General's Agent.

Your letter, dated 2nd December 1845, has been delivered to me by Moulvee Rujub Ally Khan after midnight, and I have arranged for its immediate transmission to the Durbar.

Seal of KRISHEN CHUND.

The 2nd December 1845, *after midnight, (i. e., by our reckoning*, 1 A. M. *3rd.*

The Governor-General to the Secret Committee.

Camp, Umballa, December 4th, 1845.

Major Broadfoot having reported to me that the Lahore Vakeel had joined the camp from Loodiana, I directed Major Broadfoot to see him, and to require from him the reply to his perwannah, remonstrating against the procedings which had taken place at the time it was written, and demanding the cause thereof.

The Vakeel waited upon Major Broadfoot, and in reply to his requisition asserted, that he had received no reply from the Durbar; that he had sent the communication immediately to Lahore, had received merely an acknowledgment of its safe arrival, and that he had repeatedly sent, urging that a reply should be forwarded to him, but hitherto without success; but he asserted that he fully expected the reply by that evening's post.

Major Broadfoot explicitly informed the Vakeel, as previously instructed by me, that the Governor-General would not permit the Lahore Government to trifle with him in a matter of such serious importance; that positive information had been received of the Lahore army having left the capital towards the frontier, avowedly with hostile intentions towards the British Government, to which course they had been instigated by the express and repeated orders of the Ranee and the chiefs, and that the Governor-General expected to receive, without further delay, an answer to the political agent's written remonstrance. Major Broadfoot then said, that he should report to the Governor-General the result of his interview with the Vakeel, and communicate in writing the orders he might receive. The Vakeel said very little at this interview; he protested that the had done all in his power to procure a reply to the perwannah; and on Major Broadfoot's saying that we knew positively that the Ranee and chiefs had ordered the present movement, he said *he* had no such knowledge.

When Major Broadfoot reported to me, in the evening, the result of this interview, I immediately directed him to address to the Vakeel the written communication, a copy of which is inclosed.

I considered that it was absolutely necessary on my arrival at Umballa, to take decided notice of the extraordinary proceedings that had taken place, and were stated to be still in progress. It was evident I could not permit the political agent's communications, in the face of what was going on at Lahore, to be treated with disregard. I took the mildest course in my power, consistently with the dignity, position, and interests of the British Government. I purposely left an opening to the Lahore Government to remedy, through the Vakeel, the discourtesy it had shown, by affording to that Government the facility of making any explanation it might desire. The plain construction to be put on the silence of the Lahore Government in the reply to the demand for explanation, evidently was, that the intentions of that Government were hostile, in which I did not deem it expedient to give to that Government the leisure to complete their hostile preparations; whilst, on my part, I had abstained from making any movement, expressly for the purpose of avoiding any jealousy or alarm; thus affording to the Maharajah's Government the strongest proof of the good faith and forbearance of the British Government.

Major Broadfoot entertains the impression that the reply to his demands had been sent to the Vakeel, and had either been returned by him, with a protest (as is, I understand, often done), or was, at the moment of the conference in his possession, but was withheld because the Vakeel was reluctant to deliver so unfriendly a document.

However that may be, the perwannah from Major Broadfoot of the evening of the 2nd December was received by the Vakeel the same night, and, with the reception of an acknowledgment of its receipt, no further communication has passed between him and Major Broadfoot. The Vakeel is not now in the camp.

I am satisfied that the course I have adopted was imperatively required, and before I authorise any precautionary movements to be made, I shall give full time for a reply to be received from Lahore.

This morning, news up to the 1st instant has been received. The Ranee and Sirdars are becoming more and more urgent that the army should advance to the frontier, believing that, in the present posture of affairs, the only hope of saving their lives and prolonging their power is to be found in bringing about collision with the British forces. The Sikh army moves with evident reluctance, and is calling for Gholab Singh, who is collecting forces at Jumboo, and is watching the progress of events.

My own impression remains unaltered. I do not expect that the troops will come as far as the banks of the Sutlej, or that any positive act of aggression will be committed; but it is evident that the Ranee and chiefs are, for their own preservation, endeavouring to raise a storm, which, when raised, they will be powerless either to direct or allay.

I shall, as I have before said, await the reply from Lahore to Major Broadfoot's last communication to the Vakeel.

If the reply from the ostensible Government, acting under the controul and at the dictation of the army, is hostile, I shall at once order up troops from Meerut and other stations to the support of our advanced positions, persevering up to the last moment in the sincere desire to avoid hostilities.

The Governor-General to the Secret Committee.

Camp, Ferozepore, December 31, 1845.

SINCE my last despatch to you, of the 4th instant, events of great moment have occurred.

The Sikh army, in large numbers commenced crossing the Sutlej on the 11th, and after investing Ferozepore on one side, took up an entrenched position at the village of Ferozeshah, about ten miles from Ferozepore, and about the same distance from the village of Moodkee.

In this camp the enemy had placed 108 pieces of cannon, some of large calibre, with a force exceeding 50,000 men, for the purpose of intercepting the approach of the British force, moving up from Umballa, to the relief of Ferozepore, which had been thus treacherously attacked, without provocation or declaration of hostilities.

I had ordered, on the 8th instant, that portion of our army posted at Umballa for defensive purposes, to move up on the 11th, and after a rapid march of 150 miles, it reached Moodkee on the

18th, where, on the evening of the same day, it repulsed an attack of the Sikh army, and captured seventeen guns; on the following day the army was concentrated at Moodkee, and on the 21st moved by its left on Ferozepore, and having on the march formed its junction at half-past one o'clock with 5,000 men and twenty-one guns, under Major-General Sir John Littler, which had moved from Ferozepore that morning, the Commander-in-Chief formed the army in order of battle, and attacked the enemy's entrenched camp; and on that evening and the following morning, captured seventy pieces of artillery, taking possession of the enemy's camp, with large quantities of ammunition and warlike stores.

These successful and energetic operations have been followed by the retreat of the Sikh army to the other side of the Sutlej, the British army being now encamped between Ferozepore and the fords of the Sutlej.

You will not fail to observe that these important and brilliant successes have been achieved by that portion of our army posted at and in advance of Umballa, for defensive purposes; and that, our forces from Meerut, and other stations from the rear, ordered to move up at the same time, are in reserve, and will reach this neighbourhood between the 5th and the 9th of January.

I have the honour to inclose two reports from the Commander-in-Chief, detailing the admirable manner in which these important duties have been performed; and I am convinced the Court of Directors of the East India Company, in concurrence with her Majesty's Government, will highly appreciate the eminent services rendered by the Commander-in-Chief, and by the officers, non-commissioned officers, and soldiers of the Indian army.

The Commander-in-Chief has successfully accomplished every object I had directed him to effect for the relief of Ferozepore, and the protection of these British states. No accident or failure has occurred during the complicated operations of a combined movement, and our army, whether for defence or attack, has shown, as heretofore, that its power is irresistible.

I also transmit a notification which I issued on the 25th instant, and a general order, recording the grateful acknowledgments of the Indian Government for these important services.

I now proceed to detail the events which preceded a resort to arms, and I am convinced that the forbearance manifested by me in all these transactions will meet with your approval.

My previous correspondence will show the extreme anxiety I felt to avoid hostilities, by friendly explanations required from the Lahore Durbar; and my reluctance to give any cause for jealousy or alarm to the Sikh army and Government was so strong, that, from the 18th of November up to the 8th of December, I deferred to make any movement of troops, in the hope of proving the sincerity of our professions by the moderation of our actions. This forbearance, carried to the utmost limits which prudence could allow, was not appreciated at Lahore.

In the state of anarchy and uncontrollable power usurped by the Sikh army, my reluctance to resent their hostile conduct may have been misunderstood, as the effect of conscious weakness or of timidity; but the Lahore Government, there is every reason to believe, was not influenced by any such impressions.

The Regent and her advisers courted collision for the purpose of employing their unruly soldiers against their friendly neighbour, as the safest means of extricating themselves from the personal dangers to which they were constantly exposed; the Lahore Government deceived their army by false statements of the fidelity of our native troops, whom they have in vain attempted to corrupt by emissaries employed by that Government.

And there is also reason to believe that active intrigues had for some time past been resorted to, in order to induce the chiefs of our protected Sikh territories to rise in arms against the British power, as soon as a Sikh army should cross the Sutlej.

There was no proof that such a conspiracy existed on the part of the leading Sikh chiefs on this side the Sutlej, although in a very few instances, where the personal character of the individuals accounted for the folly of their conduct, there were reasons for believing that disaffection did exist, and would be exhibited with activity on the first favourable opportunity, and particularly if any reverse should attend our arms.

I shall have occasion to advert to this subject when I notice the proclamation I issued on the 13th instant.

But will previously resume the narrative of the daily intelligence from Lahore, as affording a connected series of the events which have occurred since the 4th of December, when I informed you that I had deemed it expedient to desire the Lahore Vakeel to leave my camp, in consequence of the disregard shown by his court to my political agent's remonstrance of the 18th of November, and of the determination evinced by the Durbar to withhold all explanation of their conduct.

I had moved with my camp on the 6th of December from Umballa towards Loodiana, peaceably making my progress by the route I had announced, with the intention of visiting the Sikh protected states, according to the usual custom of my predecessors.

In common with the most experienced officers of the Indian Government, I was not of opinion that the Sikh army would cross the Sutlej with its infantry and artillery.

I considered it probable that some act of aggression would be committed by parties of plunderers, for the purpose of compelling the British Government to interfere, to which course the Sikh chiefs knew I was most averse; but I concurred with the Commander-in-Chief, and the chief secretary to the Government, as well as with my political agent, Major Broadfoot, that offensive operations, on a large scale, would not be resorted to.

Exclusive of the political reasons which induced me to carry my forbearance as far as it was possible, I was confident, from the opinions given by the Commander-in-Chief, and Major-General Sir John Littler, in command of the forces at Ferozepore, that that post would resist any attack from the Sikh army, as long as its provisions lasted; and that I could at any time relieve it, under the ordinary circumstances of an Asiatic army making an irruption into our territories, provided it had not the means of laying siege to the fort and the entrenched camp.

Up to this period no act of aggression had been committed by the Sikh army. The Lahore Government had as good a right to reinforce their bank of the river Sutlej, as we had to reinforce our posts on that river.

The Sikh army had, in 1843 and 1844, moved down upon the river from Lahore, and, after remaining there encamped a few weeks, had returned to the capital. These reasons, and above all my extreme anxiety to avoid hostilities, induced me not to make any hasty movement with our army, which when the two armies came into each other's presence, might bring about a collision.

The army had, however, been ordered to be in readiness to move at the shortest notice; and, on the 7th and 8th of December, when I heard from Lahore that preparations were making on a large scale for artillery, stores, and all the munitions of war, I wrote to the Commander-in-Chief, directing his Excellency on the 11th, to move up the force from Umballa, from Meerut, and some other stations in the rear.

Up to this time no infantry or artillery had been reported to have left Lahore, nor had a single Sikh soldier crossed the Sutlej. Nevertheless, I considered it prudent no longer to delay the forward movement of our troops, having given to the Lahore Government the most ample time for a reply to our remonstrance.

On the 9th, at night, Captain Nicolson, the assistant political agent at Ferozepore, reported that a portion of the Sikh army had approached within three miles of the river. On the other hand, the information received by Major Broadfoot on that day from Lahore was not of a character to make it probable that any Sikh movement on a large scale was meditated.

On the 10th, no intelligence was received from Lahore confirmatory of Capt. Nicolson's report, and the usual opinion continued to prevail that the Sikh army would not cross the Sutlej.

The troops, however, moved on the 10th, 11th, and 12th, in pursuance of the orders given on the 7th and 8th; and the whole of the forces destined to move up to the Sutlej were in full march on the 12th.

I did not consider the force moving up from Umballa to be

sufficient to force its way to relieve Ferozepore, if a large Sikh army, with a numerous and well-served park of artillery, should attempt to intercept it in its approach to Ferozepore, as, in such case, it could with difficulty receive any aid from that garrison. Being some days' march in advance of the Commander-in-Chief, I rode over to Loodiana; and, having inspected the fort, the cantonments and the troops, it appeared to me most advisable that the whole of this force should be moved up with the Umballa force, restricting the defence of Loodiana to the fort, which could be securely garrisoned by the more infirm soldiers of the regiments at that post, unless attacked by heavy artillery, which was a very improbable contingency.

The risk to be incurred of leaving the town and the cantonments liable to be plundered, was maturely considered, and I had no hesitation in incurring that risk to ensure the strength and sufficiency of the force which might separately be brought into action with the whole of the Sikh army. I therefore ordered Brigadier Wheeler to be prepared to march at the shortest notice.

The Umballa force, in March, was 7,500 men and 36 guns.

The Loodiana force amounted to 5,000 men and 12 guns.

The Commander-in-Chief concurred in these views: and this fine body of men, by a rapid march on Busseean, an important point, where the roads leading from Umballa and Kurnaul meet, formed the advanced column of the army, and secured the supplies which had been laid in at Busseean.

Up to the morning of the 12th, the information from Lahore had not materially varied: but, by the reports received on that day, the general aspect of affairs appeared more warlike. Still no Sikh aggression had been committed, and no artillery had moved down to the river.

On the 13th I first received precise information that the Sikh army had crossed the Sutlej, and was concentrating in great force on the left bank of the river.

The Umballa force at that time had been in movement three

days. On this date I issued the proclamation, a copy of which is enclosed.

On the 14th, the British forces moved up by double marches on alternate days, and on the 18th, reached Moodkee, 20 miles from Ferozepore, after a march of 21 miles.

On this day, and at this place, the whole British force was concentrated, with the exception of two European and two native regiments, expected on the following day.

The troops were engaged in cooking their meals, when Major Broadfoot received information that the whole Sikh army was in full march, with the intention to surprise the camp. The troops immediately stood to their arms, and advanced. The result of that short, but decisive action, was the signal defeat of the enemy at every point, and the capture of 17 guns, the details of which are given in the report of the Commander-in-Chief, herewith sent. The troops returned to their camp at midnight, and halted the 19th and 20th to refresh the men, to collect the wounded, and bring in the captured guns.

There was no objection to this delay, as it was evident, from the preparations and movements of the Sikh army, that its commander was intent upon intercepting the relieving force, and had no intention of risking an attack against Ferozepore.

On the 21st, the Commander-in-Chief, having left the baggage of the army, the wounded, and the captured guns, at Moodkee, protected by two regiments of native infantry, marched at four o'clock in the morning by his left, keeping about three or four miles from the enemy's entrenched position at Ferozeshah, in which the enemy had placed 108 pieces of cannon, protected by breast-works.

A communication had been made during the preceding night with Sir John Littler, informing him of the intended line of march, and desiring him to move out with such a part of his force as would not compromise the safety of his troops and the post.

At half-past one o'clock the Umballa force, having marched across the country disencumbered of every description of baggage, except the reserve ammunition, formed its junction with Sir John Littler's force, who had moved out of Ferozepore with 5,000 men, two regiments of cavalry, and 21 field guns.

This combined operation having been effected, the Commander-in-Chief, with my entire concurrence, made his arrangements for the attack of the enemy's position at Ferozeshah, about four miles distant from the point where our forces had united.

The British force consisted of 16,700 men, and 69 guns, chiefly horse artillery.

The Sikh forces varied from 48,000 to 60,000 men, with 103 pieces of cannon of heavy calibre, in fixed batteries.

You will observe that every soldier who could be brought into our ranks, had, by these combinations from Umballa and Loodiana to Ferozepore, been rendered available; that the force was most efficient, and, notwithstanding the difficulty of the ground, intersected with jungle, the vast superiority of the enemy's well-served artillery and the breast-works behind which their infantry fought, that our British force, particularly our infantry, surmounted every obstacle, capturing that evening and the following morning 70 pieces of artillery, and the whole of the enemy's camp-equipage and military stores.

I refer to the report of the Commander-in-Chief for the details of this brilliant exploit.

The three attempts of the Sikh army, reinforced by Tej Singh's army, to retake their position in the course of the day, were unavailing.

The Sikh army then retreated on the fords of the Sutlej, disheartened by the capture of its artillery, and the severe loss it had sustained in killed and wounded, and has since crossed over to the other side of the river.

The force thus promptly brought forward from Umballa to the frontier, has proved that it was sufficient for the protective object for which it was prepared, to repulse the treachery of the Maharajah's government, and the arrogance of the Sikh army.

It has further proved, that the military precautions taken were most necessary. It has driven the invading force from our territories, and punished the mutinous soldiery of a most unscrupulous Government.

It remains for me to advert to the proclamation, a copy of which forms an enclosure of this despatch. I have endeavoured, in that paper, to give a brief outline of our relations with the Lahore state, and of the circumstances which have preceded the present rupture. That this invasion of our territory by the Sikh army was unprovoked, must be apparent to all; and I considered it right that the forbearance I had shown, with the motives of that forbearance, should be distinctly promulgated.

The caution to the protected chiefs was necessary; for, during many months past, though no overt acts of hostility have been committed, with one exception, there was a feeling very generally prevalent among them favourable to the Lahore Government rather than to ours, which evinced itself in a backwardness to afford supplies for our army, and to attend to the requisitions of the agency. This, with the exception of the Maharajah of Puteala, was the case with perhaps all the chiefs.

Immediate measures will be taken for bringing into some order and settlement the states which have been declared confiscated on this side of the Sutlej, when it is hoped that the advantages of the British rule may, by light assessment and judicious arrangements, be made apparent to them.

I have now to conclude this despatch, by expressing my deep concern for the loss, in the action of the 21st inst., of that most invaluable officer, Major Broadfoot, my Political Agent for these states. He was wounded, and thrown off his horse, at my side, but I failed in prevailing on him to retire. He remounted his horse, and, shortly afterwards, received a mortal wound in leading on the troops against the battery in our front. I entertained the highest opinion of his abilities. He was second to none in this accomplished service, in every qualification by which the political or military interests of the East India Company could be advanced, and I shall be most gratified if, at a season of more

THE BRITISH ARMY

as drawn up at the commencement of the

BATTLE of FEROZSHAH,

at 3½ P.M on the 21st December, 1845.

Fought under the personal command of H.E. Gen.l Sir Hugh Gough Bt G.C.B. Commander in Chief.

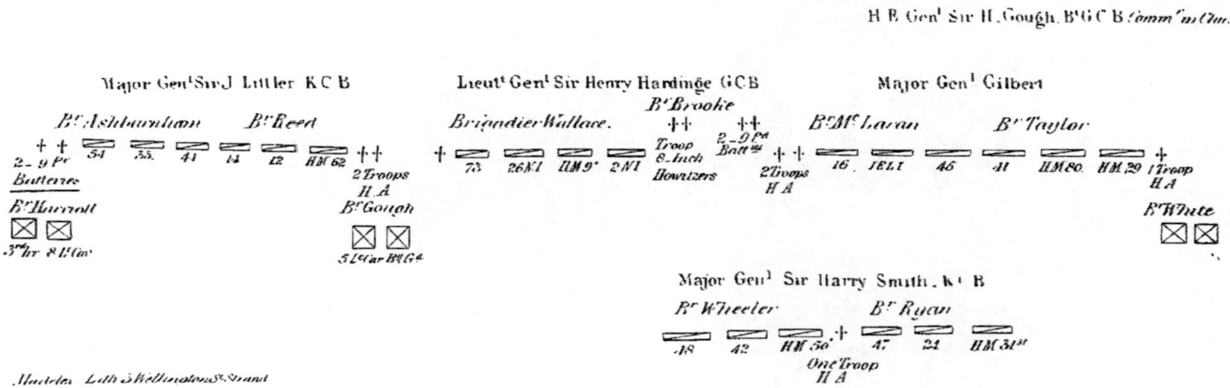

Madeley Lith 3 Wellington St. Strand

leisure, some special mark of honour can be conferred, by which his great merits and glorious death may be perpetuated.

Major George Broadfoot was the last of three brothers, who held appointments in the Company's army, and all these have fallen in battle in the service of their country.

Captain Nicolson, Assistant Political Agent from Ferozepore, was also killed in the action of the 21st inst., and was a most able and gallant officer.

Captain Abbott and Lieutenant Lake, assistants under Major Broadfoot, were wounded, and have ever since continued their exertions.

Captain Mills, Assistant Political Agent at Loodiana, took the command of a troop of horse artillery during the action, and has subsequently been of the greatest use by his intelligence and activity.

I owe great obligations to the Chief Secretary to the Government of India, Frederick Currie, Esq., who has, during all these various, and sometimes conflicting, duties, in which I have been engaged, given me his sound advice and active aid, sometimes accompanying me in the field, and at all times evincing the coolest judgment, and exhibiting the resources of his experience to the great advantage of the Company's service.

Mr. Cust, of the civil service, confidential assistant to Major Broadfoot, both in the field and in his own immediate department, has shown great intelligence in duties which were new to him, and I notice him as a most promising officer.

PROCLAMATION.

Camp, Lushkuree Khan-ke-Serai,
December 13, 1845.

" The British Government has ever been on terms of friendship with that of the Punjaub.

" In the year 1809, a treaty of amity and concord was concluded between the British Government and the late Maharajah Runjeet

Singh, the conditions of which have always been faithfully observed by the British Government, and were scrupulously fulfilled by the late Maharajah.

"The same friendly relations have been maintained with the successors of Runjeet Singh by the British Government up to the present time.

"Since the death of the late Maharajah Shere Singh, the disorganized state of the Lahore Government has made it incumbent on the Governor-General in Council to adopt precautionary measures for the protection of the British frontier; the nature of these measures, and the cause of their adoption, were at the time fully explained to the Lahore Durbar.

"Notwithstanding the disorganized state of the Lahore Government during the last two years, and many most unfriendly proceedings on the part of the Durbar, the Governor-General in Council has continued to evince his desire to maintain the relations of amity and concord which had so long existed between the two states, for the mutual interests and happiness of both. He has shown on every occasion the utmost forbearance, from consideration to the helpless state of the infant Maharajah Dhuleep Singh, whom the British Government had recognised as the successor to the late Maharajah Shere Singh.

"The Governor-General in Council sincerely desired to see a strong Sikh Government re-established in the Punjaub, able to control its army and to protect its subjects. He had not, up to the present moment, abandoned the hope of seeing that important objected effected by the patriotic efforts of the Sikhs and people of that country.

"The Sikh army recently marched from Lahore towards the British frontier, as it was alleged by the orders of the Durbar, for the purpose of invading the British territory.

"The Governor-General's agent, by direction of the Governor-General, demanded an explanation of this movement, and no reply being returned within a reasonable time, the demand was repeated. The Governor-General, unwilling to believe in the hostile intentions of the Sikh Government, to which no provocation had been given, refrained from taking any measures which might have a tendency to embarrass the Government of the Maharajah, or to induce collision between the two states.

"When no reply was given to the repeated demand for explanation, and while active military preparations were continued at Lahore, the Governor-General considered it necessary to order the advance of troops towards the frontier, to reinforce the frontier posts.

"The Sikh army has now, without a shadow of provocation, invaded the British territories.

"The Governor-General must, therefore, take measures for effectually protecting the British provinces, for vindicating the authority of the British Government, and for punishing the violators of treaties and the disturbers of public peace.

"The Governor-General hereby declares the possessions of Maharajah Dhuleep Singh, on the left or British banks of the Sutlej, confiscated and annexed to the British territories.

"The Governor-General will respect the existing rights of all ajgheerdars, zamindars, and tenants in the said possessions, who, by the course they now pursue, evince their fidelity to the British Government.

"The Governor-General hereby calls upon all the chiefs and sirdars in the protected territories to co-operate cordially with the British Government for the punishment of the common enemy, and for the maintenance of order in these states. Those of the chiefs who show alacrity and fidelity in the discharge of this duty, which they owe to the protecting power, will find their interests promoted thereby; and those who take a contrary course will be treated as enemies to the British Government, and will be punished accordingly.

"The inhabitants of all the territories on the left bank of the Sutlej are hereby directed to abide peaceably in their respective villages, where they will receive efficient protection by the British Government. All parties of men found in armed bands, who can give no satisfactory account of their proceedings, will be treated as disturbers of the public peace.

"All subjects of the British Government, and those who possess estates on both sides of the river Sutlej, who by their faithful adherence to the British Government may be liable to sustain loss, shall be indemnified and secured in all their just rights and privileges.

"On the other hand, all subjects of the British Government who shall continue in the service of the Lahore state, and who disobey this proclamation by not immediately returning to their allegiance, will be liable to have their property on this side the Sutlej confiscated, and declared to be aliens and enemies of the British Government.

"By order of the Right Hon. the Governor-General of India,

"F. CURRIE,

"*Secretary to the Government of India,*

"*with the Governor-General.*"

MOODKEE.

From General Sir Hugh Gough, Bart., G.C.B., the Commander-in-Chief of the Army in India, to the Governor-General of India.

Head Quarters, Army of the Sutlej, Camp Moodkee,
December 19th, 1845.

RIGHT HONOURABLE SIR,

It would be a superfluous form in me to address to you a narrative of the campaign which has opened against the Sikhs, and the successful action of yesterday, since you have in person shared the dangers and fatigues of our army, and witnessed its efforts and privations, but that my position at its head renders this my duty; and it is necessary, from that position, I should place these events on record, for the information of all Europe as well as of all India.

You, Sir, know, but others have to be told, that the sudden and unprovoked aggression of the Sikhs, by crossing the Sutlej with the great proportion of their army, with the avowed intention of attacking Ferozepore in time of profound peace, rendered indispensable, on our side, a series of difficult combinations for the protection of our frontier station, so unjustifiably and so unexpectedly menaced.

From the advanced and salient situation of Ferozepore, and its vicinity to the Sikh capital, its defence against a sudden attack became a difficult operation. It was always possible for the Sikh Government to throw a formidable force upon it before one sufficiently numerous could on our side be collected to support it: but when, upon the 11th instant, it became known at Umballa, where I had established my head-quarters, that this invasion had actually taken place, the efforts to repel it followed each other in rapid succession*; notwithstanding, I had the fullest confidence in Major-General Sir John Littler, commanding at Ferozepore, and in the devotedness and gallantry of the troops occupying it.

The troops from the different stations in the Sirhind division were directed to move by forced marches upon Busseean, where, by a most judicious arrangement, you had directed supplies to be collected within a wonderfully short space of time.

The main portion of the force at Loodiana was withdrawn, and a garrison thrown into the little fortress there. From this central position, already alluded to, both Loodiana and Ferozepore could be supported, and the safety of both places might be considered to be brought, in same measure, within the scope of the contingencies of a general action to be fought for their relief. All this is soon related; but most harassing have been the marches of the troops in completing this concentration. When their march had been further prolonged to this place, they had moved over a distance of upwards of 150 miles in six days, along roads of heavy sand; their perpetual labour allowing them scarcely time to cook their food, even when they received it, and hardly an hour for repose, before they were called upon for renewed exertions.

* Sic in orig.

When our leading corps reached Wudnee, a small jaghire of the late Maharajah Shere Singh, its garrison shut the gates of the fort against them; and, as our battering guns were far in the rear, it was determined to reserve it for future chastisement, and we remained content with compelling the village to furnish supplies (it could, however, provide little, except for our overworked cattle), under pain of enduring a cannonade and assault; this it did without the necessity of firing a shot.

When we reached Wudnee, it was evident that the force before Ferozepore felt the influence of our movements, as we heard that a very large portion of that force had been detached to oppose our further advance; their feeling parties retired on the morning of the 18th before our cavalry picquets, near the village and fort of Moodkee.

Soon after mid-day, the division under Major-General Sir Harry Smith, a brigade of that under Major-General Sir John M'Caskill, and another of that under Major-General Gilbert, with five troops of horse artillery, and two light field batteries, under Lieut.-Col. Brooke, of the horse artillery (Brigadier in command of the artillery force), and the cavalry division, consisting of Her Majesty's 3rd Light Dragoons, the body guard, 4th and 5th Light Cavalry, and 9th Irregular Cavalry, took up their encamping ground in front of Moodkee.

The troops were in a state of great exhaustion, principally from the want of water, which was not procurable on the road; when, about three P.M. information was received that the Sikh army was advancing; and the troops had scarcely time to get under arms, and move to their positions, when the fact was ascertained.

I immediately pushed forward the horse artillery and cavalry, directing the infantry, accompanied by the field batteries, to move forward in support. We had not proceeded beyond two miles, when we found the enemy in position. They were said to consist of from fifteen to twenty thousand infantry, about the same force of cavalry, and forty guns. They evidently had either just taken up this position, or were advancing in order of battle against us.

To resist their attack, and to cover the formation of the infantry, I advanced the cavalry under Brigadiers White, Gough, and Mactier, rapidly to the front, in columns of squadrons, and occupied the plain. They were speedily followed by the five troops of horse artillery, under Brigadier Brooke, who took up a forward position, having the cavalry then on his flanks.

The country is a dead flat, covered at short intervals with a low, but, in some places, thick jhow jungle, and dotted with sandy hillocks. The enemy screened their infantry and artillery behind this jungle, and such undulations as the ground afforded; and, whilst our twelve battalions formed from échellon of brigades into line, opened a very severe cannonade upon our advancing troops, which was vigorously replied to by the battery of horse artillery under Brigadier Brooke, which was soon joined by the two field batteries. The rapid and well-directed fire of our artillery appeared soon to paralyze that of the enemy; and, as it was necessary to complete our infantry dispositions without advancing the artillery too near to the jungle, I directed the cavalry under Brigadiers White and Gough to make a flank movement on the enemy's left, with a view of threatening and turning that flank, if possible. With praiseworthy gallantry, the 3rd Light Dragoons, with the 2nd brigade of cavalry, consisting of the body guard and 5th Light Cavalry, with a portion of the 4th Lancers, turned the left of the Sikh army, and, sweeping along the whole rear of its infantry and guns, silenced for a time the latter, and put their numerous cavalry to flight. Whilst this movement was taking place on the enemy's left, I directed the remainder of the 4th Lancers, the 9th Irregular Cavalry, under Brigadier Mactier, with a light field battery, to threaten their right. This manœuvre was also successful. Had not the infantry and guns of the enemy been screened by the jungle, these brilliant charges of the cavalry would have been productive of greater effect.

When the infantry advanced to the attack, Brigadier Brooke rapidly pushed on his horse artillery close to the jungle, and the cannonade was resumed on both sides. The infantry under Major-

Generals Sir Harry Smith, Gilbert, and Sir John M'Caskill, attacked in échellon of lines the enemy's infantry, almost invisible amongst wood and the approaching darkness of night. The opposition of the enemy was such as might have been expected from troops who had everything at stake, and who had long vaunted of being irresistible. Their ample and extended line, from their great superiority of numbers, far outflanked ours; but this was counteracted by the flank movements of our cavalry. The attack of the infantry now commenced; and the roll of fire from this powerful arm soon convinced the Sikh army, that they had met with a foe they little expected; and their whole force was driven from position after position with great slaughter, and the loss of seventeen pieces of artillery, some of them of heavy calibre; our infantry using that never-failing weapon, the bayonet, whenever they stood. Night only saved them from worse disaster, for this stout conflict was maintained during an hour and a half of dim starlight, amidst a cloud of dust from the sandy plain, which yet more obscured every object.

I regret to say, this gallant and successful attack was attended with considerable loss; the force bivouacked upon the field for some hours, and only returned to its encampment after ascertaining that it had no enemy before it, and that night prevented the possibility of a regular advance in pursuit.

I beg to congratulate you, Right Honourable Sir, on this first defeat of our invaders by the army I have the honour to command. The perseverance by which success was attained you personally witnessed; and the troops I am sure felt proud of the self-devotion with which their Governor-General exposed himself to every danger amongst them. I before said that our loss has been severe; it could not be esteemed small if we had no other to record, when I mention that, towards the conclusion of the affair, Major-General Sir Robert Sale, to whom India and England are so much indebted, had his left thigh shattered by a grape shot, and that the wound has since proved mortal. Sir John M'Caskill, an old and valued officer, who has done his country much good service, received a ball through his chest, on the advance of his division, and immediately expired. Brigadiers Bolton and Mactier, and Lieut.-Colonels Bunbury and Byrne, and other valuable officers, are amongst the wounded. These losses our country and the service will deplore, but not consider unavailing, when Ferozepore shall be rescued from the invader, and the insult to our territory and rule fitly punished.

I have every reason to be proud of, and gratified with, the exertions of the whole of the officers and troops of this army on this arduous occasion; with the conduct and dispositions of the generals of divisions, the brigadiers of the several arms, the general, personal, divisional, and brigade staff, and the commanding officers of regiments; but this despatch is necessarily completed in the utmost haste, and in the midst of most important operations,—I must, therefore, reserve to a future opportunity the pleasing task of bringing especially and by name to the notice of Government the particular merits of individual officers.

I cannot, however, refrain from expressing my deep sense of obligation to the heads of the two principal departments,—Major-General Sir James Lumley was unfortunately prevented by severe sickness from taking part in the active duties of this great crisis,—Major Grant, Deputy Adjutant General, therefore, supplied his place, and it is my duty to say how ably this has been done, and how great a loss I have endured by being deprived for the present of his services, in consequence of two wounds which he received while urging on the infantry to the final and decisive attack of the enemy's batteries. Neither must I fail to record the valuable aid which has upon this, as on a former campaign, been afforded me by the Quarter-Master General, Lieutenant-Colonel Garden; his departmental arrangements demand my highest commendation. Major-General Sir Harry Smith having been appointed to the command of a division, the charge of his office as Adjutant-General of Her Majesty's forces devolved upon Lieutenant-Colonel Barr, who, not only in the performance of these duties, but in every way in which assistance can be rendered in active operations, has been to me a most valuable staff-officer.

I have to thank you, Right Honourable Sir, for having placed at my disposal the services of the officers of your staff, and to thank them for the valuable assistance they afforded me on this arduous day. It shall be my pleasing duty to mention them individually, with the officers of my own personal staff, in the recommendation list I shall have the honour of forwarding, at an early date, to Government.——I have, &c.

H. Gough, *General, Commander-in-Chief.*

Return of the Killed and Wounded of the Army of the Sutlej, under the command of His Excellency General Sir Hugh Gough, G.C.B. Commander-in-Chief, in the Action fought at Moodkee, on the 18*th of December*, 1845.

Camp, Sultan Khan Wallah, Dec. 26, 1845.

Personal Staff—2 officers killed ; 2 officers wounded.

General Staff—1 officer killed ; 1 officer wounded.

Artillery Division—2 officers, 4 sergeants, 13 rank and file, 5 syces and grasscutters, 3 syce drivers, 45 horses—killed ; 4 officers, 1 native officer, 2 sergeants, 22 syces and grasscutters, 11 lascars, 2 syce drivers, 7 syces, 25 horses—wounded.

Cavalry Division—3 officers, 6 sergeants or havildars, 1 trumpeter, 71 rank and file, 164 horses—killed ; 9 officers, 1 native officer, 6 sergeants or havildars, 1 trumpeter, 70 rank and file, 63 horses—wounded.

1*st Infantry Division*—4 officers, 1 native officer, 4 sergeants or havildars, 69 rank and file—killed ; 18 officers, 2 native officers, 20 sergeants or havildars, 299 rank and file, 4 horses—wounded.

2*nd Infantry Division*—1 native officer, 17 rank and file, 1 horse—killed ; 4 officers, 5 native officers, 10 sergeants or havildars, 81 rank and file—wounded.

3*rd Infantry Division*—1 officer, 1 sergeant or havildar, 6 rank and file—killed; 1 officer, 4 sergeants or havildars, 73 rank, and I lascar—wounded.—Total—13 officers, 2 native officers, 15 sergeants or havildars, 1 trumpeter, 176 rank and file, 5 syces and grasscutters, 3 syce drivers, 210 horses—killed; 39 officers, 9 native officers, 42 sergeants or havildars, 1 trumpeter, 545 rank and file, 12 lascars, 2 syce drivers, 7 syces, 92 horses—wounded.

European officers, 13; native officers, 2; non-commissioned officers, drummers, rank and file, 192; syces, &c. 8; killed.—Grand total, 215.

European officers, 39; native officers, 9; non-commissioned officers, drummers, rank and file, 588; syces, &c. 21; wounded.—Grand total, 657.

Grand total of all ranks, killed and wounded, 872.

List of Officers Killed and Wounded.

Head Quarters' Staff.—Major-General Sir R. H. Sale, G.C.B. Quarter-master-General Queen's troops, killed; Major W. R. Herries, A.D.C. to the Governor-General, killed; Capt. J. Munro, killed. Major P. Grant, Deputy Adjutant-General of the army, dangerously wounded; Captain G. E. Hillier, A.D.C. to the Governor-General severely wounded; Captain H. B. Edwardes, A.D.C. to the Commander-in-Chief, slightly wounded.

Artillery Division. — Captain Jasper Trower, killed; First Lieutenant R. Pollock, killed. Captain F. Dashwood, severely wounded, since dead; First Lieutenant C.V. Cox, slightly wounded; First Lieutenant C. A. Wheelright, wounded; First Lieutenant C. A. Bowie, slightly wounded.

Cavalry Division Staff. — Brigadier W. Mactier, severely; Brevet-Captain and Brigade-Major T. L. Harrington, severely; Volunteer Mr. A. Alexander, A.D.C. to Brigadier Gough, severely.

Her Majesty's 3rd Light Dragoons.—Brevet-Captain G. Newton, killed; Cornet E. Worley, killed. Lieutenant S. Fisher, severely wounded; Lieutenant E. G. Swinton, severely wounded; Lieutenant E. B. Cureton, severely wounded.

Governor-General's Body Guard. — Lieutenant W. Fisher,

killed. Brevet-Captain C. D. Dawkins, severely wounded; Lieutenant G. R. Taylor, very severely wounded.

5th Light Cavalry.—Major Alexander, slightly; Lieutenant R. Christie, slightly.

First Division of Infantry.—Divisional and Brigade Staff.—Captain Van Homrigh, 48th N. I. Acting A.D.C., killed. Brigadier S. Bolton, C.B., dangerously wounded; Brigadier H. M. Wheeler, C.B., severely wounded; Captain E. Lugard, Deputy-Assistant Adjutant-General, slightly wounded; Lieutenant Nicolls, Engineers, Acting A.D.C. severely wounded.

First Brigade.—Her Majesty's 31st Foot.—Lieutenant H. W. Hart, killed Lieutenant-Colonel J. Byrne, severely wounded; Captain W. Willes, dangerously wounded; Captain T. Bulkeley, dangerously wounded; Captain G. D. Young, dangerously wounded; Lieutenant J. L. R. Pollard, slightly wounded; Lieutenant J. Brenchley, mortally wounded, since dead; Assistant-Surgeon R. B. Gahan, 9th Foot, dangerously wounded.

47th Native Infantry.—Lieutenant J. F. Pogson, dangerously.

Second Brigade.—Her Majesty's 50th Foot.—Assistant-Surgeon A. Graydon, killed. Captain H. Needham, severely wounded; Lieutenant W. S. Carter, slightly wounded; Lieutenant J. C. Bishop, severely wounded; Lieutenant R. E. De Montmorency, severe contusion; Lieutenant C. E. Young, severely wounded.

42nd N. Light Infantry.—Lieutenant J. Spence, killed. Ensign E. Van H. Holt, slightly wounded.

Second Infantry Division.—Divisional and Brigade Staff.—Major R. Codrington, Assistant Quarter-Master-General, severely wounded.

Second N. Grenadiers.—Captain T. W. Bolton, severely wounded. Captain J. Gifford, severely wounded; Ensign A. D. Warden, severe contusion.

Third Infantry Division.—Divisional and Brigade Staff.—Major-General Sir J. M'Caskill, K.C.B. and K.H. killed.

Fifth Brigade.—Her Majesty's 9th Foot.—Ensign J. Hanham, slightly wounded.

Sixth Brigade.—Her Majesty's 80th Foot.—Lieutenant-Colonel T. Bunbury, slightly wounded.

P. GRANT, *Major, Deputy Adjutant-General of the Army.*

Return of Ordnance captured from the Sikh Army, at the Battle of Moodkee, on the 18th of December, 1845, by the Army of the Sutlej, under the Command of His Excellency Sir Hugh Gough, G.C.B., Commander-in-Chief.

			in.	tenths	
6	Guns	Brass	4	6	12-pounders.
1	Howitzer	do.	6	5	6½ „
4	Guns	do.	4	2	9 „
3	do.	do.	3	6	6 „
1	do.	do.	2	9	3 „

Remarks.—The number of guns captured, 15. It was impossible to compute the quantity of metal in these guns, but it was evident that they were much heavier than those of a similar calibre in the Bengal Artillery.

The carriages were all in good repair, with the exception of one or two struck by our shot. The whole were destroyed, and the guns left in the fort of Moodkee.

Four more guns reported to have been dismounted by the men of the horse artillery, and left on the field from want of means to bring them away. GEO. BROOKE, *Brigadier,*

Commanding Artillery, Army of the Sutlej.

FEROZESHAH.

From His Excellency the Commander-in-Chief to the Right Honourable the Governor-General of India.

Camp, Ferozeshah, December 22nd, 1845.

RIGHT HONOURABLE SIR,

I have again to congratulate you on the success of our arms. A grand battle has been fought against the Sikh army at this place, and by the blessing of Divine Providence victory has been won, by the valour of our troops, against odds and under circumstances which will render this action one of the most memorable in the page of Indian history.

After the combat of the 18th, at Moodkee, information was received, the following day, that the enemy, in increased numbers, were moving on to attack us. A line of defence was taken up in advance of our encampment, and dispositions made to repel assault, but the day wore away without their appearing, and at night we had the satisfaction of being reinforced by her Majesty's 29th Foot, and the East India Company's 1st European Light Infantry, with our small division of heavy guns.

I must here allude to a circumstance most favourable to our efforts in the field. On this evening, in addition to the valuable counsel with which you had in every emergency before favoured me, you were pleased yet further to strengthen my hands by kindly offering your services as second in command in my army. I need hardly say with how much pleasure the offer was accepted.

On the morning of the 21st the offensive was resumed: our columns of all arms debouched four miles on the road to Ferozeshah, where it was known that the enemy, posted in great force, and with a most formidable artillery, had remained since the action of the 18th, incessantly employed in entrenching his position. Instead of advancing to the direct attack of their formidable works, our force manœuvred to their right: the second and fourth divisions of infantry, in front, supported by the first division and cavalry in second line, continued to defile for some time out of cannon-shot between the Sikhs and Ferozepore. The desired effect was not long delayed, a cloud of dust was seen on our left, and, according to the instructions sent him on the preceding evening, Major-General Sir John Littler, with his division, availing himself of the offered opportunity, was discovered in full march to unite his force with mine. This junction was soon effected, and thus was accomplished one of the great objects of all our harassing marches and privations, in the relief of this division of our army from the blockade of numerous forces by which it was surrounded.

Dispositions were now made for an united attack on the

enemy's entrenched camp. We found it to be a parallelogram of about a mile in length, and half a mile in breadth, including within its area the strong village of Ferozeshah; the shorter sides looking towards the Sutlej and Moodkee, and the longer towards Ferozepore and the open country. We moved against the last-named face, the ground in front of which was, like the Sikh position in Moodkee, covered with low jungle.

The divisions of Major-General Sir John Littler, Brigadier Wallace (who had succeeded Major-General Sir John M'Caskill), and Major-General Gilbert, deployed into line, having in the centre our whole force of artillery, with the exception of three troops of horse artillery, one on either flank and one in support, to be moved as occasion required. Major-General Sir Harry Smith's division, and our small cavalry force, moved in second line, having a brigade in reserve to cover each wing.

I should here observe, that I committed the charge and direction of the left wing to Lieutenant-General Sir Henry Hardinge, while I personally conducted the right.

A very heavy cannonade was opened by the enemy, who had dispersed over their position upwards of one hundred guns, more than forty of which were of battering calibre; these kept up a heavy and well-directed fire, which the practice of our far less numerous artillery, of much lighter metal, checked in some degree, but could not silence; finally, in the face of a storm of shot and shell, our infantry advanced and carried these formidable entrenchments; they threw themselves upon the guns, and with matchless gallantry wrested them from the enemy; but, when the batteries were partially within our grasp, our soldiery had to face such a fire of musketry from the Sikh infantry, arrayed behind their guns, that, in spite of their most heroic efforts, a portion only of the entrenchment could be carried. Night fell while the conflict was everywhere raging.

Although I now brought up Major-General Sir Harry Smith's division, and he captured and long retained another point of the position, and Her Majesty's 3rd Light Dragoons charged and took some of the most formidable batteries, yet the enemy remained in possession of a considerable portion of the great quadrangle, whilst our troops, intermingled with theirs, kept possession of the remainder, and finally bivouacked upon it, exhausted by their gallant efforts, greatly reduced in numbers, and suffering extremely from thirst, yet animated by an indomitable spirit. In this state of things the long night wore away.

Near the middle of it, one of their heavy guns was advanced and played with deadly effect upon our troops. Lieutenant-General Sir Henry Hardinge immediately formed Her Majesty's 80th Foot and the 1st European Light Infantry. They were led to the attack by their commanding officers, and animated in their exertions by Lieutenant-Colonel Wood (Aide-de-Camp to the Lieutenant-General), who was wounded in the outset, the 80th captured the gun, and the enemy, dismayed by this counter-check, did not venture to press on further. During the whole night, however, they continued to harass our troops by fire of artillery, wherever moonlight discovered our position.

But, with daylight of the 22nd, came retribution. Our infantry formed line, supported on both flanks by horse artillery, whilst a fire was opened from our centre by such of our heavy guns as remained effective, aided by a flight of rockets. A masked battery played with great effect upon this point, dismounting our pieces, and blowing up our tumbrils. At this moment Lieutenant-General Sir Henry Hardinge placed himself at the head of the left, whilst I rode at the head of the right wing. Our line advanced, and, unchecked by the enemy's fire, drove them rapidly out of the village of Ferozeshah and their encampment; then, changing front to its left, on its centre, our force continued to sweep the camp, bearing down all opposition, and dislodged the enemy from their whole position. The line then halted, as if on a day of manœuvre, receiving its two leaders as they rode along its front with a gratifying cheer, and displaying the captured standards of the Khalsa army. We had taken upwards of seventy-three pieces of cannon, and were masters of the whole field.

The force assumed a position on the ground which it had won, but even here its labours were not to cease. In the course of two hours, Sirdar Tej Singh, who had commanded in the last great battle, brought up from the vicinity of Ferozepore fresh battalions and a large field of artillery, supported by thirty thousand Ghorepurras, hitherto encamped near the river. He drove in our cavalry parties, and made strenuous efforts to regain the position at Ferozeshah. This attempt was defeated; but its failure had scarcely become manifest, when the Sirdar renewed the contest with more troops and a large artillery. He commenced by a combination against our left flank; and, when this was frustrated, made such a demonstration against the captured village, as compelled us to change our whole front to the right. His guns, during this manœuvre, maintained an incessant fire, whilst, our artillery ammunition being completely expended in these protracted combats, we were unable to answer him with a single shot.

I now directed our almost exhausted cavalry to threaten both flanks at once, preparing the infantry to advance in support, which apparently caused him suddenly to cease his fire and to abandon the field.

For twenty-four hours not a Sikh has appeared in our front. The remains of the Khalsa army are said to be in full retreat across the Sutlej, at Nuggurputhur and Tilla, or marching up its left bank towards Hurrekeeputhur, in the greatest confusion and dismay. Of their chiefs, Bahudur Singh is killed; Lal Singh said to be wounded; Mehtab Singh, Adjoodhia Pershad, and Tej Singh, the late governor of Peshawur, have fled with precipitation. Their camp is the scene of the most awful carnage, and they have abandoned large stores of grain, camp equipage, and ammunition.

Thus has apparently terminated this unprovoked and criminal invasion of the peaceful provinces under British protection.

On the conclusion of such a narrative as I have given, it is surely superfluous in me to say, that I am, and shall be to the last moment of my existence, proud of the army which I had the honour to command on the 21st and 22nd instant. To their gallant exertions I owe the satisfaction of seeing such a victory achieved, and the glory of having my name associated with it.

The loss of this army has been heavy: how could a hope be formed that it should be otherwise. Within thirty hours this force stormed an entrenched camp, fought a general action, and sustained two considerable combats with the enemy. Within four days it has dislodged from their positions, on the left bank of the Sutlej, 60,000 Sikh soldiers, supported by upwards of 150 pieces of cannon, 108 of which the enemy acknowledged to have lost, and 91 of which are in our possession.

In addition to our losses in the battle, the captured camp was found to be everywhere protected by charged mines, by the successive spring of which many brave officers and men have been destroyed.

I must bear testimony to the valour displayed in these actions by the whole of the regiments of Her Majesty's service employed, and the East India Company's 1st European Light Infantry: the native force seconded in a most spirited manner their gallant conduct.

To Lieutenant-General Sir Henry Hardinge, my second in command, my warmest thanks are due, not only for his personal exertions, which were conspicuous to all, but for the able assistance he afforded me through all the eventful scenes of this well-fought action. To the general and my personal staff, I feel deeply indebted for their unceasing exertions. Major-Generals Sir Harry Smith, Gilbert, and Sir John Littler, and Brigadier Wallace (who nobly fell in the hour of victory), fully realized the high expectations I had formed of their conduct as leaders of divisions.

With the Brigadiers, the Commandant of Artillery, and the Chief Engineer, the Commanding Officer of regiments, and with the Departmental Staff, I was also greatly pleased; their exertions were most unremitting, and highly praiseworthy.

The reports I have received from the Generals of divisions of Infantry, the Brigadiers of Cavalry, and the Commandant of Artillery, speak in the highest terms of their respective staff;

and it is my intention, as soon as possible, to forward to you, Right Honourable Sir, a list containing the names of the officers I have just enumerated, together with the names of all those who appear to me especially to merit approbation and favour.

The hurried manner in which I am forced to collect information, and prepare these numerous details, may, I fear, cause the omission of the names of some officers well deserving of notice; but I shall not fail to send in a supplementary list when I can assure myself of their individual merits, as it would be most painful to me to feel that I had not done justice to any one of the brave men who shared with me the glories and dangers of this arduous conflict.

I beg now to mention the conduct of an illustrious nobleman, Count Ravensburg*, who, with the officers of his suite, Counts Greuben and Oriola, did us the honour to accompany the force during our operations. They were present at Moodkee, and in this great battle. It is with the greatest pleasure and sincerity I can bear my testimony to their gallant conduct on these occasions, worthy of the high reputation in arms of their countrymen, and of the great ancestor of one of them. I lament to add, that Dr. Hoffmeister, the medical attendant on the Count, was killed in the action of the 21st instant.

I herewith enclose the report of Lieutenant-General the Right Honourable Sir Henry Hardinge, second in command.——I have the honour to be, &c.,

H. Gough, *General,*
Commander-in-Chief, East Indies.

* Count Ravensburg is the assumed name of Prince Waldemar of Prussia, the son of Prince William (the late King's brother), and therefore cousin to Frederick William IV., King of Prussia. The Prince is now in his twenty-ninth year, and is Colonel in the Dragoons of the Prussian Guards.

Return of Killed and Wounded of the Army of the Sutlej, under the command of His Excellency Sir Hugh Gough, Bart., G.C.B., Commander-in-Chief, in the Actions fought near Ferozeshah, on the 21st and 22nd of December, 1845.

Camp, Sultan Khan Walla, December 27, 1845.

Staff.—1 European officer killed; 3 European officers wounded.

Artillery Division.—2 European officers, 2 native officers, 1 sergeant, 26 rank and file, 4 lascars, 4 syce drivers, 2 syce grass-cutters, 118 regimental horses—killed; 4 European officers, 2 warrant officers, 10 sergeants, 61 rank and file, 7 lascars, 2 syce drivers, 2 syce grasscutters, 75 regimental horses—wounded.

Cavalry.—3 European officers, 2 native officers, 4 havildars, 1 trumpeter, 78 rank and file, 9 officers' chargers, 163 regimental horses—killed; 9 European officers, 2 native officers, 1 warrant officer, 9 havildars, 133 rank and file, 2 officers' chargers, 112 regimental horses—wounded.

1*st Infantry.*—4 European officers, 6 native officers, 5 sergeants, or havildars, 1 drummer, 119 rank and file, 9 officers' chargers—killed; 19 European officers, 21 sergeants or havildars, 8 drummers, 399 rank and file, 2 officers' chargers—wounded.

2*nd Infantry.*—8 European officers, 3 native officers, 6 sergeants or havildars, 150 rank and file, 6 officers' chargers—killed; 13 European officers, 9 native officers, 26 sergeants or havildars, 8 drummers, 365 rank and file, 2 officers' chargers—wounded.

3*rd Infantry.*—11 European officers, 1 native officer, 2 sergeants or havildars, 2 drummers, 111 rank and file, 2 officers' chargers—killed; 9 European officers, 2 native officers, 13 sergeants or havildars, 2 drummers, 315 rank and file, 1 lascar—wounded.

4*th Infantry.*—8 European officers, 3 native officers, 9 sergeants or havildars, 115 rank and file, 7 officers' chargers—killed; 21 European officers, 5 native officers, 20 sergeants or havildars, 5 drummers, 323 rank and file—wounded.

Grand total.—37 European officers, 17 native officers, 27 sergeants or havildars, 4 trumpeters or drummers, 599 rank and file,

4 lascars, 4 syce drivers, 2 syce grasscutters, 33 officers' chargers, 281 regimental horses—killed; 78 European officers, 18 native officers, 3 warrant officers, 99 sergeants or havildars, 23 trumpeters or drummers, 1,496 rank and file, 8 lascars, 2 syce drivers, 2 syce grasscutters, 6 officers' chargers, 187 regimental horses, wounded.

Names of Officers Killed and Wounded.

Personal Staff.—Lieutenant-Colonel R. B. Wood, Aide-de-Camp to the Right Honourable the Governor-General, severely wounded; Lieutenant F. P. Haines, Aide-de-Camp to his Excellency the Commander-in-Chief, severely ditto.

General Staff.—Major A. W. Fitzroy Somerset, Military Secretary to the Right Hon. the Governor-General, mortally ditto, since dead; Brevet-Captain W. Hore, Officiating Deputy Secretary to the Government, killed.

Artillery Division, Divisional Staff.—Captain W. K. Warner, Commissary of Ordnance, slightly wounded.

Brigade Staff.—Captain M. Mackenzie, Major of Brigade, slightly wounded.

2nd Troop, 1st Brigade, Horse Artillery.—Captain E. D. A. Todd, killed.

1st Troop, 3rd Brigade, Horse Artillery.—1st Lieutenant R. M. Paton, slightly wounded.

3rd Troop, 3rd Brigade, Horse Artillery.—1st Lieutenant P. C. Lambert, killed.

3rd Company, 4th Battalion.—1st Lieutenant E. Atlay, slightly wounded.

Cavalry Division.

Divisional Staff.—Lieutenant-Colonel D. Harriott, Commandant, slightly wounded; Captain C. F. Havelock, H.M. 9th Foot, D. A. Quarter-Master-General, wounded.

Brigade Staff.—Lieutenant-Colonel M. White, C.B., commanding 1st Brigade, slightly wounded.

H.M. 3rd Light Dragoons.—Brevet-Captain J. E. Codd, killed; Cornet H. Ellis, ditto; Cornet G. W. K. Bruce, H.M. 16th, ditto. Major C. W. M. Balders, slightly wounded; Lieutenant H. C. Morgan, severely wounded; Lieutenant J. G. A. Burton, slightly wounded; Cornet W. H. Orme, severely wounded; Cornet Lieutenant J. D. White, slightly wounded; Cornet J. Rathwell, ditto.

1st Division of Infantry.

Divisional Staff.—Captain E. Lugard, D. A. A. G., wounded; Lieutenant A. J. Galloway, D. A. Q. M. G., ditto; Lieutenant E. A. Holditch, A. D. C., ditto.

H.M. 31st Foot.—Lieutenant J. L. R. Pollard, killed; Lieutenant and Adjutant W. Bernard, ditto. Major G. Baldwin, severely wounded; Lieutenant T. H. Plaskett, severely wounded; Lieutenant A. Pilkington, ditto; Ensign J. Paul, slightly wounded; Ensign H. P. Hutton, ditto.

H.M. 50th Foot.—Captain W. Knowles, wounded; Lieutenant C. A. Mouat, ditto; Lieutenant E. J. Chambers, ditto; Lieutenant R. M. Barnes, ditto; Ensign A. White, ditto; Lieutenant and Adjutant E. C. Mullen, ditto.

24th Regiment N.I.—Brevet-Major J. Griffin, killed; Ensign E. A. Grubb, wounded.

42nd Light Infantry.—Lieutenant J. G. Wollen, killed; Lieutenant Adjutant C. W. Ford, wounded; Ensign J. Wardlaw, ditto.

48th Regiment N. I.—Lieutenant E. W. Litchford, slightly wounded; Lieutenant R. C. Taylor, ditto.

2nd Division of Infantry.

Brigade Staff.—Lieutenant-Colonel C. C. Taylor, Brigadier, wounded; Captain J. O. Lucas, Major of Brigade, killed; Captain J. H. Burnet, 16th N. I., ditto.

H.M. 29th Foot.—Captain G. Molle, killed; Lieutenant A. A. Simmons, ditto; Major G. Congreve, wounded; Captain A. St. G. H. Stepney, ditto.

1st European Light Infantry.—Captain T. Box, killed; Ensign P. Moxon, ditto. Captain C. Clark, severely wounded; Captain B. Kendall, dangerously ditto; Lieutenant C. T. Beatson, 14th N. I. Officiating Interpreter, severely ditto; Lieutenant R. W. H. Fanshawe, slightly ditto; Ensign F. O. Salusbury, severely ditto; Ensign C. R. Wreford, slightly ditto.

2nd Regiment N.I., Grenadiers.—Ensign G. A. Armstrong, killed. Captain T. W. Bolton, severely wounded; Ensign W. S. R. Hodsons, lightly ditto.

16th Regiment N.I., Grenadiers.—Major L. N. Hull, killed; Ensign J. J. O'Bryen, slightly wounded.

45th Regiment N.I.—Lieutenant C. V. Hamilton, wounded.

3rd Division of Infantry.

Brigade Staff.—Lieutenant-Colonel N. Wallace, Brigadier, killed.

H.M. 9th Foot.—Lieutenant-Colonel A. B. Taylor, killed; Captain J. Dunne, ditto; Captain J. F. Field, ditto. Captain A. Barton, severely wounded: Lieutenant A. Taylor, severely wounded; Lieutenant J. U. Vigors, slightly wounded; Lieutenant F. Sievwright, dangerously wounded; Lieutenant W. G. Cassidy, dangerously wounded; Ensign W. H. Forster, contused.

H.M. 80th Foot.—Captain A. D. W. Best, killed; Captain R. Scheberras, ditto; Lieutenant R. B. Warren, ditto; Lieutenant G. C. G. Bythesea, ditto. Major R. A. Lockhart, wounded; Brevet-Captain S. Fraser, since dead; Lieutenant M. D. Freeman, wounded.

26th Light Infantry, N.I.—Lieutenant G. A. Croly, killed; Lieutenant A. C. Eatwell, ditto.

73rd Regiment, N.I.—Captain R. M. Hunter, killed.

4th Division of Infantry.

Divisional Staff.—Lieutenant Harvey, Aide-de-Camp, killed; Captain J. F. Egerton, D.A.Q.M.G., wounded.

Brigade Staff.—Captain C. F. J. Burnet, Major of Brigade, slightly wounded; Lieutenant-Colonel T. Reed, slightly ditto.

H.M. 62*nd Foot.*—Captain G. H. Clarke, killed; Captain H. Wells, ditto; Lieutenant T. K. Scott, ditto; Lieutenant W. M'Nair, ditto; Lieutenant R. Gubbins, ditto; Lieutenant M. Kelly, ditto; Lieutenant and Adjutant G. Sims, ditto. Major W. T. Shortt, slightly wounded; Captain S. W. Graves, badly ditto; Captain C. W. Sibley, ditto; Captain D. G. A. Darroch, slightly ditto; Lieutenant M. J. Gregorson, badly ditto; Lieutenant W. L. Ingall, slightly ditto; Lieutenant A. S. Craig, severely ditto; Ensign C. Roberts, ditto; Ensign J. M. M. Hewett, slightly ditto.

12*th Regiment Native Infantry.*—Lieutenant-Colonel L. Bruce, very severely wounded; Captain W. B. Holmes, severely ditto; Lieutenant C. B. Tulloch, very severely ditto; Ensign J. H. C. Ewart, slightly ditto.

14*th Regiment Native Infantry.*—Captain W. Struthers, slightly wounded; Brevet-Captain C. G. Walsh, ditto; Lieutenant A. O. Wood, severely ditto; Lieutenant I. H. H. Lukin, slightly ditto; Ensign G. Weld, severely ditto.

P. GRANT, *Major*,
Deputy Adjutant-General of the Army.

Killed.—European officers, 37; native ditto, 17; non-commissioned, drummers, rank and file, 630: syces, drivers, &c. 10; total, 694.

Wounded.—European officers, 78; native ditto, 18; non-commissioned, drummers, rank and file, 1610; syces, drivers, &c. 12; warrant officers, 3; total, 1,721.

Grand total of all ranks, killed and wounded, 2,415.

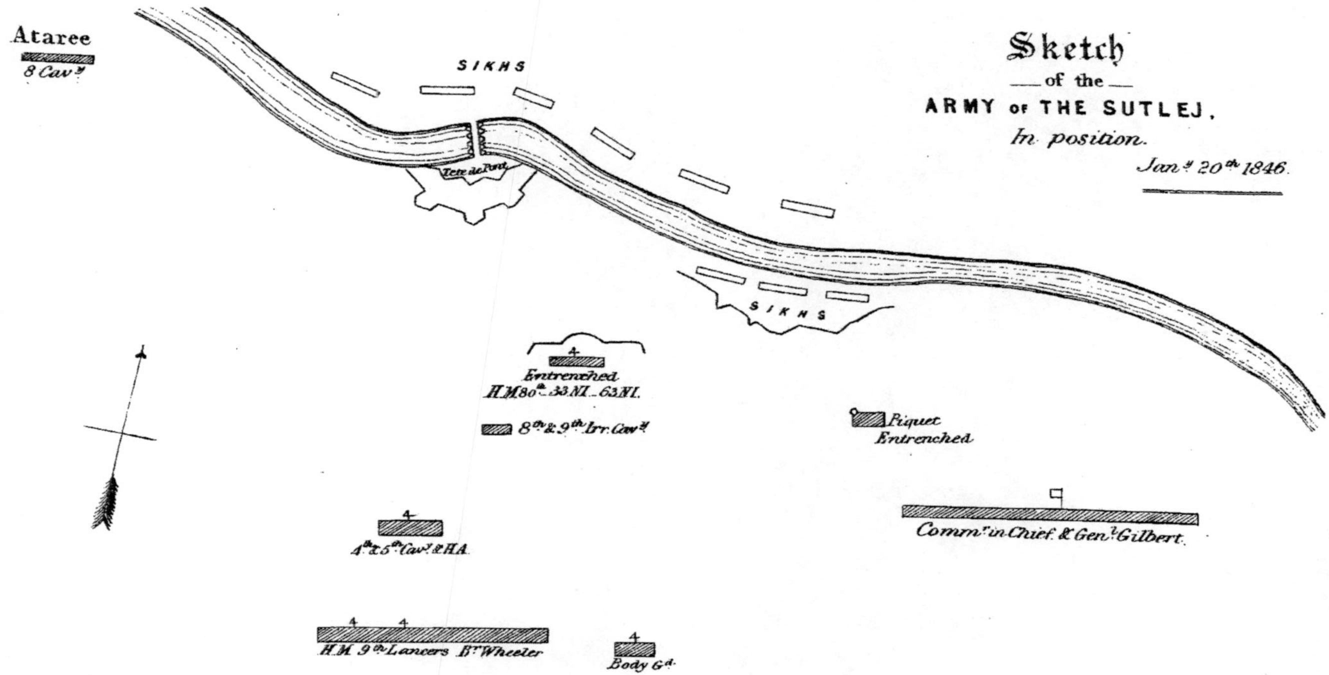
Sketch
of the
ARMY of THE SUTLEJ,
In position.
Jany. 20th 1846.
Ataree
8 Cavy.
SIKHS
Tete de Pont
SIKHS
4
Entrenched
H.M. 80th. 33 N.I. 63 N.I.
8th & 9th Irr. Cavy.
Piquet
Entrenched
4
4th & 5th Cavy. & H.A.
Commr. in Chief & Genl. Gilbert.
4
4
H.M. 9th Lancers Br. Wheeler
4
Body Gd.

Return of Ordnance captured during the Action of the 21st and 22nd instant.

Camp, Ferozeshah, 27th December, 1845.

			No.
Howitzer	.	42-pounder	1
ditto	brass	24-pounder	1
ditto	ditto	9-pounder	1
Guns	ditto	18-pounder	5
ditto	ditto	12-pounder	1
ditto	ditto	9-pounder	10
ditto	ditto	8-pounder	4
ditto	ditto	7-pounder	1
ditto	ditto	6-pounder	1
ditto	ditto	32-pounder	1
ditto	ditto	24-pounder	1
ditto	ditto	18-pounder	2
ditto	ditto	15-pounder	1

			No.
Guns	brass	12-pounder	3
ditto	ditto	11-pounder	1
ditto	ditto	10-pounder	4
ditto	ditto	9-pounder	8
ditto	ditto	8-pounder	9
ditto	ditto	7-pounder	2
ditto	ditto	6-pounder	1
ditto	ditto	3-pounder	6
ditto	iron	3-pounder	1
ditto	ditto	6-pounder	5
Mortar	brass	10-inch shell	1
ditto	ditto	24-pounder	1

Many of these guns have long Persian inscriptions on them, and very old dates; some are highly ornamented, carriages in good repair, and closely assimilating to those in use with the Bengal Artillery, the whole well fitted for post guns; the metal in these guns is much heavier than those of a similar calibre in use with the Bengal Artillery.

Two more guns were discovered at Sooltan-Khan Walla, of which no return has yet been received.

W. K. WARNER, *Lieutenant and Brevet-Captain,*
Commissary of Ordnance.

M. MC KENZIE, *Brevet-Captain, Brigade-Major Artillery,*
Army of the Sutlej.

GEO. G. DENNISS, *Brigadier of Foot Artillery,*
Army of the Sutlej.

GEORGE BROOKE, *Brigadier commanding Artillery,*
Army of the Sutlej.

From Lieutenant-General Sir Henry Hardinge, G.C.B., to His Excellency General Sir Hugh Gough, Bart., G.C.B., Commander-in-Chief of India.

Camp, Ferozepore, December 22, 1845.

SIR,

I have the honour to report to your Excellency that, when the army under your command had formed its junction with the forces fromFerozepore, under Major-General Sir John Littler, and was drawn up in order of battle, on the 21st inst., I proceeded with the two left brigades, commanded by Colonels Wallace and McLaren, to attack the enemy's entrenched position at Ferozeshah.

2.—The line advanced with great steadiness, notwithstanding the nature of the ground, intersected with jungle. When the troops had cleared these impediments, and had opened out into the plain, they continued to press on, without a check, under a very heavy fire of grape and musketry from the enemy's batteries, and having borne down all opposition, entered the enemy's camp, and captured the guns in their front.

3.—This portion of the camp was soon after on fire, compelling the troops to desist from their attack of the remainder, and as it was now dark, the troops formed on the ground, nearly on a line with the burning camp. From that period till the morning, these brave men were exposed to an incessant fire from the enemy's guns, the darkness of the night being illuminated by the explosion of mines, tumbrils, and shells.

4.—I need not dwell on the events of this night, so remarkable in military history, because your Excellency witnessed them, and with me admired the fortitude and resolution of these brave men, ready to encounter any danger, although harassed by fatigue, and suffering from thirst.

5.—I have personally reported to your Excellency my admiration of the conduct of H.M. 80th Regiment, and the 1st European Light Infantry, in obeying with alacrity the order I gave about midnight to stand to their arms and charge a battery, which bore

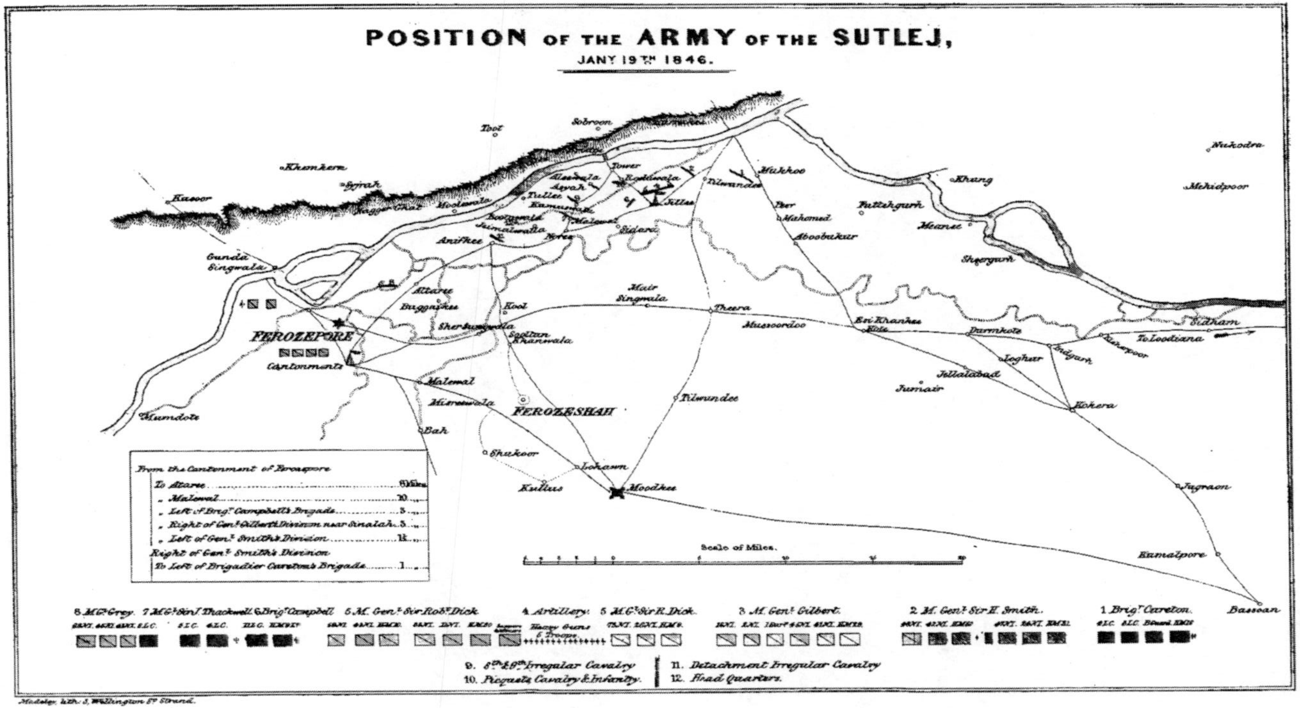

POSITION OF THE ARMY OF THE SUTLEJ,

JANY. 19TH 1846.

destructively on our ranks. Lieut.-Col. Bunbury, assisted by Lieut.-Col. Wood, my Aide-de-Camp, led the attack, on which occasion the latter officer was wounded. The guns were spiked, the enemy driven away with loss, and this part of our line left undisturbed for the remainder of the night. Their conduct in the preceding part of the action came more immediately under your Excellency's own observation.

6.—Your Excellency, having formed the troops before daylight, led the right of the attack, entrusting the left to me. The whole line instantly advanced, and, animated by your example, carried everything before them; and, having traversed the camp from one extremity to the other, drew up in a perfect line, expressing by loud cheers, as we rode up the line, their conscious pride that every man had done his duty.

7.—I again most cordially congratulate you on the brilliant success of the army under your Excellency's command.

8.—It is now my duty to report to your Excellency, that Major-General Gilbert, commanding a portion of this division of the army, gave me great satisfaction.

9.—Colonel Wallace fell bravely at the head of his troops.

10.—Colonel McLaren led his brigade with his accustomed judgment and resolution.

11.—My own personal Staff having been all disabled, with the exception of one most dear to me, and who still remained by my side, I derived, on the morning of the 22nd, the most valuable aid from Lieutenant-Colonel Birch, Judge-Advocate-General; from Lieutenant-Colonel Parsons; and from your Excellency's intelligent and brave Aide-de-Camp, Captain West. These Officers, riding several paces in front of the line, regulated the advance, animated the men, and prevented any unnecessary firing.

12.—I have great obligations, during the whole of these operations, to Colonel Benson, a Member of the Military Board, and acting as my Aide-de-Camp, who has constantly accompanied me in the field, and in whose cool judgment and experienced ability I place great reliance.

13.—My Aide-de-Camp, Lieutenant-Colonel Wood, has shown all the qualities which make a good officer.

14.—I beg to bring to your notice my Aide-de-Camp, Lieutenant Hillier, who is wounded; and Lieutenant Peel, of the 37th Native Infantry, Acting Aide-de-Camp, who is slightly wounded. Captain Becher, of the Quarter-Master-General's Department attached to my camp, also accompanied me, and I recommend him as a very promising officer.

15.—I also recommend the officers belonging to the Political Agency to these provinces, who acted as my Aides-de-Camp, Captain Abbott and Lieutenant Lake, and are both wounded. Captain Mills, Acting Aide-de-Camp, took the command of a troop of horse artillery, with his usual spirit.

16.—It is now with great pain that I have to record the irreparable loss I have sustained, and more especially the East India Company's Service, in the death of Major Broadfoot, of the Madras Army, my Political Agent. He was thrown from his horse by a shot, and I failed in prevailing upon him to leave the field. He remounted, and shortly afterwards received a mortal wound. He was as brave as he was able in every branch of the Political and Military Service.

17.—Major Somerset, my Military Secretary, much about the same time was shot through the body, conducting himself with the hereditary courage of his race. He was always foremost where difficulties required to be overcome. I deeply regret his loss.

18.—I have also lost a most promising and brave officer by the death of Captain Herries, on the night of the 18th, at Moodkee.

19.—Lieutenant Munro, of the 10th Light Cavalry, my Aide-de-Camp, a most amiable and excellent officer, I have also had the misfortune to lose, whilst placed at your Excellency's disposal, in the affair at Moodkee.

20.—Captain Hore, Assistant Military Secretary, and a valuable officer, acting as my Aide-de-Camp, was killed about the same time as Major Somerset received his wound.

21.—I have now to request your Excellency's notice to the conduct of an illustrious nobleman, Count Ravensburg, who, with the officers of his suite, Count Greuben and Count Oriola, accompanied me in the field. These Prussian officers nobly sustained the reputation of their countrymen.

22.—The Prince's surgeon was struck to the ground by a ball. I saw his Royal Highness instantly spring from his horse to his assistance. The Prince's humanity was unavailing,—death had already closed the surgeon's career.

23.—I am aware of the respectful regard which your Excellency entertains for this illustrious nobleman and his companions, travellers in the East; and I know that this brief record of their actions will be gratifying to your Excellency.

I have, &c.

H. Hardinge.

From Major-General Sir John Littler to the Adjutant-General of the Army.

Ferozepore, December 25, 1845.

Sir,

In pursuance of instructions received from the Right Honourable the Governor-General, under date the 20th instant, I moved out of my position at Ferozepore at eight A.M. on the 21st instant, with the corps as per margin*, leaving the defence of the cantonments to the 63rd Regiment Native Infantry, under the command of Lieutenant-Colonel Wilkinson, and that of the town to the 27th Regiment Native Infantry, under Lieutenant-Colonel Carnegy, together with detachments of sappers, and half a field battery in the town, and 2nd company (reserve) of artillery in the entrenchment.

I effected a junction with the troops under the personal com-

* 2 Troops Horse Artillery; 1½ Light Field Battery; 8th Light Cavalry; 3rd Irregular Cavalry; H. M. 62nd Foot, 1st brigade; 12th Native Infantry, 1st brigade; 14th ditto, 1st brigade; 33rd ditto, 2nd brigade; 44th ditto, 2nd brigade; 54th ditto, 2nd brigade; detachment of Sappers.

mand of his Excellency the Commander-in-Chief, and, agreeably to his instructions moved into position, or order of battle, on the same evening about four P.M. The first advance in line was very steady, and the approach to the enemy's works made under a most galling and destructive fire. The casualties in the ranks were awful. The troops, however, still moved on with great firmness and resolution, and approached the enemy's battery to within about 150 yards, when I considered the prize to be within their grasp.

Brigadier T. Reed gave the order to charge, supported by the left, or Brigadier the Honourable T. Ashburnham's, brigade. This charge was commenced with such determined gallantry and spirit that the result seemed certain. The enemy, however, having great confidence in their guns, continued to serve them with extraordinary activity, and to make such havoc in our ranks, as to cause an immediate panic and hesitation in Her Majesty's 62nd Foot, which of course had a similar effect on the native regiments on the flanks, notwithstanding all our exertions to induce them to advance by cheering and encouraging them, pointing at the same time to the short distance which they had to proceed, when the day would be their own. It was all in vain, and they retired out of gunshot, to where Her Majesty's 9th Foot and 26th Regiment Native Infantry were drawn up in reserve. A part of the 14th Regiment Native Infantry, with their colours, accompanied these two regiments, and entered the enemy's batteries.

At this period it was nearly dark, and, as I had heard that the divisions on the right had also been unable to obtain an entrance, I bivouacked for the night in the vicinity.

On the following morning, I obtained information of the right division having been directed to renew the attack, and I moved to co-operate, as might be necessary. I then received orders to wait until further instructions, and was moved up to the town, and directed to hold it. The result of this attack was most glorious to the British army, and I heartily congratulate his Excellency and the Governor-General on the happy termination of probably one of the most sanguinary engagements that ever took place in India.

With the conduct of the troops in general, under me, I was much gratified; their patience and perseverance in marching through the day, exposed to the sun and want of water, must have, no doubt, in some measure weakened their energies, but they notwithstanding evinced great firmness and resolution in advancing to the attack, until borne down by the furious and irresistible fire from all arms that man could be exposed to; the loss of many of their officers must have tended to relax their efforts and check their ardour, and under such circumstances only could the disappointment to Her Majesty's 62nd Regiment themselves, and to their country, have been for a moment conceived.

The native troops, under the numerous temptations to which they have been exposed for several months past by Sikh emissaries, have evinced their loyalty to the British Government in a most remarkable manner, not a single desertion having taken place, since the enemy crossed the Sutlej, that has come to my knowledge. They have maintained the character of the Bengal army in displaying courage and bravery under a heavy fire.

I have much pleasure in bringing to the favourable notice of his Excellency the Commander-in-Chief the services of those zealous and indefatigable officers, Brigadiers T. Reed, the Honourable T. Ashburnham, D. Harriott, commanding cavalry; and E. Huthwaite, commanding artillery; whose cool courage during the attack was conspicuous. To the several commanding officers of regiments and divisions, Lieutenant-Colonel Gairdner, commanding 14th Regiment Native Infantry; Lieutenant-Colonel Bruce, commanding 12th Regiment Native Infantry, who lost his arm in the action; Major Wake, commanding 44th Regiment Native Infantry; Major Shortt, commanding Her Majesty's 62nd Foot; Major Osborn, commanding 54th Regiment Native Infantry; and Captain Sandeman, commanding 33rd Regiment Native Infantry; I feel much indebted for the spirited and gallant manner in which they brought up their respective regiments during the advance.

It is with sincere regret that I have to report for his Excellency's information the death of my Aide-de-Camp, Lieutenant Harvey, of Her Majesty's 39th Foot, a very promising and intelligent young officer, and devoted to his profession. He was shot during the advance, in the act of cheering on the men, when within about 250 yards of the enemy's works. His death will be a loss to the public service, and deplored by his friends and relations.

Of Captain Egerton, my Assistant Quarter-Master-General, whose activity and zeal were conspicuous, I cannot speak too highly; he was severely wounded on the morning of the 22nd.

It is with much gratification that I also submit for his Excellency's consideration, and acknowledge the obligation to Major P. Innes, my Deputy Assistant Adjutant-General, and Captain Burnett, Major of the Brigade, for their indefatigable exertions throughout the affair, as well as for their able assistance on all occasions.

Lieutenant Goodwyn, of the Engineers, has proved himself a most zealous and indefatigable officer during the whole time that the Sikh army has been opposite Ferozepore, as well as on the evening of the 21st, during the engagement, and whom I beg to recommend to his Excellency's notice.

To Captain W. B. Thomson, Commissariat Department, who accompanied me, and to Lieutenant W. Fullerton, superintending the Sudder Bazaar, who volunteered his services as my Aide-de-Camp, and was particularly useful to me in the field, I feel indebted.

Captain Nicolson, late Assistant Governor-General's agent, and Colonel Van Courland, late of the Sikh service, who were placed at my disposal by the late Major Broadfoot, C.B., afforded me every assistance in their power during the engagement and previously, when the Sikhs first crossed the Sutlej.——I have, &c.

J. H. LITTLER, *Major-General,*
Commanding Infantry Division.

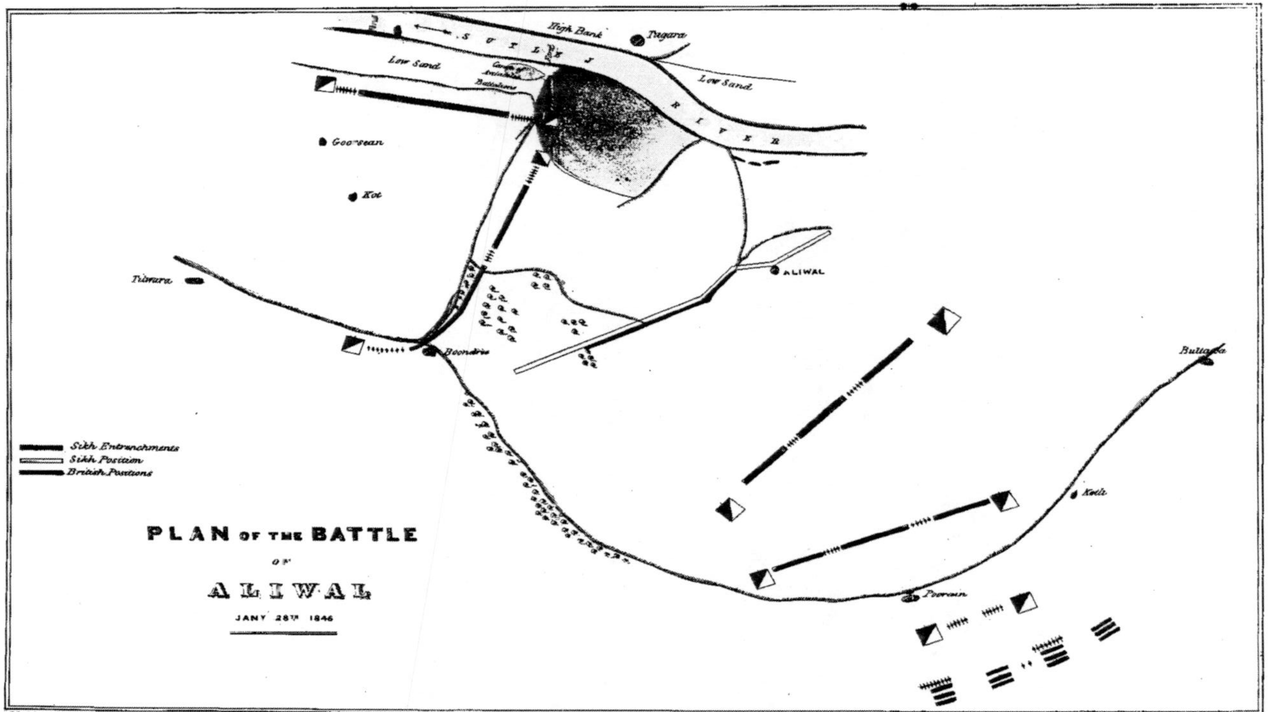

Madeley litho 3 Wellington St Strand

Despatch from Major-General Gilbert to the Commander-in-Chief, detailing the Operations of the Troops under his command at the Battle of Ferozeshah.

Camp, Sultan, December 24, 1845.

Under Br. C. Taylor, C.B.
3rd Brigade.
H. M.'s 29th Foot.
45th Regt. N.I.
H. M.'s 80th Foot.

Under Br. J. McLaren, C.B.
4th Brigade.
1st European L.I.
2nd Nat. Grenadiers.
16th Ditto.

SIR,—Agreeably to instructions just received, I have the honour to report, for the information of his Excellency the Commander-in-Chief, the operations of the 2nd infantry division in action with the enemy since that of the 18th instant at Moodkee.

My division, consisting of the troops as per margin, having been directed to lead the attack upon the enemy's entrenched camp at Ferozeshah, after steadily advancing under a heavy cannonade in échellon of regiments from the right covered by two light field batteries, commanded by Captain Horsford, came into action about four P.M., and succeeded in driving the enemy from that part of their position opposed to me, though I regret to say this was not effected without considerable loss, particularly in European officers.

In consequence of the night setting in, the fear of the troops firing on each other, and through confusion, consequent on part of the enemy's camp being on fire, not rendering it expedient that I should retain the position so gallantly won, I took up another, under instructions, about 400 yards from the camp, where I bivouacked for the night.

3rd Inf. Division.
H. M.'s 9th Foot.
26th Reg. N.I.
Two detachments of N.I.
H. M.'s 10th Foot.
H. M.'s 29th Foot.
1st European Lt. In.
16th Nat. Grenadiers.
2nd Ditto.
26th Nat. Lt. Inf.
H. M.'s 9th Foot.

Towards morning of the 22nd instant, the 3rd division, under Brigadier Wallace, consisting of the troops as per margin, having been placed under my command, in addition to my own (2nd division), I, at daybreak, under instruction from his Excellency the Commander-in-Chief, made my dispositions for again storming the enemy's entrenched post, which had been re-occupied during the night, and the troops, as per margin, advanced in line drawn up from the right, as follows:—

The front of the left of my division was led into action by his Excellency the Commander-in-Chief, and the right by the Right Honourable the Lieutenant-General, Sir H. Hardinge, and I myself leading Her Majesty's 80th Foot; and notwithstanding the advance was made under a tremendous fire of heavy guns, the enemy's entrenchment was retaken, battery after battery, at the bayonet's point; and although the troops under my immediate command required no stimulus to oppose the enemy, yet the presence of those two above-mentioned distinguished officers in the field of battle greatly animated them on this trying occasion.

The conduct of Her Majesty's 80th Regiment and the Hon. Company's 1st European Light Infantry, I cannot too highly speak of, as well as that of the 16th Grenadiers, and portions of the 2nd Grenadiers, 26th Light Infantry, and 45th Regiment Native Infantry.

It affords me great satisfaction to record the valuable services I received on this occasion and on the preceding evening from those distinguished officers, Brigadier C. Taylor, C.B., Brigadier J. McLaren, and Brigadier N. Wallace; the first-named officer, although wounded by a cannon shot in the evening, was again at the head of his brigade on the following morning; and the last-named officer (Brigadier Wallace) I regret to say was killed towards the end of the action; as well as from the general and personal staff, whose names are mentioned in the margin, particularly from the first-named officer (Captain Anson). Nor can I forbear to mention the gallant behaviour of Lieutenant and Adjutant Paton of the 14th Regiment Native Infantry, who commanded one of the detachments of native infantry on the right, which at one time hesitated to move forward, when that officer, seizing a colour,

Capt. F. W. Anson, A.A.G.
Lieut. T. S. Rawson, Offg. D. A. Q. M. G.
Capt. G. Carr, Dy. J. A. A. G.
Capt. R. Houghton, Aide-de-Camp.
Lieut. F. M. Gilbert, Offg. Extra. A.D.C.
Brevet-Capt. P. Gordon, Brig. Maj. 6th Brig.

advanced in front, and by this necessary example induced the men to regain their place in the line and move onwards.

In consequence of the death of Brigadier Wallace, commanding the 3rd division of infantry, I take leave to bring to the notice of his Excellency the Commander-in-Chief the valuable services of that zealous officer, Captain T. R. Pond, Deputy Assistant Adjutant-General of the 3rd division. A return of the killed and wounded of both actions will be forwarded as soon as possible.

I have the honour to be, &c. &c.

(Signed) W. R. Gilbert, *Major-General,*
Commanding Second Division Army of the Sutlej.

P.S.—The following of the General Staff had horses shot under them:—Major-General Gilbert, 1 killed and 1 wounded; Lieutenant T. R. Rawson, 1 killed; Captain Carr, 1 killed and 1 wounded.

Proclamation by the Governor-General of India.

Ferozepore, December 31, 1845.

The Lahore Government has, without provocation, or any declaration of hostilities, and notwithstanding the existence of a treaty of amity and alliance, made war upon the British Government. A large Sikh army has invaded the British territories, which has been repulsed and driven across the Sutlej, with the loss of 91 pieces of their artillery now in our possession. It becomes necessary, therefore, for the British Government to take measures for punishing this unprovoked aggression, and for preventing in future similar acts of treachery by the Government and army of the Punjaub. The British Government considers it right now to call upon all natives and inhabitants of Hindoostan who have taken service under the Lahore Government, to quit that service, and place themselves under the orders of the Governor-General of India. As long as relations of amity existed between the two states, there was no objection to the natives of the one territory taking service with the Government of the other; but now that the Lahore state has become the avowed enemy of the Government of Hindoostan, it is incumbent on all natives of Hindoostan, whose homes and families are under British protection, to quit the service of the common enemy, and join that of the Government of their own country. All persons of the above description are, therefore, hereby called upon to repair to the British side of the Sutlej, and to report themselves to the British authorities; their interests will, in all cases, be respected; they will, if fit for the military service, be taken into that of the British Government, with all the advantages of pay and allowances enjoyed by British soldiers.

All natives of Hindoostan who, after the promulgation of this Proclamation, continue in the service of the enemy will be considered to have forfeited all claim to British protection, and will be treated as traitors to their country, and enemies of the British Government.

By order of the Right Honourable the Governor-General of India,

F. CURRIE,

Secretary to the Government of India, with the Governor-General.

NOTIFICATION.

Ferozepore, Dec. 25, Christmas Day, 1845.

The Governor-General has the heartfelt satisfaction to announce to his Honour the President in Council, to the army, and to the people of India, the repulse of the Sikh forces in their attack on a portion of the British army near Moodkee, on the night of the 18th instant, and the capture, on the evening of the 21st and morning of the 22nd, of their entrenched camp, with seventy pieces of cannon, defended by 60,000 men, near the village of Ferozeshah. Upwards of ninety pieces of the enemy's artillery have been taken in these two operations.

These events, so glorious to the British arms, have been followed by the precipitate retreat of the enemy towards the Sutlej, his pride abated, and the unprovoked aggression on the British territory signally avenged.

The Governor-General cordially congratulates the Commander-in-Chief, General Sir Hugh Gough, Bart., G C.B., on the entire success of his Excellency's rapid and energetic operations, in which the troops, both British and native, have displayed under circumstances of long continued fatigue, since the 11th instant, their accustomed discipline and valour.

The Governor-General will rejoice in recording the gallant exploits of the army during this important campaign, by decorating the breasts of the victors with a medal, as soon as the report of these operations shall be received from the Commander-in-Chief.

Incessantly engaged in sharing with his brave troops their fatigues, and showing by his personal example at the head of his troops the value of enduring privations with patience, it has been impossible for his Excellency the Commander-in-Chief, in the midst of so many occupations, to furnish to the Governor-General a detailed report of these brilliant successes.

The Governor-General, however, cannot refrain from notifying to the Honourable the President in Council, to the army, and to the people of India, these results, so honourable to the British arms; and he directs that this Notification be carefully made known to all the troops by being read on their parades, and communicated to all the departments of the Government, civil and military, and that a salute of twenty-one guns be fired from this fort of Ferozepore, this day at one o'clock, and at every principal station of the army as soon as the notification shall be received.

These grateful and heartfelt acknowledgments to the army for its services cannot be closed without humbly remembering that our thanks are due to Him who is the only Giver of all victory, and without whose aid the battle is not to the strong.

The Governor-General therefore invites every British subject at this station to return thanks to Almighty God, this day at eleven o'clock, for the mercies He has so recently vouchsafed us, by assembling at the Governor-General's tent, where prayers and thanksgivings will be read by the Governor-General's chaplain.

By order of the Right Hon. the Governor-General of India,

F. CURRIE,

Secretary to the Government of India, with the Governor-General.

General Orders by the Right Hon. the Governor-General of India.

Camp, Ferozepore, December 30, 1845.

The Governor-General having received from the Commander-in-Chief in India the despatches, dates of which are noted in the margin*, directs that they be published for the information of the army and people of India.

The first despatch from his Excellency reports the operations of the army on the evening of the 18th inst., at Moodkee, where the enemy attempted to surprise the British camp, and were repulsed at all points with the loss of seventeen guns.

The second despatch reports the glorious successes obtained by the army under the immediate command of his Excellency, on the evening of the 21st, and the morning of the 22nd, at Ferozeshah, where the British army assaulted the entrenched camp of the Sikhs, defended by 108 pieces of cannon, some of heavy calibre, and, after driving the enemy from his position, captured seventy-four guns. Thus the enemy have been forced to relinquish to their victors on these occasions upwards of ninety pieces of artillery, with all the munitions of war in their camp.

All the objects which the Governor-General desired to effect have been accomplished by his Excellency the Commander-in-Chief. The British force posted at Ferozepore, thus suddenly and treacherously surrounded by the Sikh army, with a park of artillery, has been relieved; the brave garrison, under its able

* December 19th and 22nd.

commander Major-General Sir J. Littler, not only maintained a firm attitude of defence, but had the satisfaction, so grateful to brave soldiers, of skilfully forming a junction with the Umballa force, and gallantly taking part in the discomfiture of the enemy which had so recently invested them.

The Governor-General again cordially congratulates his Excellency General Sir Hugh Gough, G.C.B., on the great and important victories obtained by the army under his immediate command.

The Governor-General, in the name of the Government and of the people of India, gratefully acknowledges the noble services rendered to the public by his Excellency the Commander-in-Chief, by all the general and other officers, by the non-commissioned officers, and soldiers of the brave Indian army.

The Governor-General's thanks are due to all the infantry regiments of Her Majesty, and to the 1st European Light Infantry of the East India Company's service, all of which regiments distinguished themselves by the most devoted courage in braving the destructive fire of the enemy's batteries, and valiantly capturing their guns.

The Governor-General offers his thanks more especially to Her Majesty's 3rd Dragoons, who, on all these occasions, sought opportunities of useful conflict with the enemy, and fought with that superiority over their opponents, which skill and discipline impart to brave and determined men.

The European and native artillery maintained their accustomed character for steady unyielding courage, when exposed to a very heavy and galling fire.

The Governor-General's thanks are justly due to the brave infantry of the native army, whose valour so mainly contributed to these victories, and he cannot withhold his admiration for the patience and perseverance with which they endured privations inseparable from forced marches.

The artillery, cavalry, and infantry, united together by the bonds of mutual esteem, may be confident that, when they rely on each other's courage, the three arms, combined and acting together, will be ever found to be an invincible enemy.

The Government of India, as a tribute of their esteem for the meritorious conduct of the troops engaged in the recent operations, will grant to every officer and soldier in the service of the Government of India, engaged in these battles, a medal to be worn with their uniforms, on which the word "FEROZESHAH" shall be inscribed, as denoting that they have served in this important campaign.

The Commander-in-Chief will be so good as to furnish the Governor-General with lists of all the officers and soldiers engaged in the operations of this campaign.

The Governor-General is further pleased to order that the following corps be permitted to wear the word "FEROZESHAH" upon their appointments, standards, and colours, in perpetual commemoration of their gallant service:—

1st and 3rd brigades Horse Artillery; 2nd, 3rd, and 4th companies, 4th battalion; 2nd and 4th companies, 6th battalion; 2nd company, 7th battalion, Foot Artillery; Governor-General's Body Guard; 4th, 5th, and 8th regiments of Light Cavalry; 3rd, 8th, and 9th regiments Irregular Cavalry; 1st European Light Infantry; 2nd, 12th, 14th, 16th, 24th, 26th, 33rd, 42nd, 44th, 45th, 47th, 48th, 54th, and 73rd regiments of Native Infantry.

By order of the Right Hon. the Governor-General of India,

F. CURRIE.

Head Quarters, Camp, Nihalkee, January 28, 1846.

The Commander-in-Chief is pleased to direct the publication in General Orders to the army of the following General Order, issued to the army of the Sutlej.

The arrival of Her Majesty's 62nd Foot at head quarters offers to the Commander-in-Chief an opportunity, of which he gladly takes advantage, to express the satisfaction it affords him to have the services of this corps available with the force immediately opposed to the enemy.

The chance of war placed the 62nd Regiment in opposition to the strongest part of the enemy's entrenched position at the battle of Ferozeshah, on the night of the 21st ultimo.

The following day, after the enemy's position had been carried, the Commander-in-Chief, with several officers of his personal staff, minutely inspected the point attacked by the 62nd Regiment. He found it had been defended by numerous guns of heavy calibre served with grape and canister.

The very heavy fire by which the regiment was assailed, and its steady devoted gallantry under the storm, are best attested by the fact, of which his Excellency was an eye-witness, of the space in front of, and close to the enemy's battery, having been thickly strewed with the bodies of the brave officers and soldiers who fell in the assault. The Commander-in-Chief finds that seventeen officers and 185 men fell on this occasion, and that the regiment did not desist from its noble efforts to carry the position, until ordered by the brigadier commanding to fall back, as stated in the following extract from the brigadier's report only now received:—

"Under these circumstances, seeing Her Majesty's 62nd was exposed to a most destructive fire without any object, as they could not move forward, I conceived it my duty to direct them to retire, which they did in almost as good order, making allowance for the heavy loss they had sustained, as that in which they had advanced."

These are the simple facts of the case, and the Commander-in-Chief is happy to assure the 62nd Regiment, on this the first opportunity of inspecting it, that the conduct of the corps on the night of the 21st ultimo, in the battle of Ferozeshah, has received, and merits, his Excellency's most cordial approbation.

Justice to the 62nd Regiment, and to the native regiments brigaded with that corps, demands this exposition of the sentiments of the Commander-in-Chief, in correction of an erroneous impression with respect to the conduct of the brigade, which has been produced by the publication, purely through an oversight, of a despatch written exclusively for his Excellency's information.

By order of his Excellency the Commander-in-Chief,

J. R. Lumley, *Major-General,*

Adjutant-General of the Army.

ALIWAL.

General Order by the Governor-General of India.

Camp, Ferozepore, February 2, 1846.

The Governor-General announces to the army and the people of India, that he has received from his Excellency the Commander-in-Chief of the Army, a report by Major-General Sir Harry Smith, K.C.B., dated the 30th ultimo, giving the details of a complete victory gained by the troops under the immediate command of the Major-General, on the 28th January, over the Sikh forces, commanded by the Sirdar Runjoor Singh Mujethea.

In this decisive and glorious action, the enemy's infantry were dislodged from every position and village they attempted to hold, by rapid charges at the point of the bayonet. Their horsemen were driven from every part of the field by repeated charges, in which the superior valour of the European and native cavalry was most conspicuous, and the artillery moving with its accustomed celerity, was always well to the front, directing its fire with precision and effect. The result of these noble efforts of the three arms of artillery, cavalry, and infantry, in which the valour and discipline of the troops were happily combined with the skill of the commander, has been the signal defeat of the enemy, who was driven across the river with great loss, his camp being captured, and fifty-two pieces of artillery remaining in the hands of the victors.

These trophies, in addition to those taken at Ferozeshah and Moodkee, complete the number of 143 pieces of artillery taken in the field from the enemy, since the British army moved from its cantonments to repel a most unprovoked aggression on its territories.

To Major-General Sir Harry Smith, and to the brave troops he commanded, the Governor-General conveys the tribute of his admiration, and the grateful acknowledgments of the Government and the people of India. The service rendered was most important, and was accomplished by the ability of the commander and the valour of the troops.

Tha Governor-General's thanks are due to Brigadier Wheeler, who, although still suffering from the wounds received at Moodkee, energetically headed his brigade, composed of her Majesty's 50th Regiment, the 48th Native Infantry, and the Sirmoor battalion. Great praise is also due to Brigadiers Godby and Hicks, who with the 36th Native Infantry and Nusseree battalion, H. M. 31st, and the 24th and 47th Native Infantry, stormed the village of Aliwal, drove the enemy from it, and seized the guns by which it was defended.

The Governor-General has much satisfaction in observing the warm terms of admiration in which the Major-General speaks of the Nusseree and Sirmoor battalions, and the Shekawattee brigade under Brigadier Penny, Captain Fisher, and Major Forster. These corps nobly emulated the example of the regular regiments of Infantry.

In short, the conduct of the troops, European and native, regular and irregular, was, throughout the field, an honourable rivalry, in which every corps bravely did its duty.

Her Majesty's 16th Lancers, on this occasion, have added to their former reputation acquired in various fields of battle in Asia, by routing the enemy's cavalry in every direction, and by resolute charges of two of its squadrons, under Captain Bere and Major Smyth and Captain Pearson, penetrating the enemy's square of infantry, in which charges the squadrons were gallantly supported by the 3rd Light Native Cavalry under Major Angelo.

In these exploits the native cavalry distinguished itself throughout the day, and the Governor-General is happy to bear his testimony to the fact that, since the army of the Sutlej commenced its operations on the 18th December, the native cavalry has on every occasion proved its superior prowess, whether in the general actions which have been fought, or in the various skirmishes at the outposts, such as that in which Captain Becher was gallantly engaged with a small party of the 8th Irregular Cavalry at Alloowalla, on the morning of the 27th January.

The Governor-General's thanks are due, in an especial manner, to Brigadier Cureton, who commanded the Cavalry. This officer's whole life has been spent in the most meritorious exertions in Europe and Asia; and on this occasion, the skill and intrepidity with which the cavalry force was handled, obtained the admiration of the army which witnessed their movements.

The Government of India, ever desirous to mark its grateful sense of the services of the Army, will cause a medal to be presented to every officer and soldier of the East India Company's service, engaged in the battle of Aliwal, and requests, through his Excellency the Commander-in-Chief, that a nominal roll may be furnished for that purpose.

By order of the Right Hon. the Governor-General of India,

F. CURRIE,

Secretary to the Government of India with the Governor-General.

General Sir Hugh Gough, Bart., G.C.B., Commander-in-Chief in India, to the Governor-General.

Camp, Nihalkee, February 1, 1846.

After its final repulse, on the 22d of December, the Sikh army retired, in great confusion, across the ferries and fords of the Sutlej.

I established my head quarters at Sultan Khan Walla on the 24th, my divisions being encamped at that place, at Peer Khan Walla, and at Kool. On the 27th, I advanced to Hurruff; and, the same day, personally pushed a reconnoissance to the bank of the river, at the Ghat of Sobraon.

The enemy was seen stretching along the right bank in force, not half a dozen of his stragglers being surprised by our Irregular Cavalry on this side.

Major-General Sir Harry Smith's division I placed in an advanced position, with its right on the village of Mallowal, and its left on a nullah, an offset from the Sutlej.

From this point the enemy was watched by the Major-General with equal activity and circumspection, whilst the rest of our troops were held in hand ready to support him, should the Sikhs venture to resume the initiative.

On or about the 5th, our attention was directed to a predatory incursion of the enemy, in the direction of Loodiana. They burnt a few of the residences of our officers, and barracks of our soldiers at that station, but avoided the combat, when the Sirmoor battalion, and other troops, interrupted them in the work of destruction.

Rumour exaggerated the nature and extent of this inroad, and excited some alarm for our communications; but the object of this foray was, eventually, discovered to be for the purpose of favouring the escape, across the Sutlej, of the Rajah of Ladwa, who had alone, of all the principal princes and chiefs of the protected states, evinced towards us, at this conjuncture, decided hostility. With him the predatory Sikhs recrossed the Sutlej.

On the 12th of January, I determined to bring my whole force into a position, from which it might more closely observe the movements of the enemy, now posted near the greater Sobraon, on the right bank. At an early hour, it executed an oblique movement to its right and front. Major-General Sir Harry Smith, supported by a cavalry brigade, under Brigadier Cureton, (recently brought up from Meerut) was, in this new alignment, still on the right, opposite to Hurrekee Puttun: Major-General Gilbert in the centre; and Major-General Sir Robert Dick on the left, covered again by cavalry. Major-General Sir John Grey, posted at Attaree, watched the Nuggur ford. The troops of Major-General Sir John Littler occupied, or were drawn around, the cantonment and entrenchment of Ferozepore.

The enemy, on his side, reinforced his army on the right bank, completed and strengthened his bridge, and increased the force of his posts and picquets on the left bank. These parties having, on the 14th, evinced more than usual audacity, I caused that body of his infantry which held the head of the bridge, to be driven in by the fire of artillery and rockets, supported by the presence of our light troops. On the following day, a partial cannonade, which was again opened, on our side, upon the boats of the Sikhs, on their outposts on the left bank, and their encampment on the right, enabled me to ascertain, from the direction of their corresponding fire, the nature of all their defensive dispositions.

Meanwhile, the Upper Sutlej has become the scene of very interesting operations.

It is a strange feature of this war that the enemy, pressed for supplies on his own bank, has been striving to draw them from his Jaghire States on this side of the river. In the town and fort of Dhurmkote, which were filled with grain, he had, in the second week of January, a small garrison of mercenaries, Rohillas, Eusufzies, and Affghans. Major-General Sir Harry Smith was, on the 18th, sent against this place, with a single brigade of his division, and a light field battery. He easily effected its reduction, the troops within it surrendering at discretion, after a few cannot shots. But, whilst he was yet in march, I received information of a more serious character. There remained little cause to doubt that Sirdar Runjoor Singh Mujethea had crossed from Philour, at the head of a numerous force of all arms, and established himself in position at Baran Hara, between the old

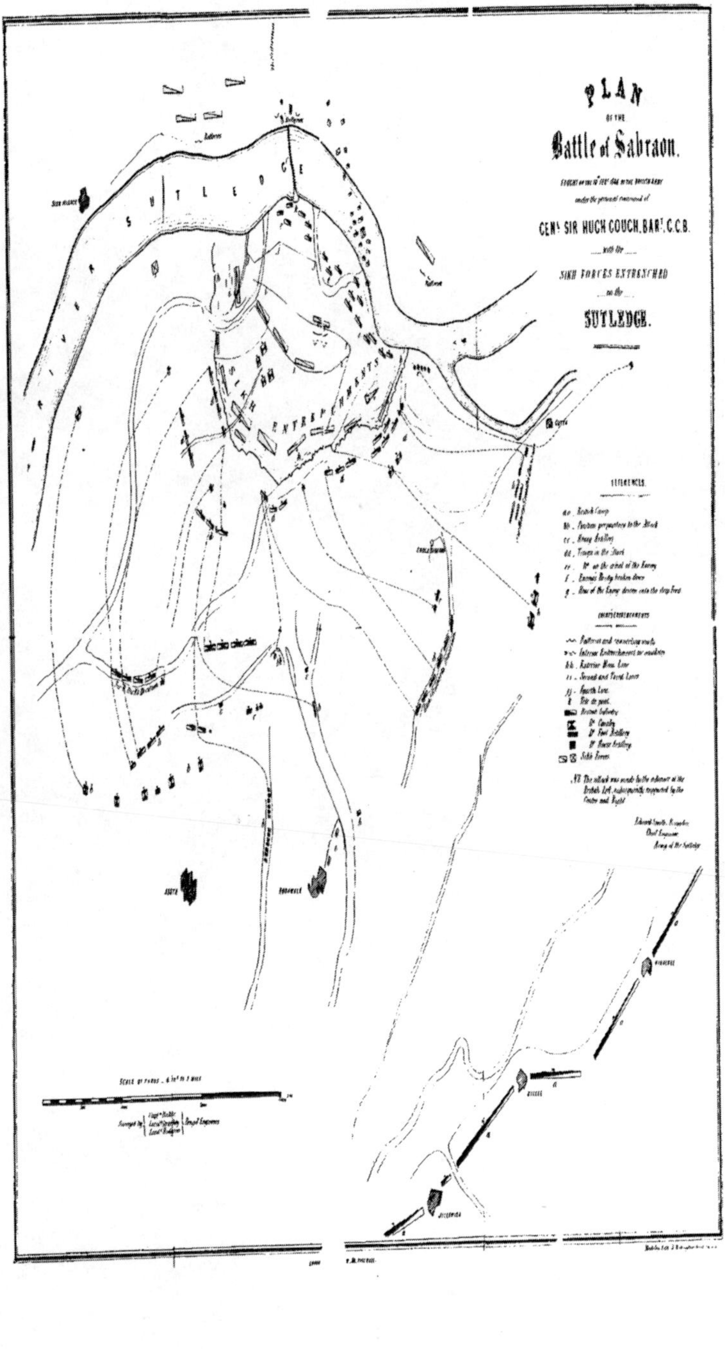
PLAN
OF THE
Battle of Sabraon.
under the personal command of
CENL. SIR HUCH COUCH, BART. G.C.B.
with the
SIKH FORCES ENTRENCHED
on the
SUTLEDGE.
RIVER SUTLEDGE
SIKH ENTRENCHMENTS
REFERENCES.
aa. British Camp
ff. Enemies Bridge broken down
Second and Third Lines
Fourth Line.
Tête de pont.
British Infantry
Do. Cavalry
Do. Foot Artillery
Do. Horse Artillery
Sikh Forces
N.B. The attack was made by the advance of the British Left, subsequently supported by the Centre and Right
Chief Engineer
Army of the Sutledge
Bengal Engineers

and the new courses of the Sutlej, not only threatening the city of Loodiana with plunder and devastation, but indicating a determination to intersect the line of our communications at Busseean and Raekote.

The safety of the rich and populous town of Loodiana had been in some measure provided for by the presence of three battalions of native infantry under Brigadier Godby: and the gradual advance of our reinforcements, amongst which was included her Majesty's 53rd Regiment, and the position of the Shekawattee brigade, near Busseean, gave breathing time to us in that direction.

But, on the receipt of intelligence which could be relied on, of the movements of Runjoor Singh, and his apparent views, Major-General Sir Harry Smith, with the brigade at Dhurmkote, and Brigadier Cureton's cavalry, was directed to advance by Jugraon towards Loodiana; and his second brigade, under Brigadier Wheeler, moved on to support him.

Then commenced a series of very delicate combinations, the momentous character of which can only be comprehended by reflecting on the task which had devolved on this army of guarding the frontier from Roopur down to Mundote.

The Major-General, breaking up from Jugraon, moved towards Loodiana; when the Sirdar, relying on the vast superiority of his forces, assumed the initiative, and endeavoured to intercept his progress by marching in a line parallel to him, and opening upon his troops a furious cannonade. The Major-General continued coolly to manœuvre; and, when the Sikh Sirdar, bending round one wing of his army, enveloped his flank, he extricated himself by retiring, with the steadiness of a field day, by échellon of battalions, and effected his communication with Loodiana, but not without severe loss.

Reinforced by Brigadier Godby, he felt himself to be strong; but his manœuvres had thrown him out of communication with Brigadier Wheeler, and a portion of his baggage had fallen into the hands of the enemy. The Sikh Sirdar took an entrenched position at Budhowal, supporting himself on his fort; but, threatened on either flank by General Smith and Brigadier Wheeler, finally decamped, and moved down to the Sutlej. The British troops made good their junction, and occupied the abandoned position of Budhowal; the Shekawattee brigade and her Majesty's 53rd Regiment also added to the strength of the Major-General, and he prepared to attack the Sikh Sirdar on his new ground. But, on the 26th, Runjoor Singh was reinforced, from the right bank, with 4,000 regular troops, twelve pieces of artillery, and a large force of cavalry.

Emboldened by this accession of strength, he ventured on the measure of advancing towards Jugraon, apparently with the view of intercepting our communications by that route.

It is my gratifying duty to announce that the presumption has been rebuked by a splendid victory obtained over him. He has not only been repulsed by the Major-General, but his camp at Aliwal carried by storm, the whole of his cannon and munitions of war captured, and his army driven headlong across the Sutlej, even on the right bank of which he found no refuge from the fire of our artillery.

I have the honour now to forward the Major-General's report which has just reached me. It is so ample and luminous that I might, perhaps, have spared some of the details into which admiration of the Major-General's conduct, and of the brave army confided to him in these operations, has led me.

It now remains for me only to congratulate you, Right Honourable Sir, and the Government of India, on the brilliant success which, under Divine Providence, the Major-General has achieved; and to record my opinion that, throughout these arduous and important operations, he has displayed all the qualities of an able commander. Most strongly, and most earnestly at the same time, I beg to bring to your notice, and to that of His Grace the Duke of Wellington, and the Honourable the Court of Directors, the officers and corps on whom he has so justly bestowed his commendations.

Major-General Sir Harry Smith, K.C.B., to the Adjutant-General of the Army.

Camp, Field of the Battle of Aliwal, Jan. 30, 1846.

SIR,

My despatches to his Excellency the Commander-in-Chief of the 23rd* instant, will have put his Excellency in possession of the position of the force under my command, after having formed a junction with the troops at Loodiana, hemmed in by a formidable body of the Sikh army under Runjoor Singh and the Rajah of Ladwa. The enemy strongly entrenched himself around the little fort of Budhowal by breast-works and "abattis," which he precipitately abandoned on the night of the 22nd instant (retiring, as it were, upon the ford of Tulwun), having ordered all the boats which were opposite Philour to that Ghat. This movement he effected during the night, and, by making a considerable detour, placed himself at a distance of ten miles, and consequently out of my reach. I could, therefore, only push forward my cavalry so soon as I had ascertained he had marched during the night, and I occupied immediately his vacated position. It appeared subsequently he had no intention of recrossing the Sutlej, but moved down to the Ghat of Tulwun (being cut off from that of Philour, by the position my force occupied after its relief of Loodiana), for the purpose of protecting the passage of a very considerable reinforcement of twelve guns and 4,000 of the regular, or "Aieen" troops, called Avitabile's battalion, entrenching himself strongly in a semicircle, his flanks resting on a river, his position covered with from forty to fifty guns (generally of large calibre), howitzers, and mortars. The reinforcement crossed during the night of the 27th instant, and encamped to the right of the main army.

Meanwhile, his Excellency the Commander-in-Chief, with that foresight and judgment which mark the able general, had rein-

* Not received by the Secret Committee.

forced me by a considerable addition to my cavalry, some guns, and the 2nd brigade of my own division, under Brigadier Wheeler, C.B. This reinforcement reached me on the 26th, and I had intended the next morning to move upon the enemy in his entrenchments, but the troops required one day's rest after the long marches Brigadier Wheeler had made.

I have now the honour to lay before you the operations of my united forces on the morning of the eventful 28th January, for his Excellency's information. The body of troops under my command having been increased, it became necessary so to organize and brigade them as to render them manageable in action. The cavalry under the command of Brigadier Cureton, and horse artillery under Major Lawrenson, were put into two brigades; the one under Brigadier MacDowell, C.B., and the other under Brigadier Stedman. The 1st division as it stood, two brigades:—Her Majesty's 53rd and 30th Native Infantry, under Brigadier Wilson, of the latter corps;—the 36th Native Infantry, and Nusseree battalion, under Brigadier Godby;—and the Shekawattee brigade under Major Forster. The Sirmoor battalion I attached to Brigadier Wheeler's brigade of the 1st division; the 42nd Native Infantry having been left at head quarters.

At daylight on the 28th, my order of advance was—the Cavalry in front, in contiguous columns of squadrons of regiments, two troops of horse artillery in the interval of brigades;—the infantry in contiguous columns of brigades at intervals of deploying distance;—artillery in the intervals, followed by two 8-inch howitzers on travelling carriages, brought into the field from the fort of Loodiana, by the indefatigable exertions of Lieutenant-Colonel Lane, Horse Artillery;—Brigadier Godby's brigade, which I had marched out from Loodiana the previous evening, on the right;—the Shekawattee infantry on the left;—the 4th Irregular Cavalry considerably to the right, for the purpose of sweeping the banks of the wet nullah on my right, and preventing any of the enemy's horse attempting an inroad towards

Loodiana, or any attempt upon the baggage assembled round the fort of Budhowal.

In this order the troops moved forward towards the enemy, a distance of six miles, the advance conducted by Captain Waugh, 16th Lancers, the Deputy Assistant Quarter-Master of Cavalry, Major Bradford, of the 1st Cavalry, and Lieutenant Strachey of the Engineers, who had been jointly employed in the conduct of patroles up to the enemy's position, and for the purpose of reporting upon the facility and point of approach. Previously to the march of the troops it had been intimated to me, by Major Mackeson, that the information by spies, led to the belief the enemy would move somewhere at daylight, either on Jugraon, my position of Budhowal, or Loodiana. On a near approach to his outposts, this rumour was confirmed by a spy, who had just left the camp, saying the Sikh army was actually in march towards Jugraon. My advance was steady; my troops well in hand; and if he had anticipated me on the Jugraon road, I could have fallen upon his centre with advantage.

From the tops of the houses of the village of Poorein, I had a distant view of the enemy. He was in motion, and appeared directly opposite my front on a ridge, of which the village of Aliwal may be regarded as the centre. His left appeared still to occupy its ground in the circular entrenchment; his right was brought forward and occupied the ridge. I immediately deployed the cavalry into line, and moved on. As I neared the enemy, the ground became most favourable for the troops to manœuvre, being open and hard grass land. I ordered the cavalry to take ground to the right and left by brigades; thus displaying the heads of the infantry columns; and, as they reached the hard ground, I directed them to deploy into line. Brigadier Godby's brigade was in direct échellon to the rear of the right; the Shekawattee infantry in like manner to the rear of my left;—the cavalry in direct échellon on, and well to the rear of, both flanks of the infantry;—the artillery massed on the right, and centre and left. After deployment, I observed the enemy's left to outflank me, I therefore broke into open column and took ground to my right. When I had gained sufficient ground, the troops wheeled into line. There was no dust, the sun shone brightly. These manœuvres were performed with the celerity and precision of the most correct field day. The glistening of the bayonets and swords of this order of battle was most imposing; and the line advanced. Scarcely had it moved 150 yards, when, at ten o'clock, the enemy opened a fierce cannonade from his whole line. At first his balls fell short, but quickly reached us. Thus upon him, and capable of better ascertaining his position, I was compelled to halt the line, though under fire, for a few moments, until I ascertained that, by bringing up my right, and carrying the village of Aliwal, I could with great effect precipitate myself upon his left and centre. I therefore quickly brought up Brigadier Godby's brigade; and, with it, and the 1st brigade under Brigadier Hicks, made a rapid and noble charge, carried the village, and two guns of large calibre. The line I ordered to advance,—Her Majesty's 31st Foot and the native regiments contending for the front; and the battle became general. The enemy had a numerous body of cavalry on the heights to his left, and I ordered Brigadier Cureton to bring up the right brigade of cavalry, who, in the most gallant manner dashed in among them, and drove them back upon their infantry. Meanwhile a second gallant charge to my right was made by the light cavalry and the body guard. The Shekawattee brigade was moved well to the right, in support of Brigadier Cureton, when I observed the enemy's encampment, and saw it was full of infantry: I immediately brought upon it Brigadier Godby's brigade, by changing front, and taking the enemy's infantry "en-reverse." They drove them before them, and took some guns without a check.

While these operations were going on upon the right; and the enemy's left flank was thus driven back, I occasionally observed the brigade under Brigadier Wheeler, an officer in whom I have the greatest confidence, charging and carrying guns and everything before it, again connecting his line, and moving on, in a manner which ably displayed the coolness of the Brigadier and the gallantry of his irresistible brigade,—Her Majesty's 50th

Foot, the 48th Native Infantry, and the Sirmoor battalion,—although the loss was, I regret to say, severe in the 50th. Upon the left, Brigadier Wilson, with Her Majesty's 53rd and the 30th Native Infantry equalled in celerity and regularity their comrades on the right; and this brigade was opposed to the "Aieen" troops, called Avitabile's, when the fight was fiercely raging.

The enemy, well driven back on his left and centre, endeavoured to hold his right to cover the passage of the river, and he strongly occupied the village of Bhoondree—I directed a squadron of the 16th Lancers, under Major Smyth and Captain Pearson, to charge a body to the right of a village, which they did in the most gallant and determined style, bearing everything before them, as a squadron under Captain Bere had previously done, going right through a square in the most intrepid manner with the deadly lance.—This charge was accompanied by the 3rd Light Cavalry under Major Angelo, and as gallantly sustained. The largest gun upon the field, and seven others, were then captured, while the 53rd Regiment carried the village by the bayonet, and the 30th Native Infantry wheeled round to the rear in a most spirited manner. Lieut.-Col. Alexander's and Capt. Turton's troops of horse artillery, under Major Lawrenson, dashed among the flying infantry, committing great havoc, until about 800 or 1,000 men rallied under the high bank of a nullah, and opened a heavy but ineffectual fire from below the bank. I immediately directed the 30th Native Infantry to charge them, which they were able to do upon their left flank, while in a line in rear of the village. This native corps nobly obeyed my orders, and rushed among the Avitabile troops, driving them from under the bank, and exposing them once more to a deadly fire of twelve guns within 300 yards. The destruction was very great, as may be supposed, from guns served as these were. Her Majesty's 53rd Regiment moved forward in support of the 30th Native Infantry, by the right of the village. The battle was won; our troops advancing with the most perfect order to the common focus—the passage of the river. The enemy, completely hemmed in, were flying from our fire, and precipitating themselves in disordered masses into the ford and boats, in the utmost confusion and consternation; our 8-inch howitzers soon began to play upon their boats, when the "débris" of the Sikh army appeared upon the opposite and high bank of the river, flying in every direction, although a sort of line was attempted to countenance their retreat, until *all* our guns commenced a furious cannonade, when they quickly receded. Nine guns were on the river by the ford. It appears as if they had been unlimbered to cover the ford. These being loaded, were fired once upon our advance; two others were sticking in the river, one of them we got out; two were seen to sink in the quicksands; two were dragged to the opposite bank and abandoned. These, and the one in the middle of the river, were gallantly spiked by Lieutenant Holmes, of the 11th Irregular Cavalry, and Gunner Scott, of the 1st troop 2nd brigade horse artillery, who rode into the stream, and crossed for the purpose, covered by our guns and light infantry.

Thus ended the battle of Aliwal, one of the most glorious victories ever achieved in India, by the united efforts of Her Majesty's and the Honourable Company's troops. *Every gun* the enemy had fell into our hands, as I infer from his never opening one upon us from the opposite bank of the river, which is high and favourable for the purpose—fifty-two guns are now in the Ordnance Park; two sank in the bed of the Sutlej; and two were spiked on the opposite bank; making a total of fifty-six pieces of cannon captured or destroyed*. Many jingalls which were attached to Avitabile's corps, and which aided in the defence of the village of Bhoondree, have also been taken, The whole army of the enemy has been driven headlong over the difficult ford of a broad river; his camp, baggage, stores of ammunition and of grain,—his all, in fact, wrested from him, by the repeated charges of cavalry and infantry, aided by the guns of Alexander, Turton, Lane, Mill, Boileau, and of the Shekawattee brigade, and by the

* Eleven guns, since ascertained to be sunk in the river, total sixty-seven; thirty odd jingalls fell into our hands.

8-inch howitzers;—our guns literally being constantly ahead of everything. The determined bravery of all was as conspicuous as noble. I am unwont to praise when praise is not merited; and I here most unavowedly express my firm opinion and conviction, that no troops in any battle on record ever behaved more nobly;—British and native, no distinction; cavalry, all vying with H. M.'s 16th Lancers, and striving to head in the repeated charges. Our guns and gunners, officers and men, may be equalled, but cannot be excelled, by any artillery in the world. Throughout the day no hesitation—a bold and intrepid advance;—and thus it is that our loss is comparatively small, though I deeply regret to say, severe. The enemy fought with much resolution; they maintained frequent rencontres with our cavalry hand to hand. In one charge, upon infantry, of H. M.'s 16th Lancers, they threw away their muskets and came on with their swords and targets against the lance.

Having thus done justice, and justice alone, to the gallant troops his Excellency entrusted to my command, I would gladly, if the limits of a despatch (already too much lengthened, I fear,) permitted me, do that justice to individuals all deserve. This cannot be; therefore must I confine myself to mention those officers, whose continued services, experience, and standing, placed them in conspicuous commands. In Brigadier Wheeler, my second in command, I had a support I could rely on with every confidence, and most gallantly did he lead his brigade. From Brigadiers Wilson, Godby, and Hicks, I had also every support, and every cause to be gratified with their exertions. In Brigadier Cureton, Her Majesty has one of those officers rarely met with; the cool experience of the veteran soldier is combined with youthful activity—his knowledge of outpost duty, and the able manner he handles his cavalry under the heaviest fire, rank him among the first cavalry officers of the age; and I beg to draw his Excellency's marked attention to this honest encomium. In Major Lawrenson, commanding the artillery, Lieut.-Col. Alexander, Captain Turton, and Lieut.-Col. Lane, the service has officers of the very first order; and I am equally satisfied with Captain Boileau, in command of the nine-pounder battery, and with Lieutenant Mill, in charge of four light guns. The two eight-inch howitzers did right good service, organized, equipped, and brought into the field by the exertions, and determination to overcome all difficulties, of Lieut.-Col. Lane, equally well served, and brought forward always with the infantry, by Lieutenant Austin.

To Brigadiers MacDowell and Stedman, commanding their gallant brigades of cavalry, the fortune of the day is greatly indebted; and to all commanding officers of cavalry and infantry, my warmest thanks are due. To Major Smyth, commanding Her Majesty's 16th Lancers, who was wounded; to Major Bradford, of the 1st Light Cavalry; to Major Angelo, of the 3rd Light Cavalry; to Major Alexander, of the 5th Light Cavalry; to Captain Hill, of the 4th Irregular Cavalry; to Major Forster, of the Shekawattee brigade; and to Captain Quin, of the Body Guard; to Lieutenant-Colonel Spence, commanding Her Majesty's 31st Foot; to Major Bird, of the 24th Native Infantry; to Captain Corfield, of the 47th Native Infantry; to Lieutenant-Colonel Ryan, K.H., of Her Majesty's 50th Regiment; to Captain Troup, of the 48th Native Infantry; to Captain Fisher, of the Sirmoor battalion; to Lieutenant-Colonel Phillips, of Her Majesty's 53rd Foot; to Captain Jack, of the 38th Native Infantry; to Captain Fleming, of the 36th Native Infantry; and to Brigadier Penny of the Nusseree battalion.

His Excellency having witnessed the glorious services of Her Majesty's 31st and 50th Regiments, and of the 24th, 47th, and 48th Native Infantry, I have only to report upon Her Majesty's 53rd, a young regiment, but veterans in daring gallantry and regularity; and Lieutenant-Colonel Phillips's bravery and coolness attracted the attention of myself and every staff-officer I sent to him. The 30th and 36th Regiments Native Infantry are an honour to any service; and the intrepid little Ghoorkhas of the Nusseree and Sirmoor battalions in bravery and obedience can be exceeded by none. I much regretted I had no brigade to give Brigadier Penny, who is in orders for one, as his Excellency is aware. I can only say, therefore, that when he gets his brigade, if he leads it as he did his gallant band of Ghoorkhas, it will be inferior to none.

The service of Her Majesty's 16th Lancers his Excellency has witnessed on a former occasion; and the exalted character of this regiment is equally before him. The 1st and 3rd Light Cavalry and the 8th Irregulars I believe he has not seen in action; and it is my duty, therefore, joyfully to report the manner they contended for the glorious prize of victory, in the many charges they this day delivered; and it will be equally gratifying when I assure his Excellency the Body Guard under Captain Quin, and the 5th Light Cavalry well did their duty. The Shekawattee brigade under Major Forster, is steady, obedient, and well-appointed—artillery, horse, and infantry, each arm striving to distinguish itself in the field.

Captain Mathias, of Her Majesty's 62nd, in charge of a detachment of convalescents of Her Majesty's service, and Lieutenant Hebbert, of the Honourable Company's Sappers and Miners, readily performed the duties assigned them in protecting the eight-inch howitzers.

To Captain Lugard, the Assistant-Adjutant-General of this force, I am deeply indebted, and the service still more so; a more cool, intrepid, and trustworthy officer cannot be brought forward; and I may say the same with great sincerity of Lieutenant Galloway, the Deputy-Assistant Quarter-Master-General of the 1st division. Captain Waugh of the 16th Lancers, Deputy-Assistant Quarter-Master-General to the cavalry, is an officer of no ordinary abilities; and the manner in which he and Major Bradford, of the 1st Light Cavalry, daily patrolled and reconnoitred, and made themselves acquainted with the position of the enemy, mainly contributed to the glorious result.

The Brigadiers all speak in high terms of their Majors of Brigade—Captain O'Hanlon of the 1st brigade, who was wounded in the action, and was replaced by Captain Palmer, of the 48th

Native Infantry; Captain Garvock, of Her Majesty's 31st Foot, of the 2nd brigade; Captain Loftie, 30th Native Infantry, of the 3rd brigade; Lieutenant Vanrenen, of the 4th brigade; Lieutenant Pattinson, of Her Majesty's 16th Lancers, of the 1st brigade of Cavalry; and Captain Campbell, of the 1st Light Cavalry, of the 2nd brigade.

Of the services of Lieutenant A. W. C. Plowden, 3rd Light Cavalry, Deputy-Assistant Adjutant-General, and my Aide-de-Camp, Lieutenant Holdich, and of Lieutenant Tombs of the Artillery, my Acting Aide-de-Camp, I am fully sensible; and with the manner in which they aided me in carrying orders I am much satisfied. Lieutenants Strachey and Baird Smith, of the Engineers, greatly contributed to the completion of my plans and arrangements, and were ever ready to act in any capacity: they are two most promising and gallant officers.

I have every reason to be satisfied with the commissariat arrangements under Captains Mainwaring and Williamson.

Owing to the judicious arrangements of Dr. Murray, Field-Surgeon, every wounded officer and soldier was placed under cover, and provided for soon after dark; and, for the zeal displayed by this able and persevering medical officer, and to the several regimental surgeons, are the wounded and our country deeply indebted. The whole of the wounded were moved yesterday to Loodiana, for the sake of accommodation and comforts, which could not be given them in the field.

If not irregular, I beg you would lay before the Commander-in-Chief, for submission to the Right Hon. the Governor-General, my just sense of the valuable services of the political officers associated with me; Major Mackeson, Captain J. D. Cunningham, and Lieutenant Lake. For the assistance I have received from them in their political capacity, I feel most grateful. On the morning of the battle each offered to aid me in his military capacity: frequently did I employ them to carry orders to the thickest of the fight; and frequently did they gallantly accompany charges of cavalry.

The reports of the several Brigadiers I inclose; a return of the officers commanding and second in command of regiments; also a return of killed and wounded; a return of ordnance captured and of ordnance stores; likewise a return of commissariat stores, grain, &c.; and a rough sketch of the field of battle of Aliwal.

The fort of Goongrana has, subsequently to the battle, been evacuated, and I yesterday evening blew up the fort of Budhowal. I shall now blow up that of Noorpoor. A portion of the peasantry, *viz.*, the Sikhs, appear less friendly to us, while the Mussulmans rejoice in being under our Government. I have, &c.

H. G. Smith,
Major-General Commanding.

(True copy).
(Signed) P. Grant, *Major,*
Deputy-Adjutant-General of the Army.

Nominal Roll of Officers Killed and Wounded, 28th January.

1st Brigade of Cavalry.

Her Majesty's 16th Lancers.—Lieutenant H. Swetenham—killed; Cornet G. B. Williams—killed. Major J. R. Smyth—severely wounded; Captain E. B. Bere—wounded; Captain L. Fyler—severely wounded; Lieutenant W. K. Orme—severely wounded; Lieutenant T. Pattle—wounded; Lieutenant W. Morris—wounded.

4th Irregular Cavalry.—Lieutenant and Adjutant Smalpage—killed.

2nd Brigade of Cavalry.

1st Regiment Light Cavalry.—Cornet W. S. Beatson—slightly wounded; Cornet T. G. Farquhar—mortally wounded.

1st Brigade Infantry.

Her Majesty's 31st Regiment.—Lieutenant Atty—slightly wounded.

24th Regiment Native Infantry.—Lieutenant Scott—wounded.

2nd Brigade Infantry.

Brigade Major.—Captain P. O'Hanlon—badly wounded.

Her Majesty's 50*th Regiment.*—Captain W. Knowles—leg amputated, dangerously wounded; Captain J. L. Wilton—severely wounded; Lieutenant Grimes—killed; Lieutenant H. J. Frampton—arm amputated, dangerously wounded; Lieutenant R. B. Bellers—slightly wounded; Lieutenant W. P. Elgee—slightly wounded; Lieutenant A. White—severely wounded; Lieutenant W. C. Vernett—severely wounded; Lieutenant J. Purcell—severely wounded; Ensign W. R. Farmer—severely wounded.

48*th Native Infantry.*—Captain Troup—slightly wounded; Captain H. Palmer, ditto; Lieutenant and Adjutant Wale—severely wounded; Ensign W. Marshall, slightly wounded.

4th Brigade Infantry.

36*th Regiment Native Infantry.*—Ensign Bagshaw—wounded.

EDWARD LUGARD, *Captain,*
Assistant-Adjutant-General.

Casualty Return of the Force under the Command of Major-General Sir H. G. Smith, K.C.B.

Camp, Aliwal, January 29, 1846.

Artillery.—3 men, 30 horses—killed; 15 men, 9 horses—wounded; 5 men, 12 horses—missing.

Cavalry.

1*st brigade.*—3 European officers, 2 native officers, 83 men, 120 horses—killed; 6 European officers, 1 native officer, 100 men, 32 horses—wounded; 1 man, 73 horses—missing.

2*nd brigade.*—11 men, 25 horses—killed; 2 European officers, 3 native officers, 34 men, 38 horses—wounded; 12 horses—missing.

Infantry.

1*st brigade.*—2 men killed; 2 European officers, 28 men—wounded; 7 men missing.

2*nd brigade.*—1 European officer, 1 native officer, 27 men, 2

Under the personal command of H.E. Genl. Sir H. Gough, B^t. G.C.B. Commander in Chief

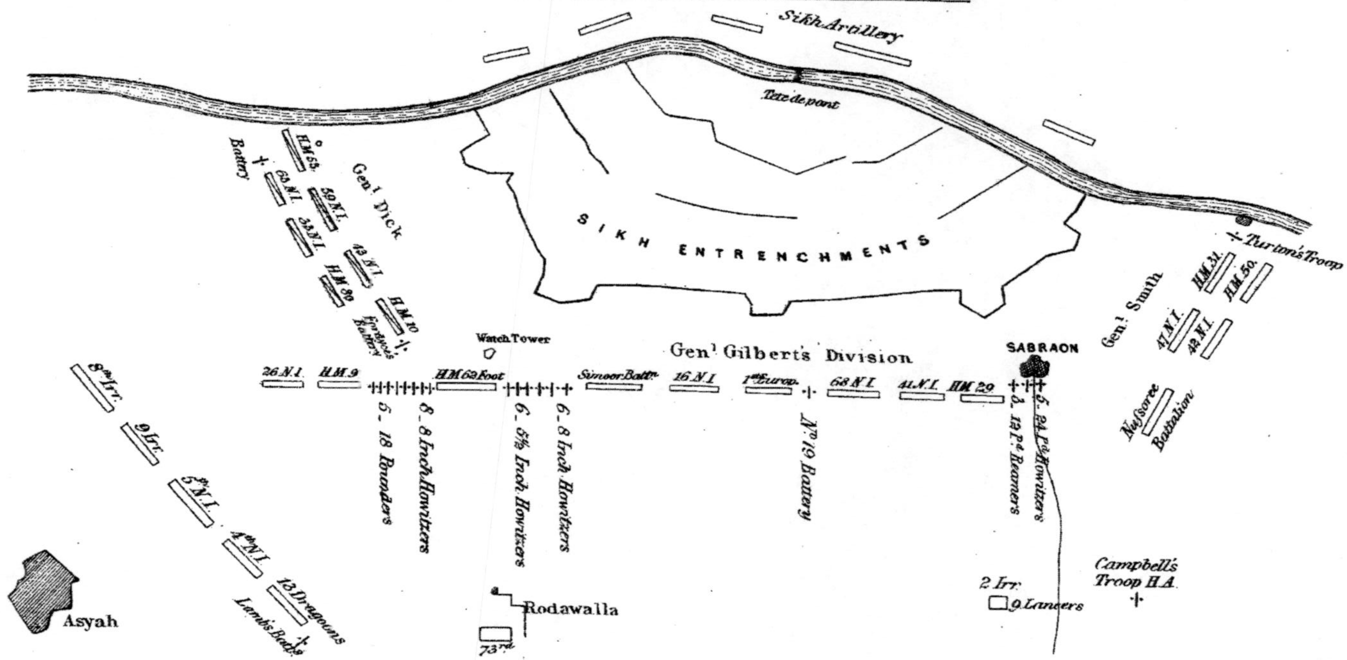

horses—killed; 14 European officers, 2 native officers, 134 men—wounded; 4 men missing.

3rd brigade.—7 men killed; 32 men wounded; 3 men missing.

4th brigade.—9 men killed; 1 European officer, 26 men—wounded; 1 man missing.

Shekawattee Infantry.—2 men killed; 13 men wounded; 4 men missing.

Sappers and Miners.—None killed or wounded.

Total killed—151 men, 177 horses; *total wounded*—413 men, 79 horses; *total missing*—25 men, 97 horses.

Grand total of killed, wounded, and missing—589 men; 353 horses.

H. G. Smith, *Major-General.*

Return of Ordnance captured from the Enemy, in action at Aliwal, by the 1st Division of the Army of the Sutlej, under the personal Command of Major-General Sir Harry Smith, K.C.B., on the 28th January, 1846.

Camp, Aliwal, January 30, 1846.

Serviceable—12 howitzers, 4 mortars, 33 guns; total—49; unserviceable—1 howitzer, 2 guns; total—3; sunk in the Sutlej, and spiked on the opposite shore—13 guns; since brought in—2 guns. Grand total, 67.

Forty swivel camel guns also captured, which have been destroyed.

G. Lawrenson, *Major, 2nd Brigade Horse Artillery,*
Commanding Artillery,
1st Division, Army of the Sutlej.

N.B.—The quantity of ammunition captured with the artillery, and found in the camp of the enemy, is beyond accurate calculation, consisting of shot, shell, grape, and small-arm ammunition of every description, and for every calibre. The powder found in the limbers and waggons of the guns, and in the magazines of the entrenched camp, has been destroyed, to prevent accidents.

Six large hackery loads have also been appropriated to the destruction of forts in the neighbourhood. As many of the shot and shell as time would admit of being collected have been brought into the Park—the shells, being useless, have been thrown into the river. The shot will be appropriated to the public service.

G. Lawrenson, *Major, 2nd Brigade Horse Artillery,*
Commanding Artillery,
1st Division, Army of the Sutlej.

Copy of a Pencil Express, written on the Field of Battle, by Sir Harry Smith, to the Commander-in-Chief.

Bank of the Sutlej, 28th January.

Hearing the enemy had received a reinforcement yesterday of twelve guns, and 4,000 men last night, I moved my troops at daylight this morning to attack. I think I have taken every gun he had, and driven him over the river. My guns are now battering him from the opposite bank. He came out to fight me. I expect fifty guns are on the field at least. My loss I hope not great. The cavalry charged several times, both black and white, like soldiers,—and infantry, vied with each other in bravery. To the God of Victory we are all indebted. God bless you, dear Sir Hugh. My Staff all right—Mackeson and Cunningham, of the Political Department, bore heavily on some villages. The enemy required all I could do with such brave fellows to teach him to swim.

(Signed) H. G. Smith, *Major-General.*

Note.—It will be observed that the publication of the despatch from Sir John Littler, at page 65, did not proceed from the Commander-in-Chief's Office, it not having been countersigned by either the Military Secretary or the Adjutant-General.

SOBRAON.

The Governor-General of India to the Secret Committee.

Camp, Kenha Cuchwa, Feb. 19, 1846.

The immediate result of the victory of Aliwal was the evacuation by the Sikh garrisons of all the forts, hitherto occupied by detachments of Lahore soldiers, on this side of the river Sutlej, and the submission of the whole of the territory on the left bank of that river to the British Government.

The Sikh army remained in its entrenched position; and, though on the first intelligence of the victory of Aliwal, and at the sight of the numerous bodies which floated from the neighbourhood of that battle-field to the bridge of boats at Sobraon, they seemed much shaken and disheartened, and though many were reported to have left them and gone to their homes, yet after a few days, the Sikh troops seemed as confident as ever of being able to defy us in their entrenched position, and to prevent our passage on the river.

The Commander-in-Chief was not in a state to take advantage of the enemy's defeat at Aliwal, by an attack on his entrenched position, at Sobraon, until the troops under Major-General Sir Harry Smith should have rejoined his Excellency's camp, and the siege train and ammunition should have arrived from Delhi. The first portion of the siege train, with the reserve ammunition for 100 field guns, reached the Commander-in-Chief's camp, on the 7th and 8th instant. On the latter day, the brigades which had been detached from the main army for the operations in the neighbourhood of Loodiana, rejoined the Commander-in-Chief. Within forty-eight hours from that time, the enemy's entrenched camp was carried by storm, his army almost annihilated, sixty-seven guns captured, and during the night of the 10th, on which this glorious victory was achieved, the advanced brigades of the British army were thrown across the Sutlej. Early on the 12th our bridge was completed, and on the 13th the Commander-in-Chief, with the whole force, excepting the heavy train, and the division left to collect and bring in the wounded to Ferozepore, with the captured guns, were encamped in the Punjaub, at Kussoor, sixteen miles from the bank of the river opposite Ferozepore, and thirty-two miles from Lahore.

For the details of these important and decisive operations, I must refer you to the enclosures of this despatch.

I cannot, however, refrain from expressing briefly the pride and gratification with which I communicate to you these results, so eminently evincing the energetic decision of the Commander-in-Chief's operations, and the indomitable courage of the British Indian army under His Excellency's command and which will, I am convinced, be met with a corresponding feeling by the Home Government and the British public.

I returned to Ferozepore from the field of Sobraon, on the afternoon of the 10th, within a few hours after the action had ceased, to superintend the passage of the Sutlej by our troops.

I joined the camp of the Commander-in-Chief at Kussoor on the morning of the 14th.

On the arrival at Lahore of the news of the complete victory of Sobraon, the Ranee and Durbar urged Rajah Gholab Singh to proceed immediately to the British camp, to beg pardon in the name of the Durbar and the Sikh Government for the offence which had been committed, and to endeavour to negociate some arrangement for the preservation of the country from utter ruin.

The Rajah first stipulated that the Durbar and the chief officers of the army, as well as the members of the Punchayets, should sign a solemn declaration that they would abide by such terms as he might determine on with the British Government. This is said to have been immediately acceded to; and, on the 15th, Rajah Gholab Singh, Dewan Deena Nath, and Fakeer Noor-ood-deen, arrived in my camp at Kussoor, with full credentials from the Maharajah, and empowered to agree, in the name of the Maharajah and the Government, to such terms as I might dictate. The Rajah was accompanied by the Barukzie Chief, Sooltan Mahomed Khan, and several of the most influential Sirdars of the nation.

I received the Rajah in Durbar as the representative of an offending Government, omitting the forms and ceremonies usually observed on the occasion of friendly meetings, and refusing to receive, at that time, the proffered Nuzzurs and complimentary offerings.

I briefly explained to the Rajah and his colleagues that the offence which had been committed was most serious, and the conduct of the chiefs and the army was most unwarrantable,—that this offence had been perpetrated without the shadow of any cause of quarrel on the part of the British Government, in the face of an existing treaty of amity and friendship,—and that, as all Asia had witnessed the injurious conduct of the Sikh nation, retributive justice required that the proceedings of the British Government should be of a character which would mark to the whole world that insult could not be offered to the British Government, and our provinces invaded by a hostile army, without signal punishment.

I told the Rajah that I recognised the wisdom, prudence, and good feeling evinced by him in having kept himself separate from these unjustifiable hostilities of the Sikhs, and that I was prepared to mark my sense of that conduct in the proceedings which must now be carried through. I stated, in the most marked manner and words, my satisfaction that he who had participated in the offence, and whose wisdom and good feeling towards the British Government were well known, had been the person chosen by the Durbar as their representative for negotiating the means by which atonement might be made, and the terms on which the Sikh Government might be rescued from impending destruction, by a return to amicable relations between the British Government and the Lahore State.

I told the Rajah and his colleagues that Mr. Currie, the Chief Secretary to Government, and Major Lawrence, my agent, were in full possession of my determination on the subject; that they were in my entire confidence; and I referred the chiefs to those officers, that they might learn from them the principles and details of adjustment which I had determined to offer for their immediate acceptance.

The chiefs remained the greater part of the night in conference with Mr. Currie and Major Lawrence; but, before they separated, a paper was signed by them to the effect that all that had been demanded would be conceded, and that arrangements would be immediately made, as far as were in the power of the chiefs, to carry out the details that had been explained to them.

The terms demanded and conceded are, the surrender, in full sovereignty, of the territory, hill and plain, lying between the Sutlej and Beas rivers, and the payment of one and a half crores of rupees as indemnity for the expenses of the war,—the disbandment of the present Sikh army, and its re-organization on the system and regulations with regard to pay which it obtained in the time of the late Maharajah Runjeet Singh,—the arrangement for limiting the extent of the force to be henceforth employed, to be determined on in communication with the British Government,—the surrender to us of all the guns that had been pointed against us,—the entire regulation and controul of both banks of the river Sutlej, and such other arrangements for settling the future boundaries of the Sikh State, and the organization of its administration, as might be determined on at Lahore.

It was further arranged that the Maharajah, with Bhaee Ram Singh, and the other chiefs remaining at Lahore, should forthwith repair to the camp of the Governor-General, and place themselves in the hands of the Governor-General, to accompany his camp to Lahore.

I had prepared, for circulation on my arrival at Kussoor, a Proclamation declaratory of my present views and intentions with regard to the Punjaub,—a translation of which was given to Rajah Gholab Singh and his colleagues, and a copy of which is enclosed for your information.

It was determined that the Maharajah should meet me at Lulleana on the 18th (yesterday), when the camp arrived at that place. On the afternoon of the 17th, it was announced to me, that the Maharajah, with Bhaee Ram Singh and other Chiefs had instantly, on receiving the summons from Rajah Gholab Singh, hastened from Lahore, and that they had arrived at Rajah Gholab Singh's camp, pitched about a mile beyond our picquets, and that His Highness was ready at once to wait upon me.

I considered it right to abide by the first arrangement, and I directed that it should be intimated to the Maharajah and the chiefs, that I would receive His Highness, on the day appointed, at Lulleana, eleven miles in advance, on the road to Lahore.

Yesterday afternoon the Maharajah, attended by Rajah Gholab Singh, Dewan Deena Nath, Fakeer Noor-ood-deen, Bhaee Ram Singh, and ten or twelve other chiefs, had an interview with me in my Durbar tent, where the Commander-in-Chief and Staff had been invited by me to be present to receive them.

As on the occasion of Rajah Gholab Singh's visit, I omitted the usual salute to the Maharajah, and curtailed the other customary ceremonies on his arrival at my tent, causing it to be explained that, until submission had been distinctly tendered by the Maharajah in person, he could not be recognised and received as a friendly prince.

Submission was tendered by the minister and chiefs, who accompanied the Maharajah, and the pardon of the British Government was requested on such conditions as I should dictate, in the most explicit terms; after which, I stated, that the conditions having been distinctly made known to the minister, Rajah Gholab Singh, and the chiefs accredited with him, it was unnecessary to discuss them in that place, and in the presence of the young Maharajah, who was of too tender an age to take part in such matters; and that, as all the requirements of the British Government had been acquiesced in, and their fulfilment promised in the name of the Maharajah and Durbar, I should consider myself justified in treating the young Maharajah from that moment, as a prince restored to the friendship of the British Government.

After some remarks, regarding the fame and character of the late Maharajah, Runjeet Singh, and hope that the young prince would follow the footsteps of his father, and my desire that such relations should henceforward exist between the two States as would tend to the benefit of both, I broke up the Durbar.

On his taking leave, I caused the customary presents to be made to the Maharajah; and, on his retiring from my tent, the usual salute was fired from our 24-pounders, drawn up at the bottom of the street of tents for that purpose.

In the course of discussion, the minister asked, if the young Maharajah should now return to the Ranee, at Lahore, or if it was my desire that he should remain at my camp, intimating that it was for me to dispose of the young chief as I pleased, and as I might consider best for His Highness's interests. I replied, that I thought it advisable that His Highness's camp should accompany mine, and that I should myself conduct him to his capital, which I purposed reaching in two marches—that is, by to-morrow morning.

The remains of the Sikh army, under Sirdar Tej Singh, and Rajah Lal Singh, on retiring from Sobraon encamped at Raebam, about eighteen miles East of Lahore. They are variously estimated at from 14,000 to 20,000 horse and foot, with about thirty-five guns. They have been positively ordered by Rajah Gholab Singh, to remain stationary; and the Mahomedan and Nujeeb battalions, in the interest of the minister, have been placed in the citadel, and at the gates of Lahore, with strict orders to permit no armed Sikh soldier to enter the town.

It was intimated to me, late last night, that the inhabitants of Lahore and Umritsur were in great alarm at the approach of our army to the capital, and were under apprehension that those cities might be sacked and plundered by our troops. I therefore caused the Proclamation, a copy of which is enclosed, to be issued to the inhabitants of those cities, informing them of the result of my interview with the Maharajah, and assuring them of protection, in person and property, if the Durbar acted in good faith, and no further hostile opposition was offered by the army.

On our arrival at this place (Kanha Kutchwa) about sixteen miles from the city of Lahore, and twelve from the cantonments), heavy firing for the best part of an hour was heard. This proved to be a salute of seven rounds from every gun in Lahore, in honour of the result of the Maharajah's meeting with me yesterday, and in joy at the prospect of the restoration of amicable relations.

PROCLAMATION,

By the Right Honourable the Governor-General of India.

Foreign Department, Kussoor, February 14, 1846.

The Sikh army has been expelled from the left bank of the river Sutlej, having been defeated in every action, with the loss of more than 220 pieces of field artillery.

The British army has crossed the Sutlej, and entered the Punjaub.

The Governor-General announces by this Proclamation that this measure has been adopted by the Government of India, in accordance with the intentions expressed in the Proclamation of the 13th of December last, as having been forced upon the Governor-General for the purpose of "effectually protecting the "British Provinces, for vindicating the authority of the British "Government, and for punishing the violators of treaties and the "disturbers of the public peace."

These operations will be steadily persevered in, and vigorously prosecuted, until the objects proposed to be accomplished are fully attained. The occupation of the Punjaub by the British forces will not be relinquished until ample atonement for the insult offered to the British Government by the infraction of the treaty of 1809, A.D., and by the unprovoked invasion of the British Provinces shall have been exacted. These objects will include full indemnity for all expenses incurred during the war, and such arrangements for the future government of the Lahore territories as will give perfect security to the British Government against similar acts of perfidy and aggression.

Military operations against the Government and army of the Lahore State have not been undertaken by the Government of India from any desire of territorial aggrandizement. The Governor-General, as already announced in the Proclamation of the 13th of December, "sincerely desired to see a strong Sikh Government re-established in the Punjaub, able to controul its army and to protect its subjects." The sincerity of these professions is proved by the fact that no preparations for hostilities had been made when the Lahore Government suddenly, and without a pretext of complaint, invaded the British territories. The unprovoked aggression has compelled the British Government to have recourse to arms, and to organize the means of offensive warfare, and whatever may now befall the Lahore State, the consequences can alone be attributed to the misconduct of that Government and its army.

No extension of territory was desired by the Government of India; the measure necessary for providing indemnity for the past and security for the future will, however, involve the retention by the British Government of a portion of the country hitherto under the Government of the Lahore State. The extent of territory which it may be deemed advisable to hold will be determined by the conduct of the Durbar, and by considerations for the security of the British frontier. The Government of India will, under any circumstances, annex to the British Provinces the districts, hill and plain, situated between the rivers Sutlej and Beas, the revenues thereof being appropriated as a part of the indemnity required from the Lahore State.

The Government of India has frequently declared that it did not desire to subvert the Sikh Government in the Punjaub; and although the conduct of the Durbar has been such as to justify the most severe and extreme measures of retribution (the infliction of which may yet be required by sound policy, if the recent acts of violence be not amply atoned for and immediate submission tendered), nevertheless the Governor-General is still willing that an opportunity should be given to the Durbar and to the chiefs to submit themselves to the authority of the British Government, and by a return to good faith, and the observance of prudent counsels, enable the Governor-General to organize a Sikh Government in the person of a descendant of its founder, the late Maharajah Runjeet Singh, the faithful ally of the British power.

The Governor-General, at this moment of a most complete and decisive victory, cannot give a stronger proof of the forbearance and moderation of the British Government than by making this declaration of his intentions, the terms and mode of the arrangement remaining for further adjustment.

The Governor-General, therefore, calls upon all those chiefs who are the well-wishers of the descendants of Runjeet Singh, and especially such chiefs as have not participated in the hostile proceedings against the British power, to act in concert with him for carrying into effect such arrangements as shall maintain a Sikh Government at Lahore, capable of controlling its army and protecting its subjects, and based upon principles that shall provide for the future tranquillity of the Sikh states, shall secure the British frontier against a repetition of acts of aggression, and shall prove to the whole world the moderation and justice of the paramount power of India.

If this opportunity of rescuing the Sikh nation from military anarchy and misrule be neglected, and hostile opposition to the British army be renewed, the Government of India will make such other arrangements for the future government of the Punjaub as the interests and security of the British power may render just and expedient.

By order, &c. (Signed) F. CURRIE,
Secretary to the Government of India, with the Governor-General.

(True copy) W. EDWARDS,
Under Secretary to the Government of India, with Governor-General.

General Order by the Right Honourable the Governor-General of India.

Camp, Kussoor, February 14, 1846.

The Governor-General, having received from his Excellency the Commander-in-Chief the despatch annexed to this paper, announces to the army and the people of India, for the fourth time during this campaign, a most important and memorable victory obtained by the army of the Sutlej over the Sikh forces at Sobraon, on the 10th instant.

On that day the enemy's strongly entrenched camp, defended by 35,000 men, and sixty-seven pieces of artillery, exclusive of heavy guns, on the opposite bank of the river, was stormed by the British army, under the immediate command of his Excellency Sir Hugh Gough, Bart., G.C.B., and in two hours the Sikh forces were driven into the river with immense loss, sixty-seven guns being captured by the victors.

The Governor-General most cordially congratulates the Commander-in-Chief and the British army on this exploit, one of the most daring ever achieved, by which, in open day, a triple line of breast-works, flanked by formidable redoubts, bristling with artillery, manned by thirty-two regular regiments of infantry, was assaulted and carried by forces under his Excellency's command.

This important operation was most judiciously preceded by a cannonade from the heavy howitzers and mortars, which had arrived from Delhi on the 8th instant, the same day on which the forces under Major-General Sir Harry Smith, which had been detached to Loodiana, and had gained the victory of Aliwal, rejoined the Commander-in-Chief's camp.

The vertical fire of the heavy ordnance had the effect intended by his Excellency; it shook the enemy's confidence in works so well and so laboriously constructed, and compelled them to seek shelter in the broken ground within their camp.

The British infantry, formed on the extreme left of the line, then advanced to the assault, and, in spite of every impediment, cleared the entrenchments, and entered the enemy's camp. Her Majesty's 10th, 53rd, and 80th Regiments, with the 33rd, 43rd, 59th, and 63rd Native Infantry, moving at a firm and steady pace never fired a shot till they had passed the barriers opposed to them, a forbearance much to be commended and most worthy of constant imitation, to which may be attributed the success of their first effort, and the small loss they sustained. This attack was crowned with the success it deserved, and (led by its gallant commander, Major-General Sir Robert Dick) obtained the admiration of the army, which witnessed its disciplined valour; when checked by the formidable obstacles and superior numbers to which the attacking division was exposed, the 2nd division, under Major-General Gilbert, afforded the most opportune assistance by rapidly advancing to the attack of the enemy's batteries, entering their fortified position after a severe struggle, and sweeping through the interior of the camp. This division inflicted a very severe loss on the retreating enemy.

The same gallant efforts, attended by the same success, distinguished the attack of the enemy's left, made by the first division under the command of Major-General Sir Harry Smith, K.C.B., in which the troops nobly sustained their former reputation.

These three divisions of infantry, concentrated within the

enemy's camp, drove his shattered forces into the river, with a loss which far exceeded that which the most experienced officers had ever witnessed.

Thus terminated, in the brief space of two hours, this most remarkable conflict, in which the military combinations of the Commander-in-Chief were fully and ably carried into effect with his Excellency's characteristic energy. The enemy's select regiments of regular infantry have been dispersed, and a large proportion destroyed, with the loss, since the campaign began, of 220 pieces of artillery taken in action.

The same evening, six regiments of native infantry crossed the Sutlej; on the following day, the bridge of boats was nearly completed by that able and indefatigable officer, Major Abbott, of the Engineers, and the army is this day encamped at Kussoor, thirty-two miles from Lahore.

The Governor-General again most cordially congratulates the Commander-in-Chief on the important results obtained by this memorable achievement. The Governor-General, in the name of the Government and of the people of India, offers to his Excellency the Commander-in-Chief, to the general officers, and all the officers and troops under their command, his grateful and heartfelt acknowledgments for the services they have performed.

To commemorate this great victory, the Governor-General will cause a medal to be struck, with "SOBRAON" engraved upon it, to be presented to the victorious army in the service of the East India Company, and requests his Excellency the Commander-in-Chief to forward the lists usually furnished of those engaged.

The Governor-General deeply regrets the loss of the brave officers and men who have fallen on this occasion. Major-General Sir Robert Dick, K.C.B., who led the attack, received a mortal wound after he had entered the enemy's entrenchments. Thus fell, most gloriously, at the moment of victory, this veteran officer, displaying the same energy and intrepidity, as when, thirty-five years ago, in Spain, he was the distinguished leader of the 42nd Highlanders.

The army has also sustained a heavy loss by the death of Brigadier Taylor, commanding the 3rd brigade of the 2nd division, a most able officer, and very worthy to have been at the head of so distinguished a corps as Her Majesty's 29th Regiment, by which he was beloved and respected.

The Company's service has lost an excellent officer in Captain Fisher, who fell at the head of the brave Sirmoor regiment, which greatly distinguished itself.

The Governor-General has much satisfaction in again offering to Major-General Sir Harry Smith, K.C.B., commanding the 1st division of infantry, his best thanks for his gallant services on this occasion, by which he has added to his well-established reputation.

The Governor-General acknowledges the meritorious conduct of Brigadier Penny and Brigadier Hicks, commanding brigades in the 1st division.

Her Majesty's 31st and 50th Regiments greatly distinguished themselves, as well as the 42nd and 47th Native Infantry and the Nusseree battalion.

The Governor-General's thanks are also due to Lieutenant-Colonel Ryan, commanding Her Majesty's 50th, who, he regrets to hear, has been severely wounded.

To Major-General Gilbert, commanding the 2nd division, the Governor-General is most happy to express his acknowledgments for the judgment, coolness, and intrepidity displayed by him on every occasion since the campaign opened; and on the present, the promptitude and energy of his attack essentially contributed to ensure the success of the day.

The Governor-General trusts that the wound received by Brigadier MacLaren will not long deprive the service of one of its best officers.

Her Majesty's 29th, and the 1st European Regiments, and the 16th, 48th, 61st Native Infantry, and the Sirmoor battalion, have entitled themselves, by their gallant conduct, to the thanks of the Government.

To Brigadier Stacy, on whom the command of the 2nd division devolved, the Governor-General's thanks are especially due, for the able manner in which the attack within the enemy's camp was directed.

The Governor-General is also glad to have this opportunity of acknowledging the services of Brigadier Wilkinson, commanding the 6th brigade of the attacking division.

The brigade composed of Her Majesty's 9th and 62nd Regiments, and the 26th Native Infantry, under the command of Brigadier the Honourable T. Ashburnham, placed in support of the attacking division, by its firm and judicious advance, contributed to the success of the assault.

The cavalry, under the command of Major-General Sir J. Thackwell, K.C.B., Brigadiers Cureton, Scott, and Campbell, were well in hand, and ready for any emergency. Her Majesty's 3rd Light Dragoons, as usual, were in the foremost ranks, and distinguished themselves under their commanding officer, Lieutenant-Colonel White.

Brigadier Smith, the commanding engineer, fully accomplished the Commander-in-Chief's instructions; and to Captain Baker and Lieutenant Becher of the Engineers, the Governor-General's acknowledgments are due, for leading the division of attack into the enemy's camp; these officers will maintain the reputation of their corps whenever gallantry or science may be required from its members.

Major Abbott, of the Engineers, exclusive of his exertions in constructing the bridge of boats, displayed much intelligence in the field. The merits of Major Reilly, commanding that most useful corps the Sappers and Miners, are acknowledged. The ability and zeal of Brigadier Irvine, the senior officer of the engineer corps, are well known to the Governor-General; and his forbearance in not assuming the command, having reached the camp on the preceding evening, is duly appreciated.

Brigadier Gowan, commanding the artillery, ably directed the practice of the heavy artillery, on the left, assisted by Lieutenant-Colonel Biddulph, Lieutenant-Colonel Brooke, Lieutenant-Colonel Wood, and Captain Pillans.

On the right, the howitzer practice was well sustained by Major Grant.

The troops of horse artillery of Lieutenant-Colonel Lane and Captain Fordyce greatly assisted the attack of our infantry on the left; and, whilst the enemy were crossing the river, the fire of Lieutenant-Colonel Alexander's troop was most effective.

The troops of Captain Horsford and Captain Swinley also did good service.

The Governor-General's acknowledgments are due to Major Grant, Deputy Adjutant-General, and to his department generally, for their ability and intelligence. To the Quarter-Master-General the service is much indebted for the judgment and zeal which mark all the proceedings of that officer, and the Governor-General offers acknowledgments to him, to the Deputy Quarter-Master-General, Lieutenant-Colonel Drummond, and the officers of that department.

To Lieutenant-Colonel Barr, Acting Adjutant-General, and to Lieutenant-Colonel Gough, Acting Quarter-Master-General, Queen's service, the Governor-General's thanks are due. He regrets the temporary privation of the services of these officers by the wounds they have received.

To Lieutenant-Colonel Birch, Judge Advocate-General, the Governor-General again has to repeat his thanks for his intelligence and gallantry.

To Lieutenant-Colonel Havelock, Persian interpreter, the Governor-General offers his best thanks.

The Governor-General desires to record his obligations to Count Ravensburg, and to the officers of His Royal Highness's Staff, Count Oriola, and Count Greuben. This gallant and amiable Prince, with his brave associates of the Prussian army, has shared all the dangers and secured for himself the respect and admiration of the British army; and the Governor-General begs to convey to His Royal Highness and to his Staff his cordial thanks for the ready offers of their services on the field of battle.

The Governor-General has now to acknowledge the services rendered by the officers attached to his own Staff.

He renews to Lieutenant-Colonel Benson, of the Military Board, his strong sense of the important services rendered by that officer during the whole of this campaign, whose general information in military details, and cool judgment in action, deserve this acknowledgment.

Lieutenant-Colonel Wood, the Governor-General's Military Secretary, displayed on the 10th instant, the same intelligence and gallantry as on former occasions.

Major Lawrence, the Governor-General's Political Agent, has, throughout these operations, afforded most useful assistance by his ability, zeal, and activity in the field, as well as on every other occasion.

Captain Mills, Assistant Political Agent, and Honorary Aide-de-Camp to the Governor-General, has shown the most unwearied devotion to the service, as well in the field as in the exercise of his personal influence in the protected Sikh states.

The Governor-General's thanks are also due to Captain Cunningham, Engineers, Assistant Political Agent.

The Governor-General's Aides-de-Camp, Captain Grant, Lord Arthur Hay, Captain Peel, and Captain Hardinge, by their gallantry and intelligence rendered themselves most useful.

In the operations of this campaign, in which officers of the civil service have accompanied the camp, and participated in the risks incidental to active warfare, the Governor-General's thanks are due for their readiness in encountering these risks, and their endurance of privations.

The Governor-General acknowledges the able assistance he has at all times received from the Political Secretary, F. Currie, Esq. His acknowledgments are also due to his Private Secretary, C. Hardinge, Esq., and to the Assistant Political Agent, R. Cust, Esq.

Lieut.-Col. Parsons, Deputy Commissary-General, has succeeded in keeping the army well supplied; and the Governor-General is much satisfied with his exertions, and those of the officers under his command. The army took the field under circumstances of great difficulty; and, by strenuous exertions, and good arrangements on the part of the Lieut.-Colonel, the army has now a large supply in reserve—a result very favourable to the Chief of the Commissariat Department. The manner in which Capt. Johnson has conducted the commissariat duties entrusted to him, has also met with the Governor-General's approbation.

To Dr. Macleod, Superintending Surgeon, and to Dr. Graham, as well as to the officers of the medical department generally, the Governor-General offers his acknowledgments.

His thanks are due to Dr. Walker, Surgeon to the Governor-General, whose ability is only to be equalled by his zeal and humanity.

A salute of twenty-one guns will be fired in celebration of the victory of Sobraon at all the usual stations of the army.

By order of the Right Hon. the Governor-General of India,

F. Currie,

Secretary to the Government of India, with the Governor-General.

General Sir Hugh Gough, Bart., G.C.B., Commander-in-Chief of the Forces in India, to the Governor-General of India.

Head Quarters, Army of the Sutlej, Camp Kussoor,
February 13, 1846.

Right Honourable Sir,

This is the fourth despatch which I have the honour of addressing to you since the opening of the campaign. Thanks to Almighty God, whose hand I desire to acknowledge in all our successes, the occasion of my writing now is to announce a fourth and most glorious and decisive victory.

My last communication detailed the movements of the Sikhs

and our counter-manœuvres since the great day of Ferozeshah. Defeated on the Upper Sutlej, the enemy continued to occupy his position on the right bank, and his formidable *tête du pont* and entrenchments on the left bank of the river, in front of the main body of our army. But, on the 10th instant, all that he held of British territory, which was comprised in the ground on which one of his camps stood, was stormed from his grasp, and his audacity was again signally punished by a blow, sudden, heavy, and overwhelming. It is my gratifying duty to detail the measures which have led to this glorious result.

The enemy's works had been repeatedly reconnoitered during the time of my head quarters being fixed at Nihalkee, by myself, my departmental staff, and my engineer and artillery officers. Our observations, coupled with the reports of spies, convinced us that there had devolved on us the arduous task of attacking a position covered with formidable entrenchments, not fewer than 30,000 men, the best of the Khalsa troops, with seventy pieces of cannon, united by a good bridge to a reserve on the opposite bank, on which the enemy had a considerable camp and some artillery, commanding and flanking his field-works on our side. Major General Sir Harry Smith's division having rejoined me on the evening of the 8th, and part of my siege train having come up with me, I resolved, on the morning of the 10th, to dispose our mortars and battering guns on the alluvial land within good range of the enemy's picquets at the post of observation in front of Kodeewalla, and at the Little Sobraon. It was directed that this should be done during the night of the 9th, but the execution of this part of the plan was deferred owing to misconceptions and casual circumstances until near daybreak. The delay was of little importance, as the event showed that the Sikhs had followed our example, in occupying the two posts in force by day only. Of both, therefore, possession was taken without opposition. The battering and disposable field artillery was then put in position on an extended semi-circle, embracing within its fire the works of the Sikhs. It had been intended that the cannonade should have commenced at daybreak; but so heavy a mist hung over the plain and river that it became necessary to wait until the rays of the sun had penetrated it and cleared the atmosphere. Meanwhile on the margin of the Sutlej, on our left, two brigades of Major-General Sir Robert Dick's division, under his personal command, stood ready to commence the assault against the enemy's extreme right. His 7th brigade, in which was the 10th Foot, reinforced by the 53rd Foot, and led by Brigadier Stacy, was to head the attack, supported, at 200 yards distance, by the 6th brigade, under Brigadier Wilkinson. In reserve was the 5th brigade, under Brigadier the Honourable T. Ashburnham, which was to move forward from the entrenched village of Kodeewalla, leaving, if necessary, a regiment for its defence. In the centre, Major-General Gilbert's division was deployed for support or attack, its right resting on and in the village of the Little Sobraon. Major-General Sir Harry Smith's division was formed near the village of Guttah, with its right thrown up towards the Sutlej. Brigadier Cureton's cavalry threatened, by feigned attacks, the ford at Hurrekee and the enemy's horse, under Rajah Lal Singh Misr, on the opposite bank. Brigadier Campbell, taking an intermediate position in the rear between Major-General Gilbert's right and Major-General Sir Harry Smith's left, protected both. Major-General Sir Thomas Thackwell, under whom was Brigadier Scott, held in reserve on our left, ready to act as circumstances might demand, the rest of the cavalry.

Our battery of nine-pounders, enlarged into twelves, opened near the Little Sobraon with a brigade of howitzers formed from the light field batteries and troops of horse artillery, shortly after daybreak. But it was half-past six before the whole of our artillery fire was developed. It was most spirited and well directed. I cannot speak in terms too high of the judicious disposition of the guns, their admirable practice, or the activity with which the cannonade was sustained. But, notwithstanding the formidable calibre of our iron guns, mortars, and howitzers, and the admirable way in which they were served, and aided by a rocket battery, it would have been visionary to expect that they could, within any limited time, silence the fire of seventy pieces behind well-constructed batteries of earth, plank, and fascines, or dislodge troops, covered either by redoubts or epaulments, or within a treble line of trenches. The effect of the cannonade was, as has been since proved by an inspection of the camp, most severely felt by the enemy; but it soon became evident that the issue of this struggle must be brought to the arbitrement of musketry and the bayonet.

At nine o'clock, Brigadier Stacy's brigade, supported on either flank by Captains Horsford's and Fordyce's batteries, and Lieutenant-Colonel Lane's troop of horse artillery, moved to the attack in admirable order. The infantry and guns aided each other correlatively. The former marched steadily on in line, which they halted only to correct when necessary. The latter took up successive positions at the gallop, until at length they were within three hundred yards of the heavy batteries of the Sikhs; but, notwithstanding the regularity and coolness, and scientific character of this assault, which Brigadier Wilkinson well supported, so hot was the fire of cannon, musketry, and zumboorucks, kept up by the Khalsa troops, that it seemed for some moments impossible that the entrenchments could be won under it; but soon, persevering gallantry triumphed, and the whole army had the satisfaction to see the gallant Brigadier Stacy's soldiers driving the Sikhs in confusion before them within the area of their encampment. The 10th Foot, under Lieutenant-Colonel Franks, now for the first time brought into serious contact with the enemy, greatly distinguished themselves. This regiment never fired a shot until it had got within the works of the enemy. The onset of Her Majesty's 53rd Foot was as gallant and effective. The 43rd and 59th Native Infantry, brigaded with them, emulated both in cool determination.

At the moment of this first success, I directed Brigadier the Hon. T. Ashburnham's brigade to move on in support; and Major-General Gilbert's and Sir Harry Smith's divisions to throw out their light troops to threaten the works, aided by artillery. As these attacks of the centre and right commenced, the fire of our heavy guns had first to be directed to the right, and then gradually to cease; but, at one time, the thunder of full 120 pieces of ordnance reverberated in this mighty combat through the valley of the Sutlej; and as it was soon seen that the weight of the whole force within the Sikh camp was likely to be thrown upon the two brigades that had passed its trenches, it became necessary to convert into close and serious attacks the demonstrations with skirmishers and artillery of the centre and right; and the battle raged with inconceivable fury from right to left. The Sikhs, even when at particular points their entrenchments were mastered with the bayonet, strove to regain them by the fiercest conflict, sword in hand. Nor was it until the cavalry of the left, under Major-General Sir Joseph Thackwell, had moved forward and ridden through the openings in the entrenchments made by our sappers, in single file, and reformed as they passed them; and the 3rd Dragoons, whom no obstacle usually held formidable by horse appears to check, had on this day, as at Ferozeshah, galloped over and cut down the obstinate defenders of batteries and field-works, and until the full weight of three divisions of infantry, with every field artillery gun which could be sent to their aid, had been cast into the scale, that victory finally declared for the British. The fire of the Sikhs first slackened, and then nearly ceased; and the victors then pressing them on every side, precipitated them in masses over their bridge, and into the Sutlej, which a sudden rise of seven inches had rendered hardly fordable. In their efforts to reach the right bank through the deepened water, they suffered from our horse artillery a terrible carnage. Hundreds fell under this cannonade; hundreds upon hundreds were drowned in attempting the perilous passage. Their awful slaughter, confusion, and dismay were such as would have excited compassion in the hearts of their generous conquerors, if the Khalsa troops had not, in the earlier part of the action, sullied their gallantry by slaughtering and barbarously mangling every wounded soldier whom, in the vicissitudes of attack, the fortune of war left at their mercy. I must pause in this narrative especially to notice the determined hardihood and bravery with which our two battalions of Ghoorkhas, the Sirmoor and Nusseree, met the Sikhs, wherever they were opposed to them. Soldiers, of small stature but indomitable spirit, they vied in ardent courage in the charge with the grenadiers of our own nation, and, armed with the short weapon of their mountains, were a terror to the Sikhs throughout this great combat.

Sixty-seven pieces of cannon, upwards of 200 camel-swivels (zumboorucks), numerous standards, and vast munitions of war, captured by our troops, are the pledges and trophies of our victory. The battle was over by eleven in the morning; and, in the forenoon, I caused our engineers to burn a part and to sink a part of the vaunted bridge of the Khalsa army, across which they had boastfully come once more to defy us, and to threaten India with ruin and devastation.

We have to deplore a loss severe in itself, but certainly not heavy when weighed in the balance against the obstacles overcome and the advantages obtained. I have especially to lament the fall of Major-General Sir Robert Dick, K.C.B., a gallant veteran of the Peninsula and Waterloo campaigns. He survived only until evening the dangerous grape-shot wound which he received close to the enemy's 80th regiment, in their career of noble daring. Major-General Gilbert, to whose gallantry and unceasing exertions I have been so deeply indebted, and whose services have been so eminent throughout this eventful campaign, and Brigadier Stacy, the leader of the brigade most hotly and successfully engaged, both received contusions. They were such as would have caused many men to retire from the field, but they did not interrupt for a moment the efforts of these heroic officers. Brigadier MacLaren, so distinguished in the campaigns in Affghanistan, at Maharajpore, and now again in our conflicts with the Sikhs, has been badly wounded by a ball in the knee. Brigadier Taylor, C.B., one of the most gallant and intelligent officers in the army, to whom I have felt deeply indebted on

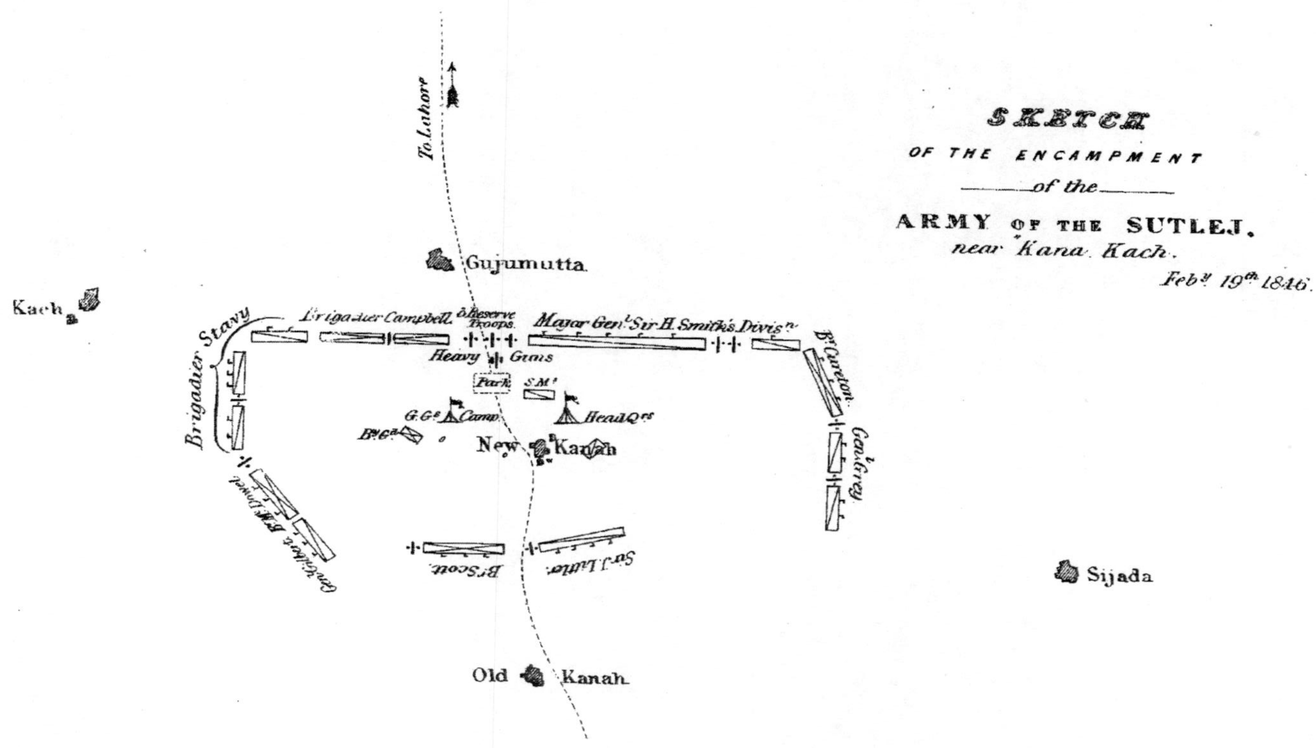
SKETCH
OF THE ENCAMPMENT
of the
ARMY OF THE SUTLEJ.
near Kana Kach.
Feby 19th 1846.
To Lahore
Gujumutta
Kach
Brigadier Stavy
Brigadier Campbell
& Reserve Troops.
Major Genl Sir H. Smith's Divisn
Br Cureton
Genl Grey
Heavy Guns
Park
S.M.
G.G.s Camp
Head Qrs
Bde G.
New Kanah
Gen Gilbert Br McDowell
Br Scott
Sir J. Littler
Old Kanah
Sijada

many occasions, fell in this fight, at the head of his brigade, in close encounter with the enemy, and covered with honourable wounds. Brigadier Penny, of the Nusseree battalion, commanding the 2nd brigade, has been wounded, but not, I trust, severely. I am deprived for the present of the valuable services of Lieutenant-Colonel J. B. Gough, C.B., Acting Quarter-Master-General of Her Majesty's troops, whose aid I have so highly prized in all my campaigns in China and India. He received a wound from a grape-shot, which is severe, but I hope not dangerous. Lieut.-Colonel Barr, Acting Adjutant-General of Her Majesty's forces, whose superior merit as a staff-officer I have before recorded, has suffered a compound fracture in the left arm by a ball. It is feared that amputation may become necessary. Lieutenant-Colonels Ryan and Petit, of the 50th Foot, were both badly wounded with that gallant regiment. Captain John Fisher, commandant of the Sirmoor battalion, fell at the head of his valiant little corps, respected and lamented by the whole army.

I have now to make the attempt, difficult, nay, impracticable I deem it, of expressing in adequate terms my sense of obligation to those who especially aided me by their talents and self-devotion in the hard-fought field of Sobraon.

First, Right Honourable Sir, you must permit me to speak of yourself. Before the action, I had the satisfaction of submitting to you my plan of attack, and I cannot describe the support which I derived from the circumstance of its having in all its details met your approbation. When a soldier of such sound judgment and experience as your Excellency assured me that my projected operation deserved success, I could not permit myself to doubt that, by the blessing of Divine Providence, the victory would be ours. Nor did your assistance stop here; though suffering severely from the effects of a fall, and unable to mount on horseback without assistance, your uncontrollable desire to see this army once more triumphant carried you into the hottest of the fire, filling all who witnessed your exposure to such peril at once with admiration of the intrepidity that prompted it and anxiety for your personal safely, involving so deeply in itself the interests and happiness of British India. I must acknowledge my obligation to you for having, whilst I was busied with another portion of our operations, superintended all the arrangements that related to laying our bridge across the Sutlej, near Ferozepore. Our prompt appearance on this side of the river, after victory, and advance to this place, which has enabled us to surprise its fort, and encamp without opposition in one of the strongest positions in the country, is the result of this invaluable assistance.

The Major-Generals of divisions engaged deserve far more commendation than I am able, within the limits of a despatch, to bestow. Major-General Sir Robert Dick, as I have already related, has fallen on a field of renown worthy of his military career and services, and the affectionate regret of his country will follow him to a soldier's grave.

In his attack on the enemy's left, Major-General Sir Harry Smith displayed the same valour and judgment which gave him the victory of Aliwal. A more arduous task has seldom, if ever, been assigned to a division. Never has an attempt been more gloriously carried through

I want words to express my gratitude to Major-General Gilbert. Not only have I to record that in this great fight all was achieved by him which, as Commander-in-Chief, I could desire to have executed; not only on this day was his division enabled, by his skill and courageous example, to triumph over obstacles from which a less ardent spirit would have recoiled as insurmountable; but, since the hour in which our leading columns moved out of Umballa, I have found in the Major-General an officer who has not merely carried out all my orders to the letter, but whose zeal and tact have enabled him in a hundred instances to perform valuable services in exact anticipation of my wishes. I beg explicitly to recommend him to your Excellency's especial notice as a divisional commander of the highest merit.

Major-General Sir Joseph Thackwell has established a claim on this day to the rare commendation of having achieved much with a cavalry force, where the duty to be done consisted of an attack on field-works, usually supposed to be the particular province of infantry and artillery. His vigilance and activity throughout our operations, and the superior manner in which our outpost duties have been carried on under his superintendence, demand my warmest acknowledgments.

Brigadier Stacy, C. B., I must commend to your special protection and favour. On him devolved the arduous duty of leading the first column to the attack, turning the enemy's right, encountering his fire, before his numbers had been thinned, or his spirit broken, and, to use a phrase which a soldier like your Excellency will comprehend, taking off the rough edge of the Sikhs in the fight. How ably, how gallantly, how successfully this was done, I have before endeavoured to relate. I feel certain that Brigadier Stacy and his noble troops will hold their due place in your Excellency's estimation, and that his merits will meet with fit reward.

Brigadier Orchard, C.B., in consequence of the only regiment under his command that was engaged in the action, being with Brigadier Stacy's brigade, attached himself to it, and shared all its dangers, glories, and success.

I beg as warmly and sincerely to praise the manner in which Brigadier Wilkinson supported Brigadier Stacy, and followed his lead into the enemy's works.

Brigadier the Hon. T. Ashburnham manœuvred with great coolness and success as a reserve to the two last-mentioned brigades.

Brigadier Taylor, of Her Majesty's 29th, fell nobly, as has already been told, in the discharge of his duty. He is himself beyond the reach of earthly praise; but it is my earnest desire that his memory may be honoured in his fall, and that his regiment, the army with which he served, and his country, may know that no officer held a higher place in my poor estimation, for gallantry or skill, than Brigadier C. C. Taylor.

Brigadier MacLaren, C.B., in whom I have ever confided, as one of the ablest of the senior officers of this force, sustained on this day, as I have before intimated, his already enviable reputation: I trust he may not long be kept by his wound out of the sphere of active exertion, which is his natural element.

Brigadiers Penny and Hicks commanded the two brigades of Major-General Sir Harry Smith's division, and overcame at their head the most formidable opposition. I beg to bring both, in the most earnest manner, to your notice, trusting that Brigadier Penny's active services will soon become once more available.

The manœuvres of Brigadier Cureton's cavalry, in attracting and fixing the attention of Rajah Lal Singh Misr's horse, fulfilled every expectation which I had formed, and were worthy of the skill of the officer employed, whose prominent exploits at the battle of Aliwal I have recently had the honour to bring to your notice.

Brigadier Scott, C.B., in command of the 1st brigade of cavalry, had the rare fortune of meeting and overcoming a powerful body of infantry in the rear of a line of formidable field-works. I have to congratulate him on the success of the noble troops under him, and to thank him for his own meritorious exertions. I am quite certain that your Excellency will bear them in mind.

Brigadier Campbell's brigade was less actively employed; but all that was required of it was most creditably performed. The demonstration on the enemy's left by the 9th Lancers towards the conclusion of the battle, was made in the best order under a sharp cannonade.

Brigadier Gowan, C.B., deserves my best thanks for his able arrangements, the value of which was so fully evinced in the first hour and a half of this conflict, when it was almost exclusively an artillery fight. Brigadiers Biddulph, Brooke, and Dennis, supported him in the ablest way throughout the day, and have given me the most effectual assistance under every circumstance of the campaign.

The effective practice of our rockets, under Brigadier Brooke, elicited my particular admiration.

Brigadier Smith, C.B., had made all the dispositions in the engineer department, which were in the highest degree judicious, and in every respect excellent. On the evening of the 9th instant Brigadier Irvine, whose name is associated with one of the most brilliant events in our military history, the capture of Bhurtpore, arrived in camp. The command would, of course, have devolved on him, but, with that generosity of spirit which ever accompanies true valour and ability, he declined to assume it, in order that all the credit of that work which he had begun might attach to Brigadier Smith. For himself, Brigadier Irvine sought only the opportunity of sharing our perils in the field, and he personally accompanied me throughout the day. Brigadier Smith has earned a title to the highest praise I can bestow.

To the General Staff I am in every way indebted. Nothing could surpass the activity and intelligence of Lieutenant-Colonel Garden and Major Grant, who are the heads of it, in the discharge of the duties of their departments, ever very laborious, and during this campaign almost overwhelming. Both yet suffer under the effects of wounds previously received. Lieutenant-Colonel Drummond, C.B., Deputy Quarter-Master-General, and Lieutenant Arthur Becher, Deputy-Assistant Quarter-Master-General, ably supported the former; and the exertions of Captains Anson and Tucker, Assistant Adjutants-General, have been most satisfactory to the latter and to myself.

Lieut.-Colonel Parsons, Deputy Commissary-General, has evinced the most successful perseverance in his important endeavours to supply the army. He has been ably aided at head quarters by Major W. J. Thompson, C.B., and Major Curtis, Sub-Assistant Commissary-General; all three of these officers were most active in conveying my orders in the battle of Sobraon in the face of every danger. I have, in the most explicit way, to record the same intelligence and ability, and the same activity and bravery, in the case of Lieutenant-Colonel Birch, Judge Advocate-

General, both as respects departmental duties and active attendance on me in the field. I have already spoken of the loss which I have sustained by Lieutenant-Colonels Gough and Barr being wounded. The exertions of both in animating our troops in moments of emergency were laudable beyond my power to praise. Lieutenant Sandys, 55th Regiment Native Infantry, Postmaster of the force, assisted in conveying my orders.

Superintending Surgeon B. Macleod, M.D., has been indefatigable in the fulfilment of every requirement of his important and responsible situation. I am entirely satisfied with his exertions and their results. I must bring to notice also the merits of Field-Surgeon J. Steel, M.D., and Surgeon Graham, M.D., in charge of the depôt of sick.

I was accompanied during the action by the following officers of my personal staff:—Captain the Hon. C. R. Sackville West, Her Majesty's 21st Foot, Officiating Military Secretary (Captain Haines, for whom he acts, still being disabled by his severe wound); Lieutenant-Colonel H. Havelock, C.B., Her Majesty's 39th Foot, Persian Interpreter; Lieutenant Bagot, 15th Native Infantry; Lieutenant Edwards, 1st European Light Infantry; and Cornet Lord James Browne, 9th Lancers, my Aides-de-Camp; and Assistant-Surgeon J. E. Stephens, M.D., my medical officer, assisted in conveying my orders to various points, in the thickest of the fight and the hottest of the fire, and to all of them I feel greatly indebted.

I have to acknowledge the services in the command of regiments, troops, and batteries, or on select and particular duties in the engineer department, of the following officers, and to recommend them to your Excellency's special favour, *viz.*:—Major F. Abbott, who laid the bridge by which the army crossed into the Punjaub, and who was present at Sobraon, and did excellent service; Captain Baker and Lieutenant John Becher, Engineers, who conducted Brigadier Stacy's column (the last of these was wounded); Lieutenant-Colonel Wood, Artillery, commanding the mortar battery; Major Lawrenson, commanding the eighteen pounder battery: Lieutenant-Colonel Huthwaite, commanding the eight-inch howitzer battery; and Lieutenant-Colonel Geddes, commanding the rockets; Captain R. Waller, horse artillery; Captain G. H. Swinley, Captain E. F. Day, Captain J. Turton, Brevet-Major C. Grant, Brevet-Lieutenant-Colonel J. Alexander, Brevet-Major F. Brind, Brevet-Lieutenant-Colonel J. T. Lane, Brevet-Major J. Campbell, Captain J. Fordyce, Captain R. Horsford, and Lieutenant G. Holland, commanding troops and batteries; Major B. Y. Reilly, commanding Sappers and Miners; Lieutenant-Colonel White, C.B., commanding the 3rd Light Dragoons; Captain Nash, 4th Light Cavalry; Major Alexander, 5th Light Cavalry; Captain Christie, 9th Irregular Cavalry; Lieutenant-Colonel Fullerton, 9th Lancers; Captain Leeson, 2nd Irregular Cavalry; Brevet-Captain Becher, 8th Irregular Cavalry; Captain Pearson, 16th Lancers; Brevet-Captain Quin, Governor-General's Body Guard; Brevet-Major Angelo, 3rd Light Cavalry; Lieutenant-Colonel Spence, 31st Foot; Captain Corfield, 47th Native Infantry; Brevet-Lieutenant-Colonel Ryan, and Brevet-Lieutenant-Colonel Petit and Captain Long, 50th Foot; Major Polwhele, 42nd Regiment Native Infantry; Captain O'Brien and Lieutenant Travers, Nusseree battalion; Captain Stepney, 29th Foot; Major Sibbald, 41st Regiment Native Infantry; Major Birrell and Brevet-Captain Seaton, 1st European Light Infantry; Brevet-Major Graves, 16th Grenadiers; Lieutenant Reid, Sirmoor battalion; Lieutenant-Colonel Davis, 9th Foot; Major Hanscomb, 26th Regiment Native Infantry; Lieutenant-Colonel Bunbury, 80th Foot; Captain Hoggan, 63rd Regiment Native Infantry; Captain Sandeman, 33rd Regiment Native Infantry; Lieutenant-Colonel Franks, 10th Foot; Brevet-Lieut.-Colonel Nash, 43rd Regiment Native Infantry; Brevet-Lieutenant-Colonel Thomson, 59th Regiment Native Infantry; Lieutenant-Colonel Phillips, 53rd Foot; Major Shortt, 62nd Foot; Brevet-Major Marshall, 68th Regiment Native Infantry; and Captain Short, 45th Regiment Infantry.

The following staff and engineer officers I have also to bring to your special notice, and to pray that their services may be favourably remembered, and the survivors duly rewarded—*viz.*, Captain E. Christie, Deputy-Assistant Adjutant-General, and Lieutenant Maxwell, Deputy-Assistant Quarter-Master-General of Artillery; and Captain Pillans and Brevet-Captain W. K. Warner, Commissaries of Ordnance; Brevet-Captain M. Mackenzie and Brevet-Captain E. G. Austen, and First Lieutenant E. Kaye, Artillery; Majors of Brigade. Napier, Major of Brigade of Engineers; Captain Tritton, 3rd Light Dragoons, Deputy-Assistant Adjutant-General; Lieutenant E. Roche, 3rd Dragoons, Aide-de-Camp to Major-General Sir J. Thackwell, and Officiating Deputy-Assistant Quarter-Master-General of Cavalry, in the place of Captain Havelock, 9th Foot, who was present in the field, but unable, from the effects of a wound, to discharge the duties of his office; Captain E. Lugard, 31st Foot, Deputy-Assistant Adjutant-General; Lieutenant A. S. Galloway, 3rd Light Cavalry, Deputy-Assistant Quarter-Master-General; Lieutenant E. A. Holdich, 80th Foot, Aide-de-Camp to Major-General Sir Harry Smith; Lieutenant F. M'D. Gilbert, 2nd Grenadiers, Acting Aide-de-Camp to Major-General Gilbert; Captain R. Houghton, 63rd Regiment Native Infanty, Officiating Assistant Adjutant-General; Lieutenant Rawson, Deputy-Assistant Quarter-Master-General—killed; Lieutenant R. Bates, 82nd Foot, Aide-de-Camp to the late Major-General Sir R. Dick; Captain J. R. Pond, 1st European Light Infantry, Deputy-Assistant Adjutant-General; Lieutenant J. S. Paton, 14th Regiment Native Infantry, Officiating Deputy-Assistant Quarter-Master-General; Brevet-Captain Harrington, 5th Light Cavalry; Captain A. Spottiswoode, 9th Lancers; Lieutenant R. Pattinson, 16th Lancers; Captain J. Garvock, 31st Foot; Lieutenant G. H. M. Jones, 29th Foot; Captain J. L. Taylor, 26th Light Infantry, Lieutenant H. F. Dunsford, 59th Regiment Native Infantry, Majors of Brigade; Captain Combe, 1st European Light Infantry, Major of Brigade, 2nd brigade; Captain Gordon, 11th Native Infantry, Major of Brigade, 6th brigade; Captain A. G.

Ward, 68th Native Infantry, Major of Brigade; and Lieutenant R. Hay, Major of Brigade—killed.

Having ventured to speak of your Excellency's own part in this action, it would be most gratifying to me to go on to mention the brilliant share taken in it by Lieutenant-Colonel Wood and the officers of your personal staff, as well as by the civil, political, and other military officers attached to you. But as these were all under your own eye, I cannot doubt that you will yourself do justice to their exertions.

We were in this battle again honoured with the presence of Prince Waldemar of Prussia, and the two noblemen in his suite, Counts Oriola and Greuben. Here, as at Moodkee and Ferozeshah, these distinguished visitors did not content themselves with a distant view of the action, but, throughout it, were to be seen in front wherever danger most urgently pressed.

The loss of the enemy has been immense; an estimate must be formed with a due allowance for the spirit of exaggeration which pervades all statements of Asiatics where their interest leads them to magnify numbers; but our own observation on the river banks and in the enemy's camp, combined with the reports brought to our intelligence department, convince me that the Khalsa casualties were between 8,000 and 10,000* men killed and wounded in action and drowned in the passage of the river. Amongst the slain are Sirdar Sham Singh Attareewalla, Generals Gholab Singh Koopta and Heera Singh Topee, Sirdar Kishen Singh, son of the late Jemadar Kooshall Singh; Generals Mobaruck Ally and Illahee Buksh, and Shah Newaz Khan, son of Futteh-ood-deen Khan of Kussoor. The body of Sham Singh was sought for in the captured camp by his followers; and respecting the gallantry with which he is reported to have devoted himself to death rather than accompany the army in its flight, I forbade

* We have since ascertained, from undoubted authority, that the Sikhs acknowledge they had 37,000 men engaged in this battle, exclusive of the large force, particularly of cavalry, at this side of the river, and that their loss on this occasion was from 13,000 to 14,000 men.

his people being molested in their search, which was finally successful.

The consequences of this great action have yet to be fully developed. It has at least, in God's providence, once more expelled the Sikhs from our territory, and planted our standards on the soil of the Punjaub. After occupying their entrenched position for nearly a month, the Khalsa army had perhaps mistaken the caution which had induced us to wait for the necessary material, for timidity. But they must now deeply feel that the blow which has fallen on them from the British arm has only been the heavier for being long delayed.

I have, &c.

H. Gough, *General,*

Commander-in-Chief, East Indies.

Return of the Killed, Wounded, and Missing of the Army of the Sutlej, under the Command of His Excellency General Sir Hugh Gough, Bart., G.C.B., Commander-in-Chief, in the Action at Sobraon, on 10th February, 1846.

Abstract.

Staff.—2 European officers wounded.

Artillery Division.—1 European officer, 3 rank and file, 3 syce drivers, 17 horses—killed; 1 European officer, 1 sergeant, 33 rank and file, 5 lascars, 5 syces, 23 horses—wounded; 5 horses missing.

Engineers and Sappers and Miners.—2 rank and file—killed; 3 European officers, 1 native ditto, 16 rank and file—wounded.

Cavalry Division.—6 rank and file, 13 horses—killed; 4 European officers, 2 trumpeters, 36 rank and file, 53 horses—wounded; 24 horses missing.

1*st Infantry Division.*—2 European officers, 1 native officer, 97 rank and file—killed; 28 European officers, 13 native officers, 489 rank and file—wounded.

2nd Infantry Division.—5 European officers, 1 native officer, 5 sergeants, 109 rank and file, 1 horse—killed; 38 European officers, 12 native officers, 46 sergeants, 2 drummers, 685 rank and file, 1 horse—wounded.

3rd Infantry Division.—5 European officers, 1 native officer, 3 sergeants, 1 drummer, 75 rank and file, 5 horses—killed; 25 European officers, 13 native officers, 27 sergeants, 3 drummers, 573 rank and file, 6 horses—wounded.

Total—13 European officers, 3 native officers, 8 sergeants, 1 drummer, 292 rank and file, 3 syces, and 36 horses—killed; 101 European officers, 39 native officers, 74 sergeants and havildars, 7 trumpeters and drummers, 832 rank and file, 5 lascars, 5 syces, 83 horses—wounded; 29 horses missing.

European officers.—13 killed, 101 wounded.

Native officers.—3 killed, 39 wounded.

Warrant and non-commissioned officers, rank and file.—301 killed, 1,913 wounded.

Lascars, syce drivers, syces, &c.—3 killed, 10 wounded.

Total—320 killed, 2,063 wounded.

Grand Total of killed, wounded, and missing, 2,383.

Names of Officers Killed and Wounded.

KILLED.

Artillery Division.

1*st Troop 2nd Brigade Horse Artillery.*—First Lieutenant H. J. Y. Faithfull.

1*st Infantry Division.*

Brigade Staff.—Lieutenant R. Hay, Major of Brigade.

Her Majesty's 50th Foot.—Lieutenant C. R. Grimes.

2nd Infantry Division.

Divisional Staff.—Lieutenant J. S. Rawson, Officiating Deputy-Assistant Quarter-Master-General.

Brigade Staff.—Lieut.-Colonel C. C. Taylor, C.B., Brigadier.

1st European Light Infantry.—Lieutenant F. Shuttleworth and Ensign F. W. A. Hamilton.

Sirmoor Battalion.—Captain J. Fisher (23rd N.I.)

3rd Infantry Division.

Divisional Staff.—Major-General Sir R. H. Dick, K.C.B. and K.C.H.

Her Majesty's 62nd Foot.—Lieutenant W. T. Bartley.

33rd Regiment Native Infantry.—Lieutenant W. D. Playfair.

Her Majesty's 10th Foot.—Lieutenant W. Y. Beale.

Her Majesty's 53rd Foot.—Captain C. E. D. Warren.

WOUNDED.

General Staff.—Lieutenant-Colonel J. B. Gough, C.B., Officiating Quarter-Master-General to Her Majesty's forces, very severely; and Lieutenant-Colonel M. Barr, Officiating Adjutant-General to Her Majesty's forces, severely and dangerously.

Artillery Division.

2nd Troop 2nd Brigade Horse Artillery.—Brevet-Major C. Grant, slightly.

Engineer Department.

Brevet-Captain W. Abercrombie, contused; First Lieutenant J. R. Becher, severely; Second Lieutenant G. P. Hebbert, slightly.

Cavalry Division.

Her Majesty's 3rd Light Dragoons.—Lieutenant J. B. Hawkes, slightly; Lieutenant H. W. White, ditto; Cornet Kauntze, severely; and Quarter-Master A. Crabtree, slightly.

1st Infantry Division.

Divisional Staff.—Lieutenant E. A. Holdich, A.D.C., severely.

Brigade Staff.—Lieutenant-Colonel N. Penny, Brigadier and Captain; J. Garvock, Major of Brigade, severely.

Her Majesty's 31*st Foot.*—Lieutenant R. Law, severely; Lieutenant G. Elmslie, severely; Lieutenant S. J. Timbrell, dangerously, both thighs broken; Lieutenant P. Gabbett, slightly; Lieutenant C. H. G. Tritton, mortally; Ensign Jones, dangerously; and Lieutenant and Adjutant Bolton, severely.

47*th Regiment Native Infantry.*—Lieutenant and Adjutant R. Renny, severely; Lieutenant H. C. James, 32nd Native Infantry, slightly; Ensign W. H. Walcot, slightly; and J. D. Ogston, slightly.

Her Majesty's 50*th Foot.*—Brevet-Lieutenant-Colonel Ryan, K.H., dangerously; Brevet-Colonel P. J. Petit, dangerously; Captain G. M'L. Tew, dangerously; Captain J. B. Bonham, dangerously; Captain Needham, dangerously; Captain J. L. Wilton, very severely; Lieutenant H. W. Hough, severely; Lieutenant J. G. Smyth, severely; Lieutenant C. A. Mouat, severely; Ensign C. H. Slessor, slightly; and Lieutenant C. H. Tottenham, slightly.

42*nd Light Infantry.*—Major T. Polwhele, slightly; and Lieutenant A. Macqueen, severely.

Nusseree Battalion.—Captain C. O'Brien, severely.

2*nd Infantry Division.*

Divisional Staff.—Major-General W. R. Gilbert, slightly; Lieut. F. M'D. Gilbert, A.D.C., slightly.

Brigade Staff.—Lieut.-Colonel MacLaren, C.B., Brigadier, dangerously; Lieut. G. H. M. Jones, Major of Brigade, very severely, right arm amputated.

H.M.'s 29*th Foot.*—Capt. A. St. G. H. Stepney, severely; Capt. J. D. Young, slightly; Capt. K. Murchison, slightly; Lieut. R. F. Henry, Lieut. J. O. Duncan, severely; Lieut. W. Kirby, very severely; Lieut. C. E. Macdonnell, severely; Lieut. H. G. Walker, slightly; Lieut. St. G. M. Nugent, severely; Lieut. G. St. J. Henderson, contusion; Lieut. E. T. Scudamore, severely; and Ensign G. Mitchell, very severely, right leg amputated.

41st Regiment Native Infantry.—Capt. W. H. Halford, severely; Captain J. Cumberlege, severely; Capt. J. W. V. Stephen, slightly; Lieut. A. W. Onslow, slightly; Lieut. M. F. Kemble, slightly; Ensign C. H. Scatcherd, severely, since dead; Ensign C. R. Aikman, slightly; and Ensign J. P. Bennett, slightly.

68th Regiment Native Infantry.—Lieutenant P. A. Robertson, slightly; and Ensign J. A. Dorin, slightly.

1st European Light Infantry.—Brevet-Captain E. Magnay, severely; Lieut. J. Patullo, severely; Lieut. J. Lambert, severely; Lieut. G. G. Denniss, severely; Lieut. A. Hume, dangerously; Lieut. T. Staples, slightly; Ensign C. O. B. Palmer, slightly; Ensign G. H. Davidson, dangerously, since dead; Ensign P. R. Innes, slightly; and Lieut. D. C. T. Beatson (14th N. I.), severely.

16th Regiment Native Infantry Grenadiers.—Capt. A. Balderston, severely; and Ensign W. S. R. Hodson, slightly.

3rd Infantry Division.

H. M.'s 9th Foot.—Lieut. R. Daunt, slightly.

26th Regiment Native Infantry.—Lieut. F. Mackenzie, severely; and Ensign M. J. White, slightly.

H. M.'s 62nd Foot.—Lieut. R. H. Haviland, severely.

H. M.'s 80th Foot.—Capt. W. Cookson, slightly; Lieut. R. Crawley, severely; Lieut. E. W. P. Kingsley, severely; and Ensign W. B. C. S. Wandesforde, severely.

33rd Regiment Native Infantry.—Lieut. T. Tulloh, severely.

63rd Regiment Native Infantry.—Capt. W. C. Ormsby, severely; Lieut. H. A. Morrison, slightly; Ensign R. T. H. Barber, slightly.

H. M.'s 10th Foot.—Lieut. H. R. Evans, slightly; and Lieut. C. J. Lindham, severely.

43rd Regiment Light Infantry.—Capt. H. Lyell, very severely; Ensign T. Munro, severely.

59th Regiment Native Infantry.—Lieutenant H. B. Lumsden, severely.

H. M.'s 53rd Foot.—Capt. T. Smart, severely; Lieut. J. Chester, severely; Lieut. A. B. O. Stokes, severely; Ensign W. Dunning, severely; Lieut.-Col. W. G. Gold, slightly; Lieut. J. Breton, slightly; Lieut. R. N. Clarke, severely; and Ensign H. Lucas, slightly.

PAT. GRANT,
Deputy-Adjutant-General of the Army.

Adjutant-General's office, Head Quarters,
Camp, Kussoor, February 13*th*, 1846.

PROCLAMATION,

By the Governor-General of India.

Camp, Lulleeanee, February 18, 1846.

The chiefs, merchants, traders, ryots, and other inhabitants of Lahore and Umritsur, are hereby informed, that his Highness Maharajah Dhuleep Singh has this day waited upon the Right Honourable the Governor-General, and expressed the contrition of himself and the Sikh Government for their late hostile proceedings. The Maharajah and Durbar having acquiesced in all the terms imposed by the British Government, the Governor-General, having every hope that the relations of friendship will speedily be established between the two Governments, the inhabitants of Lahore and Umritsur have nothing to fear from the British army.

The Governor-General and the British troops, if the conditions above adverted to are fulfilled, and no further opposition is offered by the Khalsa army, will aid their endeavours for the re-establishment of the descendants of Maharajah Runjeet Singh, and for the protection of its subjects.

The inhabitants of the cities in the Punjaub will, in that case, be perfectly safe, in person and property, from any molestation by the British troops; and they are hereby called on to dismiss apprehension, and to follow their respective callings with all confidence.

By order of the Right Hon. the Governor-General of India,

F. CURRIE,

Secretary to the Government of India, with the Governor-General.

Extract of a Letter from Sir Hugh Gough.

Head Quarters, Camp, Army of the Sutlej, Kussoor, right bank of the Sutlej, February 16, 1846.

Here let me observe one feature so highly honourable and creditable to the native army, that notwithstanding the numerous temptations held out to them by men of their own colour and religion—namely, greatly increased pay (from seven to twelve rupees a month), and immediate promotion, I had but three desertions from this large force, during the time we lay opposite to the Sikh army. Nor should I omit to mention, as a proof of their high state of discipline, that trade has been carried on as unrestrained in the towns and villages around us, and the same confidence shown by the inhabitants as if we were located in one of our long established provinces. These are features which I well know you will highly appreciate, and which make me justly proud of this noble army.

But to revert to my narrative of the battle of Sobraon, where all so signally distinguished themselves, it would be invidious, indeed, impossible to particularize. But I must—now that the field, and I hope the *great stake* for which we were fighting, has been won—mourn over the loss of many highly distinguished officers. I shall only here name those whose meed of praise can only be their country's regret at their loss—Major-General Sir Robert Dick and Colonel Taylor of the 29th, Acting Brigadiers, nobly fell in the hour of victory, esteemed, admired, and regretted by the whole army.

In the battles of Moodkee, Ferozeshah, and Aliwal, I reported upon the noble bearing of Her Majesty's army, both cavalry and infantry. At Sobraon two new regiments contended for the prize so nobly won by their comrades in former actions, and I gave them the opportunity, by placing them in the attacking columns. Nobly did they show that they would not be outdone. Her Majesty's 10th and 53rd have, by their steadiness and brilliant conduct, under Lieutenant-Colonels Franks and Phillips, established a name second to none. The former regiment never fired a shot until they were within the enemy's works, when they sent a withering volley into their densely manned trenches. These are deeds which it is my duty and my pride to report.——I have, &c.

(Signed) HUGH GOUGH.

The Letter of Sir Hugh Gough, quoted by Sir Robert Peel in the House of Commons.

Head Quarters, Camp, Army of the Sutlej,
Kussoor, February 17, 1846.

MY DEAR SIR,

My letter of the 27th of December, announcing the glorious victories of Moodkee, and Ferozeshah, by which the war with the aggressing Sikh nation was so nobly opened, would undoubtedly have led the Honourable the Court of Directors to look forward with anxiety to the future movements, on which the weal or woe of India so greatly depended.

The anxieties and cares consequent on the multiplied arrangements necessary to the ultimate success of an anticipated final blow, made it impracticable for me to report upon the brilliant success obtained by Major-General Sir Harry Smith, at Aliwal, on the 28th of January. I regretted my inability to do so, the less, as I was aware my report upon the various arrangements, which led to this brilliant victory, made to the Right Honourable the Governor-General on the 2nd instant, would have been laid before that honourable body.

It is now with pride and with pleasure I enclose you a copy of my despatch, detailing one of the most splendid and decisive victories upon record—the Waterloo of India.

I have entered so fully both into detail and commendation in my despatch to the Governor-General, that it would be impossible for me to enlarge upon a subject embracing the warmest feelings of my heart. Policy, however, precluded me publicly recording my sentiments on the splendid gallantry of our fallen foe, or to record the acts of heroism displayed, not only individually, but almost collectively by the Sikh Sirdars and army; and I declare, were it not from a deep conviction that my country's good required the sacrifice, I would have wept to have witnessed the fearful slaughter of so devoted a body of men.

Never in the page of military history has the hand of an All-wise Being been so signally manifested: to Him, therefore be the glory! we, as his instruments, feel the pride!

But I cannot pass over, I cannot too strongly record, facts which, while they add lustre to the native army, afford to me, as its head, inexpressible pride and pleasure. For upwards of a month, when the two armies were close in front of one another, notwithstanding the numerous temptations held out to our sepoys, by men of their own colour and religion—namely, greatly increased pay (from seven to twelve rupees a month), and immediate promotion, I had but three desertions from this large force. Nor should I omit to mention, as a proof of the high state of discipline of this splendid army, that trade has been carried on unrestrainedly since we crossed the Sutlej, in the several Sikh towns around which our divisions have been necessarily placed for the procurance of water, and the same confidence has been shown as though we were in one of our long established provinces.

* * * * * *

Believe me, my dear Sir,

Very faithfully yours,

(Signed) H. Gough.

General Order by the Right Hon. the Governor-General of India.

Foreign Department, Camp of Lahore, February 20th, 1846.

The Right Hon. the Governor-General requests that the Commander-in-Chief will cause the following arrangements to be made for escorting his Highness the Maharajah Dhuleep Singh to his palace in the citadel of Lahore, this afternoon. The escort will consist of two regiments of European cavalry, two regiments of native cavalry—the body guard to be one; one regiment of irregular horse, two troops of horse artillery, one European and one native.

The Secretary to the Government of India, F. Currie, Esq., will take charge of his Highness and his suite, and will be accompanied by the Political Agent, Major Lawrence, the Governor-General's Private Secretary, Charles Hardinge, Esq., the Aide-de-Camp of the Governor-General; two Aides-de-Camp of the Commander-in-Chief, one Aide-de-Camp from each General officer of division, in uniform.

The escort will be formed at the nearest convenient spot to the Governor-General's camp, at two o'clock, and proceed to his Highness's camp, and thence to his palace.

On alighting from his elephant, a salute of twenty-one guns will be fired by the horse artillery.

His Highness the Maharajah of the Sikh nation, selected by the chiefs as their sovereign, having on the 18th instant, intimated his intention to proceed to the Governor-General's camp at Lulleeanee, attended by his Highness's Wuzeer, the Rajah Gholab Singh, and other chiefs, was received in Durbar on the afternoon of that day by the Governor-General, the Commander-in-Chief and the Staff being present. His Highness's ministers and chiefs there tendered his submission, and solicited the clemency of the British Government.

The Governor-General extended the clemency of the British Government to a prince the descendant of the Maharajah, the late Runjeet Singh, for so many years the faithful ally and friend of the British Government, as the representative of the Sikh nation selected by the chiefs and the people to be their ruler, on the condition that all the terms imposed by the British Government, and previously explained to his Highness's ministers and chiefs, should be faithfully executed.

On withdrawing from the Durbar, the Maharajah received the usual salutes due to his Highness's exalted rank.

His Highness has since remained near the Governor-General's camp, and as it will be conducive to his Highness's comfort, that he should rejoin his family, the Governor-General desires that he may, with all honour and in safety, be conducted by the British troops to the gates of his palace this day.

The following Proclamation was issued on the 18th instant, by the Governor-General, promising protection to all persons at Lahore and elsewhere who peaceably continue in their usual employment of trade and industry.

The Governor-General is satisfied, after the experience of this campaign, that he can rely on the discipline of this invincible army, as fully and securely as he has always been, confident that the day of battle, under their distinguished Commander, would be one of victory.

He trusts at present that no officers or soldiers will pass the advanced sentries of their encampment to enter the town of Lahore, and he requests his Excellency the Commander-in-Chief to give the necessary instruction to carry this order strictly into effect, as well as to protect all persons bringing provisions into the camp.

By order, &c. F. Currie,

Secretary to the Government of India,
with the Governor-General.

To the Right Hon. Sir Henry Hardinge, G.C.B. Governor-General of India.

RIGHT HONOURABLE SIR,

I have the honour to state, for the information of your Excellency, that, in accordance with the instructions contained in the order of the Governor-General of yesterday's date, I proceeded in the afternoon with the escort ordered, and accompanied by the officers mentioned below, on elephants, to conduct the Maharajah Dhuleep Singh to his palace in the citadel of Lahore.

Major Lawrence, the Governor-General's Political Agent.
W. Edwards, Esq., Under Secretary of the Foreign Department.
R. Cust, Esq., Assistant Secretary to the Foreign Department.
C. Hardinge, Esq., Private Secretary to the Governor-General.
Lieut.-Col. Wood, Military Secretary to the Governor-General.
Captain Cunningham.
Captain Hardinge, Aide-de-Camp to the Governor-General.
Captain Grant, ditto.
Lord Arthur Hay, ditto.
Captain Mills, ditto.
Captain Bagot, Aide-de-Camp to the Commander-in-Chief.
Captain Edwards, ditto.
Captain Gilbert, Aide-de-Camp to General Gilbert.
Capt. Tottenham, Aide de-Camp to General Smith.
Lieut.-Colonel Irvine, Engineers.
Lieut.-Colonel Smith, ditto.
Captain Napier, ditto,
Captain Smith, ditto.

The procession was arranged in the following order:—

9th Irregular Cavalry.
3rd Light Cavalry.
Her Majesty's 16th Lancers.
Troop Horse Artillery, Europeans.
Troop Horse Artillery, natives.
Her Majesty's 9th Lancers.
The Secretary with the Maharajah and Suite.
The Governor-General's Body Guard.

The escort was formed in open column of troops left in front, commanded by Brigadier Cureton, C.B.

We proceeded in this order to the encampment of the Maharajah's camp, about one and a half miles from our picquets, and nearly the same distance from the citadel gate of the city.

At about three-quarters of a mile from the Maharajah's camp, I was met by the minister, Rajah Gholab Singh, and some of the chiefs.

Intimation of our approach was then sent on to the Maharajah, that he might be ready on his elephant upon our arrival.

On reaching the Maharajah's camp, the troops of our escort drew up, and the Maharajah, with Bhaee Ram Singh on the same elephant, came forward from his tent, accompanied by several chiefs.

After the usual salutation, and complimentary questions and replies, I placed the Maharajah's elephant next to mine, and the troops having fallen in, as at first, proceeded round the walls of the city to the gate of the citadel.

On arriving, Brigadier Cureton drew up the escort in line in front of the gateway, and I took the Maharajah, accompanied by the officers enumerated in the former part of this letter, with Rajah Gholab Singh and the other chiefs, into the interior of the citadel, and to the inner door of his palace.

I then observed to the Maharajah and chiefs that, by order of the Right Hon. the Governor-General, I had thus brought the Maharajah, conducted by the British army, to his palace, which his Highness had left for the purpose of tendering submission to the British Government, and for placing himself, his capital, and his country, at the mercy of the Governor-General, and requesting pardon for the insult that had been offered; and that the Governor-General had thus restored him to his palace as a mark of the favour which he desired to show to the descendant of the late Maharajah Runjeet Singh.

A salute of twenty-one guns was then fired by the horse artillery.

We then took leave of the Maharajah at the gate of his palace, and returning to the outside of the city, we, continuing our progress round Lahore, thus returned to our camp.

As our camp is situated opposite to the south-east end of the city-face, and the citadel is immediately within the city walls at the north-west angle, we made the entire circuit of Lahore. I considered this preferable to going through the city, the streets of which are narrow, and would have much impeded the progress of our large escort.

We did not see one gun upon any part of the walls: all the embrasures were empty.

I have the honour to be, &c.,

F. CURRIE,

Secretary to the Government of India, with the Governor-General.

From his Excellency the Commander-in-Chief to the Right Hon. Sir Henry Hardinge, G.C.B., Governor-General of India, &c.

Head Quarters, Army of the Sutlej, in front of Lahore, Feb. 22, 1846.

RIGHT HONOURABLE SIR,

I have now to offer my congratulations on some of the earliest fruits of our victory of the 10th instant. About noon on the 20th, a day henceforth very memorable in our Indian annals, the army under my command pitched its tents on the plain of Myan Meer, under the walls of the Sikh capital. The entire submission of the Maharajah and his advisers to the will of the British Government had been before personally tendered to you, and graciously accepted; and this morning, in fulfilment of one of the conditions which your wisdom had dictated for the real interests of the ruler and people of the Punjaub, I had the honour to conduct a brigade of troops to the city, which took formal possession of the Badshahee Musjid and Hoozooree Bagh, forming a part of the palace and citadel of Lahore. I trust, by the observance of a strict discipline, to preserve unshaken that confidence which the people of the city and country around it evidently repose in the generosity, clemency, and good faith of their conquerors. Supplies of all sorts are willingly brought to our camp and punctually paid for; and I believe that by every class of persons in this vicinity the presence of our troops is felt to be a national benefit; none, certainly, have had real cause to lament it as a calamity.

I have, &c.,

HUGH GOUGH, *General,*

Commander-in-Chief, East Indies.

General Order by the Right Hon. the Governor-General of India.

Foreign Department, Camp Lahore, February 22, 1846.

The British army has this day occupied the gateway of the citadel of Lahore, the Badshahee Mosque, and the Hoozooree Bagh.

The remaining part of the citadel is the residence of his Highness the Maharajah, and also that of the families of the late Maharajah Runjeet Singh, for so many years the faithful ally of the British Government. In consideration of these circumstances, no troops will be posted within the precincts of the palace gate.

The army of the Sutlej has now brought its operations in the field to a close, by the dispersion of the Sikh army and the military occupation of Lahore, preceded by a series of the most triumphant successes ever recorded in the military history of India. The British Government, trusting to the faith of treaties and to the long subsisting friendship between the two states, had limited military preparations to the defence of its own frontier.

Compelled suddenly to assume the offensive by the unprovoked invasion of its territories, the British army, under the command of its distinguished leader, has, in sixty days, defeated the Sikh forces in four general actions, has captured 220 pieces of field artillery, and is now at the capital, dictating to the Lahore Durbar the terms of a treaty, the conditions of which will tend to secure the British Provinces from the repetition of a similar outrage.

The Governor-General being determined, however, to mark with reprobation the perfidious character of the war, has required and will exact, that every remaining piece of Sikh artillery which has been pointed against the British army during this campaign shall be surrendered.

The Sikh army, whose insubordinate conduct is one of the chief causes of the anarchy and misrule which have brought the Sikh State to the brink of destruction, is about to be disbanded.

The soldiers of the army of the Sutlej have not only proved their superior prowess in battle, but have on every occasion, with subordination and patience, endured the fatigues and privations inseparable from a state of active operations in the field. The native troops of this army have also proved that a faithful attachment to their colours and to the Company's service is an honourable feature in the character of the British sepoy.

The Governor-General has repeatedly expressed, on his own part, and that of the Government of India, admiration and gratitude for the important services which the army has rendered.

The Governor-General is now pleased to resolve, as a testimony of the approbation of the Government of India of the bravery, discipline, and soldier-like bearing of the army of the Sutlej, that all the generals, officers, non-commissioned officers, and privates, shall receive a gratuity of twelve months' batta.

Every regiment which, in obedience to its orders, may have remained in posts and forts between Loodiana and Ferozepore, and was not present in action, as in the case of the troops ordered to remain at Moodkee to protect the wounded, and those left in the forts of Ferozepore and Loodiana, shall receive the gratuity of twelve months' batta.

Obedience to orders is the first duty of a soldier, and the Governor-General, in affirming this principle, can never admit that absence, caused by the performance of indispensable duties, on which the success of the operations in the field greatly depended, ought to disqualify any soldier placed in these circumstances from participating in the gratuity given for the general good conduct of the army in the field.

All regiments and individuals ordered to the frontier and forming part of the army of the Sutlej, which may have reached Loodiana or Busseean before the date of this order, will be included as entitled to the gratuity.

By order of the Right Hon. the Governor-General of India,

F. Currie,
Secretary to the Government of India with the Governor-General.

Arrangements were fast making for the occupation of the conquered country, which is exceedingly fertile, and will yield an annual revenue of £.400,000. The chief town is Jullinder, with 40,000 inhabitants; Phulloor, Pugwarra, and Sultanpore are also of note. The cantonments of the British will not be far distant from Lahore, so as to be able to keep down all attempts at insurrection.

GOVERNMENT NOTIFICATION.

Foreign Department, Camp, Umritsir, March 16.

The Right Hon. the Governor-General of India has been pleased to direct the publication, for general information, of the subjoined extracts from the proceedings of the Government of India, relative to the re-establishment of amicable relations between the British Government and the State of Lahore, and the recognition of the independence of Maharajah Gholab Singh.

No. 1.

Note of Conference between F. Currie, Esq., and Major H. M. Lawrence, on the one part, and the Ministers and Chiefs of the Lahore Durbar on the other, 8th March, 1846.

The Ministers and chiefs having assembled at the tent of the Governor-General's agent, for the purpose of signing the treaty, the conditions of which had been previously discussed and determined, produced, on the part of the Maharajah, a letter addressed to Major Lawrence, the Governor-General's agent, of which the following is a translation:—

"The feelings of consideration, kindness, and generosity which have been evinced towards the Lahore State by the Right Hon. the Governor-General, and his Excellency's respect for the former friendship of the British Government with the late Maharajah Runjeet Singh, have been communicated to me through Mr. Secretary Currie and yourself, and have caused me to feel most grateful.

"Certain important matters will now be represented to you by the following confidential personages:—Bhaee Ram Singh, Rajah Lal Singh, Sirdar Tej Singh, Dewan Deena Nath, Fakeer Noor-ood-Deen, and you, who are the guardian of the perpetual friendship of the two Governments, will represent these matters to the Governor-General, and will, doubtless, use your endeavours to procure a favourable decision regarding them.

"The Lahore Government, it is known, is endeavouring to arrange its affairs, and it is necessary that effectual measures should be taken to prevent the recurrence of any disturbances. With this view it is very desirable that some British regiments, with artillery and officers, should be directed to remain at Lahore for a few months, for the protection of the State. After affairs have been satisfactorily settled, and the period which may be fixed upon expired, the British troops will then return."

To the above paper the following reply was made verbally, and was, at the request of the Minister and chiefs, written down and given to them:—

"The letter from the Maharajah to Major Lawrence, expressing gratitude to the Governor-General, has been read in presence of the Minister and chiefs of the Durbar. At the close of that letter, it is requested that a British force may be left at Lahore for a limited period.

"Upon this, it is to be observed, that from the wording of the letter, it is not evident that the retention of a British force at Lahore is sincerely and urgently desired by the Lahore Government, and the nature of the disturbances which are to be provided against are not specifically described. In so important a matter, general expressions are out of place. The British Government desires to exercise no interference with the Government of Lahore after the treaty of peace is concluded, and the Governor-General is not willing to have any concern with the Lahore Government, or to accede to any measure not provided for by the treaty. This has been repeatedly explained to the Lahore Durbar. If, therefore, for any special reason, and on any particular account, the assistance and intervention of the British Government are desired by the Lahore Durbar, the fact should have been more distinctly stated in the Khurreeta, and the causes which render such aid indispensable should have been given in detail. However, as the Maharajah has authorised the chiefs named in the Khurreeta, and who are present, to make known all the particulars of the case, they should now state all the circumstances in full."

The Minister and chiefs, after consultation, read aloud the substance of the paper, of which the following is a translation, but requested that it might be put in the form of a Khurreeta from the Maharajah, and sent in the evening. A communication was then made to the Governor-General who, determined that a British force should, under certain conditions, to be entered in a separate engagement, occupy Lahore for a limited time; the treaty was then signed by the Commissioners, and the meeting broke up.

Translation of Document alluded to in preceding paragraph afterwards sent from the Durbar as a formal Khurreeta, with the seal of the Maharajah.

"All the circumstances regarding the disorganization of the Government of Lahore since the demise of the late Maharajah Runjeet Singh until the present time are well known to the British Government.

"The satisfactory settlement of affairs, the discharge of the disturbers of public peace, and the reorganization of the army under the stipulations of the new treaty, are now engaging consideration. But lest, after the departure of the British forces, the evil disposed of should create fresh disturbances, and endeavour to ruin the State, it is the earnest and sincere desire and hope of the Lahore Durbar that British troops with intelligent officers should, for some months, as circumstances may seem to require, be left at Lahore for the protection of the Government and the Maharajah and the inhabitants of the city. When affairs have been satisfactorily settled, and the period prescribed for the stay of the British force shall have expired, the troops may then be withdrawn.

"True note and translation,

"F. CURRIE,

"*Secretary to the Government of India, with the Governor-General.*"

No. 2.

General Order by the Right Hon. the Governor-General of India.

Foreign Department, Camp, Lahore, March 8.

The treaty of peace between the British Government and that of his Highness the Maharajah Dhuleep Singh has been signed.

The treaty will be ratified by the Governor-General, in presence of the Maharajah and the Sikh chiefs to morrow afternoon, the 9th instant, at four o'clock, in the Governor-General's tent.

The Governor-General invites his Excellency the Commander-in-Chief, his Excellency the Governor of Scinde, with their present staff, to attend on this occasion, also the Generals of division, the Brigadiers, the head of each department, and all officers commanding corps, with one native officer from every regiment.

His Highness the Maharajah Dhuleep Singh will be received by a salute of twenty-one guns. The street leading to the Governor-General's tent will be lined by detachments of regiments according to the orders which his Excellency the Commander-in-Chief will be pleased to issue.

The following day the Governor-General will pay his Highness the Maharajah a visit of congratulation on the restoration of peace between the two Governments, and will leave the camp for that purpose at three o'clock. The escort will be fixed in the General Order of his Excellency the Commander-in-Chief.

The thirty-six pieces of Sikh artillery which were pointed against the British army have been surrendered and brought into camp. The disbandment of the Sikh army, its reorganization, on the same rate of pay as in the time of the late Maharajah Runjeet Singh, and the limitations of its numbers, have been settled by the treaty.

At the earnest solicitation of the Government of the Maharajah Dhuleep Singh, the Governor-General has consented to occupy the citadel and town of Lahore by British troops for a limited period, that opportunity may be afforded the Lahore Government of completing the reorganization of its army, according to the stipulations of the treaty.

If by the good offices of the British Government peace and order can take the place of the military anarchy and misrule by which the Sikh nation has been brought to the verge of dissolution, the Governor-General will rejoice that the co-operation of the British Government, by the aid of its faithful army, shall have been successful in effecting that object. It is the strongest proof which the British Government can give of the sincerity of its desire to see a Sikh Government re-established. The British Government having afforded the protection desired, the troops will be withdrawn before the end of the year. The details of the force will be determined between the Governor-General and his Excellency the Commander-in-Chief. During the period of occupation the native troops will continue to receive Scinde pay and allowances.

It is by the valour and discipline of the British troops, led by their distinguished commander, that these important and complete successes have been gained, and the Governor-General is confident that, during the temporary occupation of the fortified town of Lahore, the troops will prove, by their good conduct, that they are as generous and humane after victory, as they are brave and invincible in the field of battle.

By order of the Right Hon. the Governor-General of India,

F. Currie,

Secretary to the Government of India, with the Governor-General.

No. 3.

Memorandum of the Proceedings of a Durbar held at Lahore, on the 9th March, 1846.

At four P.M., of the 9th March, a public Durbar was held in the state tent of the Right Honourable the Governor-General, at which his Excellency the Commander-in-Chief and Staff, his Excellency the Governor of Scinde and Staff, with the British and native officers invited in the Governor-General's order, dated 8th instant, attended.

The young Maharajah of Lahore, attended by the Minister Rajah Lal Singh, Rajah Gholab Singh, the Commander-in-Chief of the Lahore army, Sirdar Tej Singh, and about thirty other Sirdars and civil officers, with their suites, were present.

After the treaty of peace was ratified and exchanged with the usual ceremonies, the Governor-General addressed the chiefs in the following terms, the address being translated, sentence by sentence, by the Secretary to the Government of India, Mr. F. Currie:—

" On this occasion of ratifying the treaty of peace between the British Government and the Maharajah Dhuleep Singh, in the presence of his Excellency the Commander-in-Chief, his Excellency the Governor of Scinde, and the officers of the British army on the one hand, and of the Sikh chiefs on the other, I have to repeat the assurances which have so often been given by me and by my predecessors of our desire that peace and friendship may always subsist between the two Governments.

" The British Government desires to see a Sikh Government re-established which may be able to controul its army, protect its subjects, and willing to respect the rights of its neighbours.

" By this treaty the Lahore Government has sufficient strength to resist and punish any native power which may venture to assail it, and to put down all internal commotions.

" Wisdom in council and good faith in fulfilling its engagements will cause the Sikh Government to be respected, and enable it to preserve its national independence.

" For forty years it was the policy, in Runjeet Singh's time, to cultivate friendly relations between the two Governments, and during the whole of that period the Sikh nation was independent and happy. Let the policy of that able man towards the British Government be the model for your future imitation.

" The British Government in no respect provoked the late war. It had no objects of aggrandizement to obtain by hostilities. The proof of its sincerity is to be found in its moderation in the hour of victory.

"A just quarrel, followed by a successful war, has not changed the policy of the British Government. The British Government does not desire to interfere in your internal affairs. I am ready and anxious to withdraw every British soldier from Lahore. At the earnest solicitation of the Sikh Government, I have reluctantly consented to leave a British force in garrison at Lahore, until time shall have been afforded for the reorganization of the Sikh army, by which assistance the stipulations of the treaty may be more easily carried into effect.

"In no case can I consent that the British troops shall remain in garrison for a longer period than the end of this year.

"I state this publicly, that all the world may know the truth, and the motives by which I am actuated in this matter.

"The Sikh army must, according to the treaty, be immediately reorganized by reverting to the same system and rate of pay as in Runjeet Singh's time.

"If the friendly assistance now afforded by the British Government be wisely followed up, and honest exertions made by the chiefs without delay, you will become an independent and prosperous state.

"The success or failure is in your own hands; my co-operation shall not be wanting: but, if you neglect this opportunity, no aid on the part of the British Government can save the state.

"I leave my political agent, Major Lawrence, assisted by Major M'Gregor, and a most able General officer, Sir John Littler, to command the British troops. These officers possess my entire confidence.

"Again I repeat, my anxious desire is to see a Sikh Government strong and respected, an obedient army, patriotic chiefs, and a happy people.

"I trust the reign of the Maharajah will be long and prosperous, and celebrated for the happiness of his people under a just and pacific Government."

At the close of this address the Sirdars expressed in warm

terms their gratitude to the Governor-General, and their resolution to follow the advice his Excellency had given them.

The usual presents were then given, after which the Durbar broke up.

F. CURRIE,
Secretary to the Government of India, with the Governor-General.

No. 4.

Treaty between the British Government and the State of Lahore.

Whereas the treaty of amity and concord, which was concluded between the British Government and the late Maharajah Runjeet Singh, the ruler of Lahore, in 1809, was broken by the unprovoked aggression, on the British Provinces, of the Sikh army in December last, and whereas, on occasion, by the Proclamation dated 13th of December, the territories then in the occupation of the Maharajah of Lahore on that, the left or British bank of the river Sutlej, were confiscated and annexed to the British Provinces, and since that time hostile operations have been prosecuted by the two Governments, the one against the other, which have resulted in the occupation of Lahore by the British troops; and whereas it has been determined that, upon certain conditions, peace shall be re-established between the two Governments, the following treaty of peace between the Hon. English East India Company and Maharajah Dhuleep Singh Bahadoor and his children, heirs, and successors, has been concluded on the part of the Honourable Company by Frederick Currie, Esq., and Brevet-Major Henry Montgomery Lawrence, by virtue of full powers to that effect, vested in them by the Right Honourable Sir Henry Hardinge, G.C.B., one of her Britannic Majesty's Most Honourable Privy Council, Governor-General, appointed by the Honourable Company to direct and controul all their affairs in the East Indies, and on the part of his Highness the Maharajah Dhuleep Singh by Bhaee Ram Singh, Rajah Lal Singh, Sirdar Tej Singh, Sirdar Chuttur Singh Attareewalla, Sirdar Runjoor Singh Majethea, Deewan Deena Nath, and

Fakeer Noor-ood-Deen, vested with full powers and authority on the part of his Highness.

Article 1.—There shall be perpetual peace and friendship between the British Government on the one part, and Maharajah Dhuleep Singh, his heirs and successors, on the other.

Art. 2.—The Maharajah of Lahore renounces for himself, his heirs and successors, all claim to, or connexion with, the territories lying to the south of the river Sutlej, and engages never to have any concern with those territories or the inhabitants thereof.

Art. 3.—The Maharajah cedes to the Honourable Company, in perpetual sovereignty, all his forts, territories, and rights, in the doab or country, hill and plain, situate between the rivers Beeas and Sutlej.

Art. 4.—The British Government having demanded from the Lahore State, as indemnification for the expenses of the war, in addition to the cession of territory described in Article 3, payment of one and a half crores of rupees, and the Lahore Government being unable to pay the whole of this sum at this time, or to give security satisfactory to the British Government for its eventual payment, the Maharajah cedes to the Honourable Company, in perpetual sovereignty, as equivalent for one crore of rupees, all his forts, territories, rights, and interests, in the hill countries which are situate between the rivers Beeas and Indus, including the provinces of Cashmere and Hazarah.

Art. 5.—The Maharajah will pay to the British Government the sum of fifty lacs of rupees on or before the ratification of this treaty.

Art. 6.—The Maharajah engages to disband the mutinous troops of the Lahore army, taking from them their arms; and his Highness agrees to reorganize the regular, or Aeen regiments of infantry, upon the system and according to the regulations as to pay and allowances observed in the time of the late Maharajah Runjeet Singh. The Maharajah further engages to pay up all arrears to the soldiers that are discharged under the provisions of this article.

Art. 7.—The regular army of the Lahore State shall henceforth be limited to twenty-five battalions of infantry, consisting of 800 bayonets each, with 12,000 cavalry: this number at no time to be exceeded without the concurrence of the British Government. Should it be necessary at any time, for any special cause, that this force should be increased, the cause shall be fully explained to the British Government, and when the special necessity shall have passed, the regular troops shall be again reduced to the standard specified in the former clause of this article.

Art. 8.—The Maharajah will surrender to the British Government all the guns, thirty-six in number, which have been pointed against the British troops, and which, having been placed on the right bank of the river Sutlej, were not captured at the battle of Sobraon.

Art. 9.—The controul of the rivers Beeas and Sutlej, with the continuation of the latter river, commonly called the Gurrah and the Punjnud, to the confluence of the Indus at Mithunkote, and the controul of the Indus from Mithunkote to the borders of Beloochistan, shall, in respect to tolls and ferries, rest with the British Government. The provisions of this article shall not interfere with the passage of boats belonging to the Lahore Government on the said rivers for the purposes of traffic or the conveyance of passengers up and down their course. Regarding the ferries between the two countries respectively, at the several ghats, of the said rivers, it is agreed that the British Government, after defraying all the expenses of management and establishments, shall account to the Lahore Government for one-half of the net profits of the ferry collections. The provisions of this article have no reference to the ferries on that part of the river Sutlej which forms the boundary of Bahawulpore and Lahore respectively.

Art. 10.—If the British Government should, at any time, desire to pass troops through the territories of his Highness the Maharajah for the protection of the British territories, or those of their allies, the British troops shall, on such special occasion, due notice being given, be allowed to pass through the Lahore territories. In such case the officers of the Lahore State will afford facilities in providing supplies and boats for the passage of the rivers, and the British Government will pay the full price of all such provisions and boats, and will make fair compensation for all private property, that may be endamaged. The British Government will moreover observe all due consideration to the religious feelings of the inhabitants of those tracts through which the army may pass.

Art. 11.—The Maharajah engages never to take, or retain in his service, any British subject nor the subject of any European or American state, without the consent of the British Government.

Art. 12.—In consideration of the services rendered by Rajah Gholab Singh, of Jummoo, to the Lahore State, towards procuring the restoration of the relations of amity between the Lahore and British Governments, the Maharajah hereby agrees to recognize the independent sovereignty of Rajah Gholab Singh in such territories and districts in the hills as may be made over to the said Rajah Gholab Singh by separate agreement between himself and the British Government, with the dependencies thereof, which may have been in the Rajah's possession since the time of the late Maharajah Kurruk Singh, and the British Government, in consideration of the good conduct of Rajah Gholab Singh, also agrees to recognize his independence in such territories, and to admit him to the privileges of a separate treaty with the British Government.

Art. 13.—In the event of any dispute or difference arising between the Lahore State and Rajah Gholab Singh, the same shall be referred to the arbitration of the British Government, and by its decision the Maharajah engages to abide.

Art. 14.—The limits of the Lahore territories shall not be, at any time, changed without the concurrence of the British Government.

Art. 15.—The British Government will not exercise any interference in the internal administration of the Lahore State, but in all cases or questions which may be referred to the British Government, the Governor-General will give the aid of his advice and good offices for the furtherance of the interests of the Lahore Government.

Art. 16.—The subjects of either state shall, on visiting the territories of the other, be on the footing of the subjects of the most favoured nation.

This treaty, consisting of sixteen articles, has been this day settled by Frederick Currie, Esq., and Brevet-Major Henry Montgomery Lawrence, acting under the directions of the Right Honourable Sir Henry Hardinge, G.C.B., Governor-General, on the part of the British Government, and by Bhaee Ram Singh, Rajah Lal Singh, Sirdar Tej Singh, Sirdar Chuttur Singh Attareewalla, Sirdar Runjoor Singh Majethea, Dewan Deena Nath, and Fakeer Noor-ood-Deen, on the part of the Maharajah Dhuleep Singh, and the said treaty has been this day ratified by the seal of the Right Honourable Sir Henry Hardinge, G.C.B., Governor-General, and by that of his Highness Maharajah Dhuleep Singh.

Done at Lahore, this 9th day of March, in the year of our Lord 1846, corresponding with the tenth day of Rubbeeoolawul; 1262, Hijree, and ratified on the same date.

MAHARAJAH DHULEEP SINGH, (L.S.)
BHAEE RAM SINGH, (L.S.)
RAJAH LAL SINGH, (L.S.)
SIRDAR TEJ SINGH, (L.S.)
SIRDAR CHUTTUR SINGH ATTAREEWALLA, (L.S.)
SIRDAR RUNJOOR SINGH MAJETHEA, (L.S.)
DEWAN DEENA NATH, (L.S.
FAKEER NOOR-OOD-DEEN, (L.S.)
H. HARDINGE, (L S.)
F. CURRIE.
H. M. LAWRENCE.

By order of the Right Honourable the Governor-General of India,

F. CURRIE,

Secretary to the Government of India,
with the Governor-General.

No. 5.

Memorandum of a State Visit paid by the Governor-General to the Maharajah of Lahore in his Highness's Palace, on the 10th March, 1846.

On the afternoon of the 10th of March, the Governor-General, attended by his Excellency the Commander-in-Chief, his Excellency the Governor of Scinde, and the British officers who were present at the ratification of the treaty on the 9th instant, paid a visit of congratulation to the Maharajah Dhuleep Singh at the Palace in Lahore. On this occasion Dewan Deena Nath, by direction of the Minister and assembled chiefs, read from a written paper an address, of which the following is a translation:—

"It is impossible for us adequately to express the gratitude which we feel to the Governor-General, for his having determined to continue the ancient relations which existed with the late Maharajah Runjeet Singh, and for his generosity, kindness, and mercy in maintaining this Government.

"For the excellent advice which was given yesterday, through kindness and friendship, to the assembled Sirdars, exhorting them to unanimity, prudence, and good government, we are also most grateful. We consider this good advice as having a direct tendency to effect the re-establishment of the Government of the country. We have further to express our gratitude for arrangements having generously been made, in compliance with our solicitations, for leaving a garrison in Lahore of British troops, with Major Lawrence and other trustworthy officers, for our protection and that of the city.

"These troops will assuredly be honourably dismissed towards the Sutlej, upon a satisfactory settlement of affairs being effected within the period prescribed for their stay.

"The various acts of generosity shown by the Governor-General on the present occasion entirely satisfy us that his Excellency will ever maintain the same magnanimous and generous policy towards this State, and that, taking compassion on the extreme youth of the Maharajah, his Excellency will maintain all those friendly relations which existed in the time of the late Maharajah Runjeet Singh."

After the presentation by the Maharajah of the usual offerings, the Governor-General and suite returned to camp.

True memorandum and translation,

F. CURRIE,
Secretary to the Government of India, with the Governor-General.

No. 6.

Note of the proceedings of a Meeting of the Minister and Chiefs of the Lahore Durbar and the British Commissioners, held at the tent of the Governor-General's Agent, on the 11*th of March,* 1846.

On the forenoon of the 11th instant, the Minister and chiefs of the Durbar attended at the tent of the Governor-General's agent, when the following agreement was concluded, and subsequently confirmed by the Right Hon. the Governor-General:—

Articles of Agreement concluded between the British Government and the Lahore Durbar, on the 11*th of March*, 1846.

Whereas the Lahore Government has solicited the Governor-General to leave a British force at Lahore for the protection of the Maharajah's person, and of the capital, till the reorganization of the Lahore army, according to the provisions of article 6 of the treaty of Lahore, dated the 9th instant; and whereas the Governor-General has, on certain conditions, consented to this measure; and whereas it is expedient that certain matters concerning the territories ceded by articles 3 and 4 of the aforesaid treaty should be specifically determined, the following eight articles of agreement have this day been concluded between the afore-mentioned contracting parties:—

Art. 1.—The British Government shall leave at Lahore, till the close of the current year A.D. 1846, such force as shall seem to the Governor-General adequate for the purpose of protecting the person of the Maharajah and the inhabitants of the city of Lahore during the reorganization of the Sikh army, in accordance with the provisions of article 6 of the treaty of Lahore. That force to be withdrawn at any convenient time before the expiration of the year, if the object to be fulfilled shall, in the opinion of the Durbar, have been attained; but the force shall not be detained at Lahore beyond the expiration of the current year.

Art. 2.—The Lahore Government agrees that the force left at Lahore for the purpose specified in the foregoing article shall be placed in full possession of the fort and city of Lahore, and that the Lahore troops shall be removed from within the city. The Lahore Government engages to furnish convenient quarters for the officers and men of the said force, and to pay the British Government all the extra expenses in regard to the said force which may be incurred by the British Government in consequence of their troops being employed away from their own cantonments, and in a foreign territory.

Art. 3.—The Lahore Government engages to apply itself immediately and earnestly to the reorganization of its army according to the prescribed condition, and to communicate fully with the British authorities left at Lahore as to the progress of such reorganization, and as to the location of the troops.

Art. 4.—If the Lahore Government fails in the performance of the conditions of the foregoing article, the British Government shall be at liberty to withdraw the force from Lahore at any time before the expiration of the period specified in article 1.

Art. 5.—The British Government agrees to respect the *bonâ fide* rights of those Jaghirdars within the territories ceded by articles 3 and 4 of the treaty of Lahore, dated 9th instant, who were attached to the families of the late Maharajah Runjeet Singh, Kurruck Singh, and Shere Singh, and the British Government will maintain those Jaghirdars in their *bonâ fide* possessions during their lives.

Art. 6.—The Lahore Government shall receive the assistance of the British local authorities in recovering the arrears of revenue justly due to the Lahore Government from their Kardars and managers in the territories ceded by the provisions of articles 3 and 4 of the treaty of Lahore, to the close of the Khurreef harvest of the current year, viz., 902 of the Sumbut Bikramajeet.

Art. 7.—The Lahore Government shall be at liberty to remove from the forts in the territories specified in the foregoing article all treasure and state property, with the exception of guns. Should, however, the British Government desire to retain any part of the said property, they shall be at liberty to do so, paying for the same at a fair valuation, and the British officers shall give their assistance to the Lahore Government in disposing on the spot of such part of the aforesaid property as the Lahore Government may not wish to remove, and the British officers may not desire to retain.

Art. 8.—Commissioners shall be immediately appointed by the two Governments to settle and lay down the boundary between the two states, as defined by article 4 of the treaty of Lahore, dated March 9, 1846.

MAHARAJAH DHULEEP SINGH, (L.S.)
BHAEE RAM SINGH, (L.S.)
RAJAH LAL SINGH, (L.S.)
SIRDAR TEJ SINGH, (L.S.)
SIRDAR CHUTTER SINGH ATTAREEWALLA, (L.S.)
SIRDAR RUNJOOR SINGH MAJETHEA, (L.S.)
DEWAN DEENA NATH, (L.S.)
FAKEER NOOR-OOD-DEEN, (L.S.)
H. HARDINGE, (L.S.)
F. CURRIE.
H. M. LAWRENCE.

By order of the Right Hon. the Governor-General of India,

F. CURRIE,

Secretary to the Government of India, with the Governor-General.

No. 7.

Treaty between the British Government and Maharajah Gholab Singh, concluded at Umritsir on the 16*th of March,* 1846.

Treaty between the British Government on the one part, and Maharajah Gholab Singh, of Jummoo, on the other, concluded on the part of the British Government by Frederick Currie, Esq., and Brevet-Major Henry Montgomery Lawrence, acting under the orders of the Right Honourable Sir Henry Hardinge, G.C.B., one of Her Britannic Majesty's Most Honourable Privy Council, Governor-General, appointed by the Honourable Company to direct and controul all their affairs in the East Indies, and by Maharajah Gholab Singh in person.

Art. 1.—The British Government transfers and makes over, for ever, in independent possession, to Maharajah Gholab Singh, and the heirs male of his body, all the hilly or mountainous country, with its dependencies, situate to the eastward of the River Indus, and westward of the River Ravee, including Chumba and excluding Lahool, being part of the territory ceded to the British Government by the Lahore State, according to the provisions of Article 4 of the treaty of Lahore, dated 9th March, 1846.

Art. 2.—The eastern boundary of the tract transferred by the foregoing article to Maharajah Gholab Singh shall be laid down by commissioners appointed by the British Government and Maharajah Gholab Singh respectively for that purpose, and shall be defined in a separate engagement after survey.

Art. 3.—In consideration of the transfer made to him and his heirs, by the provisions of the foregoing articles, Maharajah Gholab Singh will pay to the British Government the sum of 75 lacs of rupees (Nanuckshahee), 50 lacs to be paid on ratification of this treaty, and 25 lacs on or before the 1st of October of the current year, 1846.

Art. 4.—The limits of the territories of Maharajah Gholab Singh shall not be at any time changed without the concurrence of the British Government.

Art. 5.—Maharajah Gholab Singh will refer to the arbitration of the British Government any disputes or questions that may arise between himself and the Government of Lahore, or any other neighbouring state, and will abide by the decision of the British Government.

Art. 6.—Maharajah Gholab Singh engages for himself and heirs to join with the whole of his military force the British troops when employed within the hills, or in the territories adjoining his possessions.

Art. 7.—Maharajah Gholab Singh engages never to take or retain in his service any British subject, nor the subject of any European or American state, without the consent of the British Government.

Art. 8.—Maharajah Gholab Singh engages to respect, in regard to the territory transferred to him, the provisions of articles 5, 6, and 7, of the separate engagement between the British Government and the Lahore Durbar, dated March 11, 1846.

Art. 9.—The British Government will give its aid to Maharajah Gholab Singh in protecting his territories from external enemies.

Art. 10.—Maharajah Gholab Singh acknowledges the supremacy of the British Government, and will, in token of such supremacy, present annually to the British Government, one horse, twelve perfect shawl goats of approved breed (six male and six female), and three pairs of Cashmere shawls.

This treaty, consisting of ten articles, has been this day settled by Frederick Currie, Esq., and Brevet-Major Henry Montgomery Lawrence, acting under the directions of the Right Honourable Sir Henry Hardinge, G.C.B., Governor-General, on the part of the British Government, and by Maharajah Gholab Singh in person, and the said treaty has been this day ratified by the seal of the Right Honourable Sir Henry Hardinge, G.C.B., Governor-General.

Done at Umritsir, this 16th day of March, in the year of our

Lord 1846, corresponding with the 17th day of Rubbeeoolawul 1262, Hijree.

GHOLAB SINGH, (L. S.)
H. HARDINGE, (L. S.)
F. CURRIE.
H. M. LAWRENCE.

By order of the Right Hon. the Governor-General of India,

F. CURRIE,
Secretary to the Government of India, with the Governor-General.

(True extracts)

F. CURRIE,
Secretary to the Government of India, with the Governor-General.

THANKS TO THE ARMY IN INDIA.

VICTORIES OF MOODKEE AND FEROZESHAH.

HOUSE OF LORDS.

The resolutions which follow the report of the speech of the Right Honourable Sir Robert Peel, Bart., in the House of Commons, were proposed in the House of Lords by the Right Honourable the Earl of Ripon, in a most effective speech; but which, in a great measure, was to the same purport as that of the Right Honourable Baronet at the head of Her Majesty's Government.—The motion was seconded by the Right Honourable the Marquis of Lansdowne, who was succeeded in the debate, in the following words, by his Grace

The DUKE of WELLINGTON :—My Lords, I could not hear a motion of this description discussed without adding, to what has been stated, my unqualified approbation of the conduct of the troops on this occasion, and also of the officers who commanded them; and particularly of my Right Honourable and gallant friend, the Governor-General, who, after having made all the arrangements appertaining to his duty as Governor-General, in order to collect all the resources of the country for the purpose of the great contest impending, having collected all the troops and made all the arrangement for the security of the country, volunteered his services in his rank in the army, in order to give his assistance to the officer commanding the army in chief in carrying on those operations which remained for him to carry on in order to secure the public interests and the possession of the country. There is no obligation on an officer placed in his situation to take that course; you can hardly point to a single instance of a man being placed in that situation; but he has given us an example which I hope will always be followed. When he found his services could be useful, he laid aside his position and even his power as Governor-General; for it should not be forgotten that he would have carried with him into the field the power over the military operations of the army; he laid that aside—which indeed it is true, according to the usual practice, could not in that way be exercised, and most particularly in his case could not, because Her Majesty, when he went to India, and the Court of Directors, gave him his commission to succeed the command of the army after the death or coming away of the present Commander-in-Chief; but he volunteered his service and his assistance to the Commander-in-Chief in the great contest which was impending. But it has been said truly, that all exerted themselves and did everything in their power to obtain the great result which has crowned their efforts. It is not generally known, my Lords, but I know it, that the enemy's position was completely closed in by entrenchments, so closed around, that it deserved rather the name of a fortress than a fortified position; and notwithstanding the advantages our troops in India have, of having water carriages and persons attached to each company whose duty it is to supply them with water, they laboured in this action under the singular disadvantage of being deprived even of that refreshment for nearly twenty-four hours, because the country happened to be so much dried up, and the villages so distant. Under these circumstances it was that the troops carried this position, certainly with very great loss, but which I hope has not left them in a state otherwise than efficient, if their services should be called for on military duty. I really must say, that I have not for a length of time heard of an action that has given me so much unqualified satisfaction as this, excepting in one particular. I have read with pain of one regiment, to which the word "panic" was applied; and I considered it my duty, in the position in which I am placed, to examine particularly into the circumstances. I see, in the returns, that that regiment is stated to have lost five-twelfths of its number, and a vast number of officers and non-commissioned officers. I have seen an account which states, that in the first quarter of an hour from the time when the regiment first entered into action, one-third of its officers fell. I cannot question the accuracy of the report of the operations made by the commanding officer, but I wish that this officer, when he sat down to write an elaborate report of the conduct of the troops under his command, had referred to the list of killed and wounded; and if he had inquired into the loss sustained by that regiment, I believe he would have found that they were absolutely mowed down by the fire under which they were advancing. I have made inquiries respecting that regiment, and I find that it has been sixteen years in the East Indies; that in the course of forty years it has served thirty-three years abroad, and only seven in the United Kingdom; that in the course of the sixteen years during which it has served in the East Indies, it has been in all parts of India; that its numbers have been recruited twice over since it has been in that country; and that at this moment, of these men who made that attack and suffered that loss, three-fourths had not been seven years in the service. I considered it my duty to examine into the state of this regiment, seeing that word "panic;" and I believe I have with me a most extraordinary report of their good conduct from this very General officer on a former occasion; and it will convince your Lordships that if the list of killed and wounded had been brought before him on that occasion it would have been impossible for him to apply that word to them. I cannot find the paper now, but it contains the expression of unqualified approbation of the state of this very regiment, by this same General officer, Sir John Littler, upon the last inspection at Christmas last. I was anxious to read it to your Lordships to show that to the accident of the dreadful fire kept up upon them, and their being mowed down, you ought to attribute what occurred, and not to a deficiency or failure on their part*.

House of Commons.

Sir R. Peel rose and spoke as follows:—I am about to propose that one of the highest rewards that can be bestowed upon successful valour shall be conferred by this House. I am about to propose that the thanks of the Commons of this great empire shall be given to the officers and men, who recently on the banks of the Sutlej, under very trying circumstances, by their discipline, by their fortitude, by their brilliant valour, have sustained the reputation of their country, and proved themselves worthy of the service to which they belong. The resolutions with which I shall conclude will not touch upon any matter of purely political concern, but are framed in conformity with established usage—that usage being consonant with reason and justice. * * * The state of the country and the history of the Punjaub are probably well known to all whom I am addressing, from the relation in which we stood towards it, during our operations in the neighbouring county of Affghanistan. The House is probably well aware that by the ability and energy of an individual (Runjeet Singh), supremacy was established by him in the Punjaub; and that for many years, through that ability and energy, he ruled the destinies of that great country, and kept in subjection and subordination a powerful army. Since his death, which took place in the year 1839, the Government of the Punjaub has pre-

* The reader is referred to the General Order, issued by the Commander-in-Chief, at page 40.

sented a series of acts of cruelty, of intrigue, of a rapid succession of governors, in consequence of the murder of the predecessor by the successor; it has exhibited a picture of licentiousness and debauchery so extravagant, that it might be calculated to provoke a smile, if it were not for the influence such licentiousness and debauchery must exercise over the welfare of millions. The acts of that Government have been mainly directed by that powerful soldiery over which Runjeet Singh established his sway; but which since his death has been in the constant habit of controlling the conduct of the civil authorities, and even of the military commanders, by repeated acts of insubordination, and repeated murders, for the purpose of extorting increased pay. Perhaps the best idea one can give of the anomalous condition of affairs, and of the difficulties of speculating upon any acts that may be committed, or upon any measure that may be resorted to is this—that it is quite clear that the main object of the governors of that country, and of the principal landed proprietors, and chiefs, has been to provoke collision with the British army, not for the purpose of resenting any wrong, or of sustaining the military reputation of the country, but of freeing themselves from subjection to an insubordinate and licentious force, by provoking a conflict with Great Britain, in which that force should fall a sacrifice, That has been the main object, and the strange principle of public policy, that has for some time guided the decisions and regulated the acts of the rulers of the Punjaub. I well know what was the object of my friend, Sir Henry Hardinge, in undertaking the government of India. He made great sacrifices from a sense of public duty; my gallant friend held a prominent place in the Councils of Her Majesty: he was, I believe, without any reference to party divisions, held in general esteem in this House, as well by his political opponents as by his political friends. He was regarded by the army of this country as its friend, because he was the friend of justice to all ranks of that army. It was proposed to him at a time of life when, perhaps, ambition is a less powerful stimulus than it might have been at an earlier period—it was proposed to him to relinquish his place in the Councils of his Sovereign—to forego the satisfaction he must have felt at what he could not fail to see, that he was an object of general respect and esteem. He separated himself from that family which constituted the chief happiness of his life, for the purpose of performing a public duty he owed to his Sovereign and his country, by taking the arduous and responsible situation of Chief Governor of our Indian possessions. He went out with a high military reputation. Solicitous to establish his fame in connexion with our Indian Empire, not by means of conquest, or the exhibition of military skill and valour, but by obtaining for himself a name in the annals of India as the friend of peace, and through the promotion of the social interests and welfare of the inhabitants. It was mainly on account of the military character and high reputation of my gallant friend that he was enabled to controul and keep in check the aspirations of more ardent and impetuous minds bent upon the invasion and conquest of the Punjaub.

The view which the Governor-General took of the policy to be pursued in regard to the Punjaub, was shortly this: he thought the dominions of the British Crown in India were sufficient for every purpose—that the interests of the Empire would not be promoted by the addition of the Punjaub to the possessions already subject to our own rule. He was determined, therefore, to resist any temptation to territorial aggrandizement. His desire was to see a native Government established in the Punjaub capable of maintaining its independence, of restoring subordination in the ranks of a great army, composed of men of high natural courage, of great physical strength, accustomed to discipline, and trained to military habits by European officers of distinguished reputation. His wish was, that a Sikh Government should be established. He deprecated the formation of a Mussulman Government, or the domination of any other than Sikh authorities. At the same time that he was determined to resist the temptations to direct aggression, he refused repeated proposals that were made to him to interfere in the domestic affairs of the Punjaub. Although nothing could have been more easy; although but a word from him would have been necessary to induce the Mussulman inhabitants of the Punjaub to rise against the Sikh authorities, who were conducting themselves in a manner so irreconcilable with sound policy or common sense, he resolved steadily to adhere to the line he had chalked out; to abstain from all interference in the domestic affairs of the Punjaub, and to observe literally every obligation of good faith.

But while that was his view of the policy that ought to be pursued, he was not insensible to the danger to which our Indian empire was constantly exposed, from the maintenance on its frontiers of a profligate and debauched Government, controlled by an insubordinate and licentious army. My gallant friend, therefore, took all precautions. He had to guard a frontier extending on the banks of the Sutlej at least 100 miles. The frontier from Ferozepore to Roopur was at least 100 miles; from Ferozepore to Loodiana about 77 miles. My gallant friend, cautiously abstaining from the collection of any force on the frontier which could justify aggression, or even remonstrance, on the part of the Lahore Government, took those precautions which would effectually prevent successful attack on their part. At Ferozepore he stationed a force of about 8,000 men, consisting of one European regiment, seven regiments of native infantry, two regiments of native cavalry, twenty-four light guns, and had mounted in position at Ferozepore thirty or thirty-five pieces of heavy artillery. He intended this to be the advanced post of the British army on the western side of the frontier.

At a distance of about seventy-six miles to the eastward, higher up the Sutlej, at Loodiana, he collected a force of about 500 men. He thought that these two armies, or two divisions of an army, stationed about seventy-six miles from each other, acting on the flanks of any force from the Punjaub, induced by caprice or by the temerity of their rulers to invade the British territory, would be sufficient to keep it in effectual controul. At a distance more in the interior—namely, at Umballa, he stationed another division of 7,500 men at the least. My gallant friend was undoubtedly under the impression that it was highly improbable that any attack would be made by the army of the Punjaub upon the British positions. He knew that no conduct on his part could provoke or justify such an attack; and he felt every assurance that could be felt, so far as justice and reason sanctioned the inference, that the army of the Punjaub would not be mad enough to seek a conflict with the British forces on the left bank of the Sutlej.

There were good reasons why Sir Henry Hardinge did not keep together for the last two or three years an immense British and native army on the banks of the Sutlej. Constant efforts were made by the Government and by the military leaders of the army of the Punjaub to corrupt our native troops. The constitution of the army of the Punjaub is purely democratic: the private soldiers elect representatives, five in number from each company, to controul their officers, to depose them when they think fit, or to subject them to death when it is deemed expedient. The pay of an infantry soldier of the Punjaub is about twenty-five shillings a month; while the pay of a sepoy in Her Majesty's service is only about fourteen or fifteen shillings a month. Constant exertions were made, by direct and indirect means, aided by community of language and of religion, to shake the fidelity of the native troops; but I rejoice to say that they were made without success. The loyalty of the sepoys, with scarcely a single exception, has been untainted. All the offers of a profligate Government and a licentious soldiery were unavailing; but still it was prudent in my gallant friend, not to bring together on the frontier, for an indefinite time and for no specific object, an immense native force, seeing that within a few miles they would be exposed to the injurious example of a soldiery free from all restraint, and constantly resorting to threats of actual violence towards their leaders. There were, therefore, political reasons for not keeping our troops, as it were, in immediate contact with such an enemy, and there were military reasons equally powerful.

It was, in the first place, impossible, if aggressions were

intended, to foresee at what point an invasion would be made. On the left bank of the Sutlej were many states belonging to the Punjaub, and some of the chiefs of those states men of doubtful fidelity. In those dominions on the left bank of the Sutlej are many forts of considerable size and strength. A force controlled by no Government, impelled by the fear of losing its pay, or the hope of extorting more, is not governed by ordinary considerations of prudence like the armies of regular states; and if the army of the Punjaub meditated a sudden irruption into the British territory, it was difficult to see at what point the descent would be made. Between Ferozepore and Roopur there are not fewer than twenty fords available for the passage of troops; nor is it easy to ascertain their exact position, since from the nature of the river, they are constantly changing. My gallant friend thought, therefore, that true military policy recommended the course he has pursued, not that his whole army should be concentrated on the banks of the Sutlej, but that our territory should be guarded by a sufficient force stationed at Ferozepore and Loodiana. Seeing the superior force of cavalry in the army of the Punjaub, the desperate rashness of a licentious army not governed by the ordinary rules of conduct, it was within the limit of possibility that a dash might be made at Delhi, or some vital part of the Indian empire. My gallant friend, therefore, most wisely and prudently, kept a considerable force at Umballa, seventy-six miles to the south-east from Loodiana, and a still larger body of troops in the neighbourhood of Delhi. This whole force was assembled by way of precaution against the possible attempts of the Lahore army; and it consisted in the whole of not fewer than thirty regiments of native infantry, of nine regiments of European infantry, of twelve regiments of native cavalry, and of three regiments of European cavalry. All this was quite consistent with forbearance on the part of the Governor-General, and with his determination to be seduced by no temptation to aggression on the enemy.

It is quite clear that my gallant friend the Governor-General did take every precaution to ensure the safety of the British dominions in India, in case of sudden and unprovoked attack. In the early part of the year, at the time he was occupied with his functions as Governor-General, and when it was most material that he should perform them in conjunction with his Council at Calcutta: in a minute, dated on the 16th of June, he submitted to the Council his opinion, that our relations with the Court of Lahore became so doubtful, that, great as was the inconvenience of separating the Governor-General and his Council, it was desirable, with reference exclusively to Indian interests, that he should proceed to the left bank of the Sutlej, in order that on the spot he might be enabled to give such directions as appeared necessary, and which, if given at the distance of a thousand miles, might be inappropriate. The unanimous opinion of the members of the Council was, that it was for the public interest that the Governor-General should proceed to join the army; and, in conformity with this advice, in the month of October he took his departure for the left bank of the Sutlej. Up to an early period in December, the opinion of my gallant friend, Sir Henry Hardinge, was, that there would be no irruption from the right bank of the Sutlej into the British territory. He felt confident that the Sikhs must be convinced that such an attempt could only end in signal defeat, and therefore that it would not be made. So far as he could reason from experience, he had a right to arrive at this conclusion. In 1843, the army of Lahore left the capital and advanced to the Sutlej; but after remonstrance on our part, it retired again, and abandoned the enterprize. In 1844, exactly the same conduct was observed; the Punjaub army, eager for pay, or for booty, if pay could not be obtained, and, instigated by the Government and the chiefs, appeared to contemplate an irruption; but in 1844, as in 1843, the army withdrew to the interior. Accounts, however, reached my gallant friend towards the end of November last, which led him to believe that an invasion of the British territory was seriously menaced.*

* * * * * *

* See the Despatches of Major Broadfoot, page 15.

On the 9th of December, the Governor-General, thinking our relations with the Punjaub very critical, and that it was desirable to take every precaution against any sudden irruption, gave orders that the division of troops at Umballa, consisting of 7,500 men, should move towards the Sutlej. On December 11, the very day on which the Lahore army crossed the Sutlej, the British and native troops of that division were on their march from Umballa to the frontier. The whole proceedings of the Governor-General and the Commander-in-Chief, subsequently to that day, as well as before it, were characterized by the greatest prudence, skill, and foresight. From Umballa the troops marched to a place called Busseean, where, owing to the prudent precautions of the Governor-General, they found an ample supply of food and stores. It was resolved that a junction should be effected with the Loodiana division, and that it would be better to incur some risk at Loodiana, rather than forego the advantage of a junction with the Loodiana division of the army. Those troops advanced accordingly towards Ferozepore, and learned by the way that the army of Lahore, amounting to not less than 60,000 men, had crossed the river, and were prepared to attack the British army. The expectations of the Governor-General were entirely justified by the result. There were in Ferozepore 7,500 men, 35 heavy guns in position, and 24 pieces of field artillery, in addition to the heavy ordnance. The army of Lahore shrunk from the attack of so formidable a post, and Ferozepore was entirely safe, according to the anticipations which had been entertained by the Governor-General. The army of Lahore not venturing to attack Ferozepore, determined to give battle to the British forces on their march from Umballa, and on the 18th of December made a sudden attack on them. On that day the troops had reached Moodkee, after having marched 150 miles by forced marches. The men were suffering severely from want of water, and from exhaustion, and yet such was their discipline and gallantry, that they repelled the whole of the attacking army, though greatly superior to them in number, defeating a force treble their amount, and succeeding in the capture of seventeen of their guns. The army of Lahore, thus repulsed by our forces advancing from Umballa, retired within very formidable entrenchments at Ferozeshah. Those entrenchments, consisting of strong breast-works, were in the form of a parallelogram, of which the opposite faces were a mile, and half a mile in length respectively. In the face of those formidable works, protected by 150 guns of heavy calibre and excellent workmanship, and defended by near 60,000 men, the Governor-General and the Commander-in-Chief determined to effect a junction with the division of the army which was stationed at Ferozepore. The troops advanced accordingly within three miles of the enemy's position, and manœuvred on his left flank; but the Commander-in-Chief having given previous notice to Sir John Littler, made a march to his left, and on the 21st December effected a junction with the Ferozepore division, which thus gave an addition of 7,500 men. At this time there remained but three hours to sunset. It was resolved, however, to attack the position of the enemy. My gallant friend (the Governor-General) offered his services as second in command, services which were cheerfully and promptly accepted by the Commander-in-Chief. Determined not to wait till next morning, the instant they effected their junction with the division under Sir John Littler, the commanders resolved to make an attack upon the entrenched camp. The result, Sir, of that attack proved the valour of our European and Indian forces in a pre-eminent degree, and has entitled them to the warmest acknowledgments of this House, and of the country. The night of the 21st December was one of the most memorable in the military annals of the British empire. The enemy were well defended within strongly fortified entrenchments—their guns were served with the greatest precision, and told on our advancing columns with great effect. The right of the British army was led by the Commander-in-Chief, whilst the left centre was headed by Sir H. Hardinge. Our forces made an attack on the enemy's camp during the three hours which as yet remained of daylight; but they had not sufficient time to complete that victory, which was gloriously achieved on the following day. The British army, however, made good their attack, and occupied a part of the enemy's camp. In the middle of the night the camp took fire, and further conflict was for a time suspended in consequence; but as soon as it had ceased, the army of Lahore brought forward their heavy artillery, and poured a most destructive fire upon our troops. The details of those occurrences have been given with admirable clearness in the despatches of both commanders. Perhaps the House will excuse me if I read an extract from a private letter from the Governor-General to a member of his own family. The Right Hon. Baronet then read as follows:—

> "The night of the 21st was the most extraordinary of my life. I bivouacked with the men, without food or covering, and our nights are bitter cold. A burning camp in our front, our brave fellows lying down under a heavy cannonade, which continued during the whole night, mixed with the wild cries of the Sikhs, our English hurrah, the tramp of men, and the groans of the dying. In this state with a handful of men, who had carried the batteries the night before, I remained till morning, taking very short intervals of rest by lying down with various regiments in succession, to ascertain their temper, and revive their spirits."

My gallant friend, as you see, spent that eventful night passing from regiment to regiment, cheering the men by his own example of constancy and courage—doing all that human means could do to ensure victory to our arms. "I found," my gallant friend goes on to say—"I found myself again with my old friends of the 29th, 31st, 50th, and 9th, all in good heart"—(regiments with which he had served in the Peninsula)—and with them that regiment which has earned immortal fame in the annals of the British army—Her Majesty's 80th Regiment—

> "My answer to all and every man was, that we must fight it out, attack the enemy vigorously at daybreak, beat him, or die honourably in the field. The gallant old general, kind-hearted and heroically brave, entirely coincided with me."

Let the House observe how anxious my gallant friend is to do justice to his companions in arms.

> "During the night, I occasionally called on our brave English soldiers to punish the Sikhs when they came too close and were impudent; and when morning broke we went at it in true English style. Gough was on the right. I placed myself, and dear little Arthur [his son] by my side, in the centre, about thirty yards in front of the men, to prevent their firing, and we drove the enemy, without a halt, from one extremity of

the camp to the other, capturing thirty or forty guns as we went along, which fired at twenty paces from us, and were served obstinately. The brave men drew up in an excellent line, and cheered Gough and myself as we rode up the line, the regimental colours lowering to me as on parade. The mournful part is the heavy loss I have sustained in my officers. I have had ten aides-de-camp, *hors de combat*, five killed and five wounded. The fire of grape was very heavy from 100 pieces of cannon; the Sikh army drilled by French officers, and the men the most warlike in India."

From my affectionate regard for that gallant man, I am proud to be enabled to exhibit him on such a night as that of the 21st of December—going through the camp—passing from regiment to regiment—keeping up the spirits of the men—encouraging them —animating their ardour—and having lost ten aides-de-camp out of twelve—placing his young son, a boy of seventeen or eighteen years of age, in the front of the line, in order that the British troops might be induced not to fire on the enemy, but drive them back by the force of the British bayonet. It was characteristic of the man to read these details. He had two sons present, one of whom was a civilian, and the other in the army. On the night of the 21st he sent the civilian to the rear of the army, saying that his presence disturbed him, and that if he refused to retire, he would send him away in arrest as a prisoner; but the presence, he said, of his younger son, an officer, whose duty called him to the field, only made the father more desperately resolute in the discharge of his duty. On the 22nd, after the battle was over, he took his eldest son, when visiting the sepoys and the wounded, and he showed them a Governor-General of India who had lost his hand, and the son of a Governor-General who had lost his foot, and endeavoured to console them in their sufferings by proving to them that men in the highest rank were exposed to the same casualties as themselves.

As I before observed, the accounts of all the military operations are given with admirable clearness in the despatches laid before the House. They must have been read with such attention by every Member of the House, that I will not weaken their effect by minute reference to military details. The pride and satisfaction we must all derive from those gallant exploits are no doubt counterbalanced by deep regret for the loss of so many men of the highest distinction and promise. We have had the misfortune—the great misfortune—of losing that gallant officer who on former occasions has so frequently distinguished himself—Sir Robert Sale. He, Sir, has closed a long career of glory by that death to which I believe he himself looked forward and which he coveted—that death in the field, which entitles me to say, that even in his own estimation, he was "*felix etiam opportunitate mortis.*" Sir, I do hope that this House will, on no distant day, mark their esteem and respect for the memory of Sir Robert Sale by humbly representing to Her Majesty their unanimous wish that she may be pleased to record the gratitude of the country by the erection of a monument to Sir Robert Sale.

We have, Sir, also to deplore the loss of Sir John M'Caskill, to whom a brief but touching testimony of approbation is borne in the despatch of the Commander-in-Chief, as well as one of the most eminent men in the civil and military services of India—Major Broadfoot. In that gentleman the highest confidence was placed by every one who came in contact with him. He obtained the applause of every civil and military authority in the country; and his prudence and skill as a civilian were only equalled by his ardour and bravery in the field. He was, I believe, the last of three brothers, all of whom have died in the service of their country on the field of battle. Major Broadfoot was present with Sir Robert Sale during the siege of Jellalabad, and took a most conspicuous part in its defence. It is mournful, Sir, that we should have to deplore the loss in the same conflict of two gallant men so devoted to their country's service as Sir Robert Sale and Major Broadfoot.

I shall not refer by name to officers of lower rank who have fallen in this conflict; for, where all were so distinguished, it must be invidious to particularize; but whatever their rank, I can assure their surviving relatives that their country will do justice to their memory. I hope the thanks of the House will be conveyed to all the men of every regiment engaged in this brilliant exploit, without exception. If there were occasions on which the reputation for valour of some regiments may appear not to have been upheld, considering their former services—their known gallantry—their severe losses—the remembrance of one moment's default is altogether obliterated by the recollection of their former eminent conduct, and of the services they rendered on that very day. I am quite certain, Sir, that the men of Her Majesty's 62nd Regiment, of the 14th Native Infantry, and the other gallant native regiment on the flank of Her Majesty's 62nd Regiment, will not suffer in the estimation of the country; that the willing thanks of this House will be given, without exception, to all the regiments engaged in this action. * * * * There never has been a greater example of extreme forbearance, strict justice, and a resolve to resist all the temptations to which the army was exposed—there never was a greater combination of those high qualities with the most brilliant talent and valour in defence of the British empire in India. The gallantry of those who fell in that conflict will not be without its fruits. Their lives will not have been sacrificed in vain. The remembrance of their conduct constitutes one of the brightest possessions—one of the great defences of this country. When we reflect what can be effected by discipline and valour, such as was manifested by our countrymen on these memorable days, we feel that in a just cause our country must be victorious. The memory of those men who have fallen through their devotion to their country will long serve to animate the British army. It will make us proud of that name which we bear, and encourage us, if need be, to emulate their heroic exertions, and exhibit equal devotion, equal perseverance, equal courage, in the cause of our common country. (Great and enthusiastic cheering greeted the Right Hon. Baronet from all sides of the House in the progress, and at the conclusion of his speech.) He moved the first of the following series of resolutions:—

That the thanks of this House be given to the Right Honourable Lieutenant-General Sir Henry Hardinge, Governor-General of India, Knight Grand Cross of the Order of the Bath, for the energy and ability with which he directed the military means at his disposal, to the repelling of the unprovoked invasion of the Sikh army of the dominions of the British Government, and of the Protracted States upon the left bank of the Sutlej; and also, for the firmness and gallantry with which he directed the operations of that portion of the army under his immediate command, in the afternoon and night of December 21st, 1845, and on the morning of the 22nd, upon which occasion the enemy's defences were carried by storm, the greater part of their artillery captured, and their subsequent attempts to regain what they had lost repeatedly defeated.

That the thanks of this House be given to General Sir Hugh Gough, Baronet, Knight Grand Cross of the Order of the Bath, Commander-in-Chief of the Forces in the East Indies, for the distinguished valour with which he directed and led the several attacks upon the enemy, and for the eminent services rendered by him in the battles of the 18th, 21st, and 22nd of December, 1845, displaying, as he did, in conjunction with the Governor-General, a brilliant example to the troops, of perseverance and courage in critical circumstances, and of irresistible ardour in the several attacks made upon the enemy.

That the thanks of this House be given to Major-General Sir Harry George Smith, Knight Commander of the Order of the Bath, to Major-General Walter Raleigh Gilbert, and to Major-General Sir John Hunter Littler, Knight Commander of the Order of the Bath, and to the several officers, European and native, under their command, for the eminent services rendered by them in the recent arduous and successful operations.

That the thanks of this House be given to the non-commissioned officers and private soldiers, European and native, for the perseverance and fortitude maintained by them at Moodkee on the 18th of December, 1845, and for the daring valour with which they forced the enemy's entrenchments at Ferozeshah on the 21st and 22nd of December, captured most of his guns, and finally compelled the Sikh army, of greatly superior numbers, to retire within their own frontier.

That this Resolution be signified to them by the commanders of the several corps.

Ordered—That the said Resolutions be transmitted by Mr. Speaker to the Governor-General of India, and that he be requested to communicate the same to the several officers referred to therein.

The motion was seconded by the Right Honourable Lord John Russell, and, after speeches by Sir Robert Inglis, Mr. Hogg, Captain Layard, Sir Howard Douglas, and other honourable members, the resolutions were put *seriatim* and carried *nem. con*.

At a Special Court of Proprietors of East India Stock, the Chairman (Sir Henry Willock, K.L.S.), stated that the Court had been especially summoned, in order to lay before it certain papers relating to the war in India, and to offer the thanks of the Court to the officers and men employed in that war. The Chairman, in a brief but affecting speech, submitted a motion, couched in the same terms as those adopted by the Houses of Parliament, and which will be found in that report; which having been seconded by the Deputy-Chairman (J. W. Hogg, Esq. M.P.), was unanimously agreed to.

ALIWAL AND SOBRAON.

The Thanks of Parliament.

On the evening of the 2nd of April, the thanks of the House of Lords were proposed by the Right Honourable the Earl of Ripon, who concluded a most effective speech with the following words:—" I have purposely abstained from specifying the acts of those to whose victories I have called your attention. I felt that I could not have done justice to them; and I beg now simply to propose the motions, the objects of which I have explained. They are as follow:"—

That the thanks of this House be given to Major-General Sir Harry George Smith, Knight Commander of the Most Honourable Military Order of the Bath, for his skilful and meritorious conduct when in command of the British troops employed against a large portion of the Sikh army, of greatly superior numbers, and for the signal valour and judgment displayed by him in the battle of the 28th of January, when the enemy's force was totally defeated, and new lustre added to the reputation of the British arms.

That the thanks of this House be given to the several officers, European and native under the command of Sir Harry Smith, for the distinguished services rendered by them at the battle of Aliwal.

That this House doth highly approve of and commend the intrepidity and exemplary discipline displayed by the non-commissioned officers and private soldiers, European and native, on the 28th of January, in their attack on the enemy's position, by which the Sikhs were completely routed and driven in confusion across the Sutlej, with the loss of all their artillery and military equipment; and that the same be signified to them by the commanders of the several corps, who are desired to thank them for their gallant behaviour.

That in requesting the Governor-General of India to communicate these resolutions to the several officers referred to therein, this House desires to acknowledge the zeal and judgment evinced by the Right Honourable Lieutenant-General Sir Henry Hardinge, Knight Grand Cross of the Order of the Bath, Governor-General of India; and also by General Sir Hugh Gough, Bart., Knight Grand Cross of the Order of the Bath, Commander-in-Chief of the Forces in India, in supplying Major-General Sir Harry Smith with such reinforcements and military means as enabled him, under Divine Providence, to overcome all the obstacles thrown in his way by a brave and determined enemy.

That the thanks of this House be given to the Right Honourable Lieutenant-General Sir Henry Hardinge, Knight Grand Cross of the Most Honourable Military Order of the Bath, Governor-General of India, for the judgment, energy, and ability with which the resources of the British empire in India have been applied in repelling the unjust and unprovoked invasion of the British territory by the Sikh nation; and for the valour and indefatigable exertions which he displayed on the 10th of February, at the battle of Sobraon, when, by the blessing of Almighty God, which we desire most humbly to acknowledge, this hostile and treacherous invasion was successfully defeated.

That the thanks of this House be given to General Sir Hugh Gough, Bart., Knight Grand Cross of the Most Honourable Military Order of the Bath, Commander-in-Chief of the Forces in India, for the signal ability and valour with which, upon the 10th of February, he directed and led the attack, when the enemy's entrenchments were stormed, their artillery captured, their army defeated and scattered, and the Punjaub laid open to the advance of our victorious troops.

That the thanks of this House be given to Major-General Sir Harry George Smith, Knight Commander of the most Honourable Military Order of the Bath, Major-General Walter Raleigh Gilbert, and Major-General Sir Joseph Thackwell, Knight Commander of the most Honourable Military Order of the Bath; and to the other officers, European and native, for the distinguished services rendered by them in the eminently successful operations at the battle of Sobraon.

That this House doth highly approve of and commend the invincible intrepidity, perseverance, and steady discipline displayed by the non-commissioned officers and private soldiers, European and native, on the 10th of February, by which the glory of the British arms has been successfully maintained against a determined and greatly superior force; and that the same be signified to them by the commanders of the several corps, who are desired to thank them for their gallant behaviour.

They were seconded by the Right Hon. the Earl of Auckland; and in the course of the debate the following remarks fell from his Grace the Duke of Wellington:—In the meantime the distant points of the frontier were threatened; Loodiana was threatened—I believe it was even attacked, and the cantonments were burned: and then it was that Sir Harry Smith was sent with a detachment of troops towards Loodiana, taking possession of various points on his road—Durrumkote and other places, of which the enemy had taken possession by bodies of troops which had crossed the Sutlej. And I beg your Lordships to observe that, when Sir Harry Smith was sent, he had three objects in view: one to give security to the post at Loodiana, already reinforced by the arrival there of General Godby after the battle: the others to keep up his communications with the rear by the town of Busseean, a point of great strength and importance, with a view to the communication between Ferozepore and Loodiana, in the front line, and Ferozepore and Delhi in the rear, the point from which the heavy train and the means of carrying on the siege in the ultimate operations were to come. These must have passed between twenty and thirty miles of the enemy, while the main body of the army at Ferozepore was not less distant than fifty. These were the objects, to secure which Sir Harry Smith was detached from the army. He marched upon Loodiana, and communicated with the British commander there, who endeavoured to move out to his assistance. While he was engaged with the enemy on this march, which he made in order to perform a part of his instructions—namely, to maintain the communication with Loodiana, they came out from the entrenched camp and carried off his baggage. I desire to explain that, because it was the only check which the gallant officer met with throughout the whole of this operation, and in fact it is the only misfortune, trifling as it is, which has happened during the whole operations that have taken place in that part of the country. This loss of the baggage, such as it is, has been written up as a great misfortune; but, in point of fact, it could not be otherwise. He was obliged to march within sight of the entrenched camp, from which the enemy had an opportunity of attacking him on his march. I beg your Lordships to observe that Sir Harry Smith had not only to secure his communication with Loodiana, but likewise to secure his junction with General Wheeler, who, alone, was not able to contend against the enemy. He performed all those objects, was joined by General Wheeler, and then moved on to attack the new position which the enemy had taken up near the river. And, my Lords, I will say upon this, I have read the account of many a battle, but I never read the account of one in which more ability, energy, and experience have been manifested than in this. I know of no one in which an officer ever showed himself more capable than this officer has in commanding troops in the field. He brought every description of troops to bear, with all arms in the position in which they were most capable of rendering service;

the nicest manœuvres were performed under the fire of the enemy with the utmost precision, and at the same time with an energy and gallantry on the part of the troops never surpassed on any occasion whatever in any part of the world. I must say of this officer, that I never have seen any acconnt which manifests more plainly than his does, that he is an officer capable of rendering the most important services, and of ultimately being an honour to this country.

House of Commons.

A vote to the same effect was proposed by Sir Robert Peel in the House of Commons, from whose speech we extract the following:—The great battle was fought on the 28th of January, but earlier in that month Sir Harry Smith had sustained what some may consider a reverse. I allude to a period before his junction with Colonel Wheeler, and with the five regiments from Loodiana. In the absence of all intelligence he encountered the enemy, and was exposed to serious hazard. Writing to Sir Hugh Gough on the 21st, after he had succeeded in relieving Loodiana, he said that he had accomplished that object, but under circumstances not quite so fortunate as he desired, and he used these expressions: "When within a mile and a half to my left of Buddowal, moving parallel with my column (which was right in front ready to wheel into line), and evidently for the purpose of interrupting my advance, I saw the enemy. Nothing could be stronger for the enemy than the continued line of villages. He was moving by roads, while I was moving over very heavy sand-beds. He was in advance far beyond, on my right flank; so far did he extend, and so numerous did he show his infantry and guns, and so well chosen for him was this line of villages, that with my force he was not to be assailed; and he opened a furious cannonade of from thirty-five to forty guns of very large calibre, and, as usual, right well served. My object being to unite myself with the force from Loodiana, which every moment I expected to appear in sight, for it was nine o'clock, I moved parallel with the enemy, resolving to attack the moment the Loodiana troops reached me. He, however, so pressed upon me, that I opened in one body my eleven guns upon him with considerable effect, and moved up the 31st, and was preparing to form line upon this regiment, when the enemy most rapidly formed a line of seven regiments, with their guns between, at right angles with the line I was about to attack, while a considerable force was moving round my right and front. Thus enveloped and overwhelmed by numbers, and such a superiority of guns, I had nothing for it but to throw back my line on its right, which represented a small line on the hypotenuse of a triangle. The enemy thus outflanked me and my whole force. I therefore gradually withdrew my infantry in échellon of battalions, the cavalry in échellon of squadrons, in the direction of Loodiana, momentarily expecting to see the approach of that force—viz., one regiment of cavalry, five guns, and four regiments of infantry, when I would have made a vigorous attack. The ground was very deep and sandy, and, therefore, very difficult to move on. The enemy continued to move on as described for upwards of an hour, and until I knew the Loodiana force was moving, not a musket was fired. Nothing could exceed the steadiness of the troops. The line was thrown back, under this cannonade, as if on parade, native as well as British, and the movements of the cavalry, under Brigadier Cureton, were, without any exception, the most perfect thing I ever saw, and which I cannot describe." * * * *

Of the battle itself I will not speak; the victory was complete, and it has been so admirably described by the illustrious commander, that I will not weaken the effect of his narrative. And what, let me ask, have been the services of this gallant officer? These recent events have given new lustre to his glory; but he was at the capture of Monte Video—at the attack upon Buenos Ayres; he served during the Peninsula war, from the battle of Vimeira to that of Corunna. He was then wounded in another action, but he was at the battles of Sabagal and Fuentes d'Onor, and the sieges of Ciudad Rodrigo and Badajos, at the battles of

Salamanca, Vittoria, Orthes, the Pyrenees, and Toulouse. He was at Washington and at New Orleans, and finally he was at Waterloo. What a series of noble services, and how rejoiced I am that there should be an opportunity, through this new and signal victory, of bringing before the gladdened eyes of a grateful country a long life of military exertion, and an unbroken series of military honours. After he had achieved that success for which we are about to give him our special thanks—after he had driven back the enemy across the Sutlej, he instantly returned to rejoin his commanding officer, Sir Hugh Gough. He arrived on the 8th, two days before the decisive victory gained by the forces under Sir Hugh Gough and Sir Henry Hardinge. But for his services in the victory of the 28th of January, I propose that there should be a distinct and separate vote—distinct and separate from that which I shall recommend for that not more glorious, though perhaps more important achievement accomplished at a later date by the whole British army. * * * * *

There is much to adorn and nothing to sully our victory, and I do hope that now it has been achieved, it will give lasting peace to India; that a general conviction will be felt of our power—a conviction of the superiority of British arms that will ensure a long enjoyment of tranquillity to that country, and the application of all our efforts for the improvement of its natural resources. I trust that this may be our last battle, and that hereafter we shall have nothing to do but to direct our attention to the amelioration of the condition of our Indian fellow-subjects. In that anticipation I am sure the House will permit me to refer to some events and some circumstances which may well fill our hearts with joy and exultation. The two leaders of our victorious army, the Governor-General and the Commander-in-Chief, have throughout these operations set an example of cordial concert and communion—an utter forgetfulness of themselves—to which the happy result is greatly to be attributed. All matters of punctillio were sacrificed, and Sir Henry Hardinge consented to serve as second in command. On the other hand, there was not a suggestion offered by Sir Henry Hardinge which was not thankfully accepted by Sir Hugh Gough. * * * * I will now refer to a document, not of a public character, that has been put into my hand since I entered the House this evening—it is a letter from Sir Hugh Gough, which was never intended to meet the public eye, but it does him so much honour that I cannot refuse myself the pleasure of reading it.* * * * * * * * * * *

I am sure the House will permit me, among expressions of gratitude to the surviving conquerors, to mingle some of deep regret at the loss we have sustained. On this occasion I have to deplore the loss of several officers of the highest reputation; and the first I shall name, is Sir Robert Dick. He entered the service in 1800. He embarked with the 78th Regiment for Sicily in 1806, and was wounded in battle. He accompanied the expedition to Egypt, and was present at the taking of Alexandria. He embarked with the 42nd Regiment in 1829, and was again wounded at Fuentes d'Onor. He commanded the second battalion of the 42nd Regiment at Ciudad Rodrigo. He was at the battle of Salamanca, at the storming of St. Michel, and was present during the siege of Burgos. In 1815 he was severely wounded, and, after a life of honour, he at last fell in the battle, for the happy result of which we are about to make our grateful acknowledgments. On the day which deprived us for ever of the services of Sir Robert Dick, there also fell Lieutenant-Colonel Taylor, of the 29th Regiment. When the father of this gallant officer was Lieutenant-Colonel of the 20th Light Dragoons, he lost his life in the Peninsula. The father fell at Vimiera—the son met an equally glorious death in India, and thus did those heroic men establish an hereditary and double claim to the gratitude of the country. Lieutenant-Colonel C. J. Taylor commanded the light company of the 30th Foot, in the expedition against Khalapore, in 1827-8; served on the frontier during the

* The document here referred to will be found in full at page 137.

Canadian rebellion, where, in the successful attack of a village occupied by the rebels, he rendered an important service; commanded a brigade of infantry in the actions of the 18th, 21st, and 22nd of December, 1845, wherein he was wounded; the troops sent to keep up the communication between Sir Harry Smith and the main army, whilst the former was engaged in the operations which led to the battle of Aliwal; and a brigade of infantry at the battle of Sobraon, where he fell.

How many there are who have lost their sons and relatives in this conflict I need not say; but I have been thrown into intercourse I could not avoid with one, the life of whose gallant son has been sacrificed in this encounter; it has been my duty, my painful duty in some respects, to hold constant communication with Lord Fitzroy Somerset, whose brave offspring, had he survived, would have supported the honour of his family, and the military glory of his father. Lord Fitzroy Somerset himself has run an illustrious career. He accompanied the Duke of Wellington throughout all the battles of the Peninsula, but his pleasure in awarding honour to the living and the dead is now clouded by the loss of his son, who, had his life been spared, would have added to his own and to his country's reputation. Although the rank of Major Somerset hardly entitles him to special notice, yet recollecting the services of his father and the long connexion between him and his illustrious chief, the House will perhaps permit me to offer this poor consolation to the sorrows of a parent. I wish I could do justice to my own feelings by naming many others scarcely less distinguished or less lamented; but the list is so numerous of those entitled to grateful remembrance that I trust it will not be imputed to any want of a due sense of their claims and merits.

Sir Robert Peel then moved the votes of thanks, a copy of which is given under the report of the House of Lords. The motion was seconded by Sir John Cam Hobhouse, and, after a few words from other hon. members, the resolutions were put and severally agreed to *nem. con.*

The East India Company.

On the same day, a Special General Court of the Proprietors of Stock was held at the East India House, for the purpose of passing a vote of thanks to Major-General Sir Harry Smith, for his victory at Aliwal, over the Sikh army; and to General Sir Henry Hardinge, and General Sir Hugh Gough, and to the European and native troops who were engaged in the war of the Sutlej.

Sir Henry Willock, the Chairman, again presided, and proposed the two separate resolutions which we have already given, under the report of the proceedings of the Houses of Lords and Commons. They were seconded by J. W. Hogg, Esq., M.P., and unanimously adopted.

The Court of Common Council.

At a Special Court of the Court of Common Council of the City of London, the thanks and congratulations of the Court were awarded, together with the freedom of the City in gold boxes of the value of 100 guineas, to Lieutenant-General Sir Henry Hardinge, G.C.B., General Sir Hugh Gough, Bart., G.C.B., and Major-General Sir Harry Smith, K.C.B., for the valour, judgment, and ability displayed by them in the recent battles of Aliwal and Sobraon. Also the thanks of the Court to the other officers, European and native, for the intrepidity, perseverance, and discipline evinced by them upon both of these memorable occasions.

Her Majesty has since been graciously pleased to direct Letters Patent to be passed under the Great Seal, granting the dignity of Viscount to Lieutenant-General Sir Henry Hardinge, G.C.B., that of a Baron to General Sir Hugh Gough, Bart., G.C.B., as well as to confer the dignity of a Baronet upon Major-General Sir Harry Smith, G.C.B.

House of Commons.

May 4, 1846.

The order of the day for going into committee of the whole House, to consider Her Most Gracious Majesty's messages having been read—

Sir Robert Peel moved that in accordance with that message, the annual sum of £.3,000 be granted to Viscount Hardinge, and £.2,000 to Lord Gough, and the two next heirs male of their bodies.

The motion having been seconded by Lord John Russell, was immediately adopted.

In the course of his speech Sir Robert Peel announced that, in the event of the East India Company conferring a pension upon these two illustrious individuals during their lives, the Government grants would be confined to their successors.

Mr. Hogg subsequently announced that, at a Court of Directors of that Honourable Company, he had the honour of proposing, what had been unanimously adopted, that a pension of £.5,000 per annum be granted to Viscount Hardinge during his lifetime, in addition to his salary as Governor-General of India; and that a pension of £.2,000 per annum be likewise granted to Lord Gough—both to commence from the period when our troops arrived under the walls of Lahore. Mr. Hogg remarked, this was the first instance of the Company granting a pension to a Commander-in-Chief.

We extract also from Sir Robert Peel's speech the following testimony to the services of these distinguished officers:—

"It is now forty-eight years since my gallant friend, Lord Hardinge, entered the British army. During his long military service it has been the good fortune of my gallant friend to be present at numerous actions in the Peninsula,—at Roleia, at Vimiera (where he was wounded), and, under the command of that most gallant, distinguished, and lamented officer, Sir John Moore, during the retreat to Corunna, and at the battle of Corunna. At the battle of Corunna, at an early period of his life, Captain Hardinge was near Sir John Moore when that gallant officer received his death-wound upon the field. Of Lord Hardinge it is said by the eloquent historian of the Peninsula campaign, when describing the battle of Corunna, that Captain Hardinge, a staff-officer, who was near Sir John Moore, attempted to take off his sword, which had entered the deep wound in his shoulder made by the cannon shot by which he was struck; that Captain Hardinge proposed to Sir John to unbuckle the sword, that the torment occasioned by its entry into the wound might be relieved; but that Sir John Moore stopped him with this affecting speech, " It is as well as it is. I had rather it should go out of the field with me." The historian adds that, in this manner, so becoming a soldier, Sir John Moore was borne from the field, refusing to part with his sword in the moment of death. After the battle of Corunna, Sir H. Hardinge was present at the battle of the Douro, at the battle of Busaco, in the lines of Torres Vedras, at the battle of Albuera, at the three sieges of Badajoz, at the siege and capture of Ciudad Rodrigo, at Salamanca, at Vittoria, where he was severely wounded, at Pampeluna, at the battles of the Pyrenees at Nivelle, at Nive, and at Orthez. It will be remembered, that my gallant friend was at Ligny, two days before the battle of Waterloo, and he was only prevented from taking his share in that great action by the severe wounds he received at the battle of Ligny. We cannot forget what a distinguished part my gallant friend took in the battle of Albuera; and it is possible that he learned in that action what confidence could be justly placed in the desperate valour of British soldiers. It is probable that the recollection of the battle of Albuera, and of the change in the fortunes of that day, accomplished chiefly through the valour of the British infantry, may have induced my gallant friend to persevere under all discouragements in his latter and equally glorious battles, and to place a just and not disappointed confidence in the enduring valour of the British troops.

So much for the services of my gallant friend, Sir H. Hardinge. As I said before, he has now completed forty-eight years of military service. The career of that other gallant officer, whom her Majesty has elevated to the British peerage, has not been less distinguished. For fifty-two years has Lord Gough served in the British army; and no one would have supposed from the vigour, the energy and the heroism of his conduct, that fifty-two years of active service could have passed over his head. Sir Hugh Gough was at the capture of the Cape of Good Hope, at the attack on Porto Rico, and at the capture of Surinam. During the Peninsula war he commanded the 87th Regiment at Talavera, where he was severely wounded, at Barossa, at Vittoria, at Nivelle, where he was also severely wounded; at the sieges of Cadiz, and at Tarifa. He also commanded the British army at Canton, and during almost all the operations in China; and he was with the right wing of the army of Gwalior, which fought and gained the battle of Maharajpore. These are the services rendered by that gallant officer previous to the late campaign, when he was Commander-in-Chief of the army in India. It would be presumptuous in me to attempt to do justice to his signal services. I believe he is known to the British army as a man of the most heroic valour, and that his valour and skill inspire confidence in all those whom he commands. I will not speak merely of his valour and his skill,—these are admitted by all who are acquainted with the history of our Peninsula and Indian wars. But, I must take this opportunity of placing upon record an instance of his devotion to the service of his country, which he, probably, little thought would ever be mentioned within the walls of Parliament, but which I conceive to be at least as honourable to him as any services he has rendered in the field. After the termination of the Chinese campaign, Lord Gough was nominated to the command of the forces in Madras. It was thought expedient, at a period subsequent to his nomination to this command, that the military and civil command should be united in the hands of one person—that person having the advantage of previous personal communication with her Majesty's servants. Lord Tweeddale was selected for the government of Madras; and, as I have said, it being thought desirable in the circumstances in which that presidency was then placed to unite the military and civil commands, Lord Tweeddale superseded Lord Gough in the military command. That was a severe trial to a British officer—a severe trial to one who had been victorious in China. Now, what was the answer returned by Lord Gough to the Commander-in-Chief, on its being intimated to him that the public service required the union of the two commands? Many officers would have felt deeply mortified; but I consider the answer of Lord Gough to be so honourable to him, and to set so striking an example of what is the duty of a British soldier under such circumstances as I have mentioned, that I have determined to present to the House the letter written by the gallant officer on that occasion:—

"*Head-quarters, Ship Marion, off Nankin,*
"*September* 15, 1842.

"My Lord,

"I have the honour to acknowledge the receipt of your Lordship's letter of the 30th of April. However mortifying it may be to me to find myself deprived of the appointment to which I had been so graciously nominated, I beg to assure your Lordship that I bow, without repining, to any measure that may be considered beneficial to the interests of my country. To serve that country in the higher walks of a profession which I entered as a child, I came to India, and especially to China, and I trust your Lordship will believe, that while my Sovereign considered my services useful, they were, as they ever shall be, freely, and, I hope, energetically rendered; but when they are no longer required, or when the public exigencies in such an important portion of our foreign possessions as Madras are deemed to clash with my individual advantage, I hope I may say, that I am one of the last men in the army who would not readily sacrifice self-interest. My gracious Sovereign's unsolicited nomination of me to the chief command at Madras was received by me with thankfulness; and whenever, for the furtherance of Her Majesty's service, it became expedient to place another in that situation, whether in a single or a conjoint capacity, I should not have wished my private interests to stand in the way of the public good. That I feel rather disappointed, I cannot deny; but I am not the less grateful to my Sovereign for her gracious kindness towards me; or the less sincerely and warmly thankful to your Lordship for the renewed proof of kind consideration which your letter conveys. With the earnest and anxious prayer that the union of the civil government and military command at Madras may fully meet the expectations of the Government,

"I have, &c.,
"H. Gough, *Lieutenant-General,*
"*Commanding Expeditionary Land Force.*"

This, in my opinion, is one of the most creditable letters ever written by a military man; and proved, I think, that the writer was worthy of a higher trust than that of Commander at Madras. I trust that these instances of apparent self-sacrifice, and of devotion to the true interests of the military service, will ever meet with their just rewards; and though Sir Hugh Gough, when he wrote that letter, never contemplated that a consequence of this might be his appointment to the chief command in India, yet I rejoice that such a noble devotion to the public service was followed by a reward to which he has proved himself to be fully entitled.

The following Statistical Account of the result of the several General Actions in which Lord Gough has commanded in chief, is computed from official despatches.

Engagements.	Date.	British Force.	Chinese Force.	Ordnance in action.		Ordnance captured.		Captures and Remarks.
				British.	Chinese.	Iron.	Brass.	
Height above Canton	25 May, 1841	2,400 including the brigade of seamen.	40 to 50,000, besides upwards of 20,000 militia	10 guns, 3 mortars.	42 in the four captured forts, besides those in the well armed fortified towns of Canton.	42		Captured a large number of gingals, and a considerable quantity of powder.
Amoy	26 Aug. 1841	No official return published		Ditto		393	1	Guns not mounted 157, and a vast quantity of military stores.
Chusan	1 Oct.	Ditto		Ditto		100		Matchlocks in considerable numbers, 584 gunpowder tubs, 30 rockets, 100 leaden ball boxes and tubs.
Chinhae	10 Oct.	Ditto		Ditto		90	67	A large quantity of copper metal taken and embarked.
Ningpo	13 Oct.	Ditto		Ditto		25		1,047 gunpowder tubs, 100,000 lbs. of powder, 50 tons of shot, 405 boxes of leaden ball.
Heights of Segoan	Mar. 15, 1842	865 soldiers, 350 seamen and —— marines 1215	About 8,000 (killed 1,000)	Ditto		No return		
Chapho	May 18	2,210 including seamen	8,000, 12 to 1500 killed	Ditto		many destroyed	11 brought away	Several arsenals, all kinds of arms and amunition, a foundry and gunpowder manufactory.
Woosing	June 16	No returns		Ditto		167	42	This does not include ordnance captured on the right bank of the river, which is not known.
Shanghae	June 19	Ditto		Ditto		120	51	About 18,000 lbs. of powder taken, and destroyed large quantities of gingals, matchlocks, &c.
Between Woosing, Shanghae, and above the river Suyshan. Battery opposite Silver Island	July 14 — 16	Ditto		Ditto		167		

Chinkeangfoo	July 21	Ditto		Ditto		20		60,000 dollars captured in the arsenal, and paid over to the military chest. A large quantity of matchlocks and gingals, and a large quantity of powder destroyed.
Maharajpore	29 Dec. 1843	3,066 Infantry 350 Artillery —— 3,416 engaged 1,341 Cavalry 1,754 Infantry reserved	11,200 Infantry 500 Artillery —— 11,700 engaged 3,000 Cavalry Infantry reserved	30	58	15	43	
Punniar under Gen. Sir J. Grey detached	Do.	2007	12,000		24	24	Iron or brass	
Moodkee	18 Dec. 1845	No official return published	15 to 20,000 Infantry 15 to 20,000 Cavalry		40		15, and 4 dismounted during action	
Ferozeshah	21 & 22 Dec.	Do.	60,000		108	27	48	
Aliwal under Maj.-Gen. Sir H. Smith, detached	28 Jan.	Do.	No official return				67	
Sobraon	10 Feb.	Do.	35,000		70 ex. of heavy guns on opposite bank of Sutlej		67	
					Total—Guns captured in India	66	244	
					Captured in China	1124	172	
					Total number of guns captured by the forces under Sir H. Gough, exclusive of those given up by treaty . . .	1190	416	
					Woosing was properly a naval action, as were those of Shinghae and Suyshan. There are to be deducted therefore . .	334	42	
					Leaving a gross total of .	856	374 taken in action by the armies under his command.	

ABSTRACT,

Showing the disposition of the Sikh Army.

1st *July*, 1844.

STATION.	Infantry.	Cavalry.	Artillery.		
			Men.	Guns.	Swivels.
Lahore	16,820	14,075	2475	238	395
On furlough	19,600	5300	560	50	50
Mitha Towana (Dera Ismael Khan)	2500	1500	20	4	..
Jummoo Hills	8000	2750	600	50	300
Poonchh Hills	500	..	..	..	..
Bhimbur Hills	500	..	..	..	..
Nowshehra Hills	1500	..	40	10	..
Reeasee Hills	3000	..	100	22	..
Ludakh	2000	..	40	10	..
Syed Ghur (foot of hills)	2000	500	50	10	..
Pind dadul Khan (on Jehlum)	500	..	..	..	..
Ramnuggur Hills	2000	..	30	8	..
Samba Hills	3000	400	60	8	25
Jesrota Hills	5000	500	60	8	..
Jalundhur Dooab Beeas and Sutlej	1000	200	40	4	..
Cashmeer	2300	400	100	14	..
Muzzufferabad, (near to Cashmere)	500	..	..	..	..
Hussoora (N. W. of Cashmere)	500	..	..	..	..
Ghilghit	1000	..	20	4	..
Shahdura (Lahore)	100	100	..	..	..
Attok	..	100	..	..	..
Hussun Ubdal (near Attok)	..	900	60	..	50
Peshawur	5700	400	140	14	..
Yoosufzaees (N. E. of Peshawur)	400	100	60	6	..
Huzara (E. of Attok)	3100	..	80	8	..
Tank (Dera Ismael Khan)	1500	400	30	..	25
Mooltan	3500	500	235	40	70
Kote Mithun (Junction of Indus and Sutlej)	500	..	..	..	..
Rojhan (near Sukkur)	500	..	..	..	..
Syedwata } near Dera Ghazee Khan	..	250	..	..	..
Sunghur } near Dera Ghazee Khan	400	250	..	..	..
In the neighbourhood of Mooltan	1500	500	..	..	..
Koonjah (near Vuzeerabad)	200	300	20	4	..
Kohat (Peshawur)	600	500	45	4	25
Dooaba, (near Peshawur)	500	300	25	2	15
Husht nuggur (Peshawur)	600	400	40	8	15
In the Kanggra Hills	5000	..	..	..	..
Suraj (Kooloo Hills)	1000	..	..	..	..
Mujethea (Umritsir)	..	400	15	2	..
Teelook Nath (Hills)	200	..	..	..	..
With Sirdar Lehna Singh Mujeetheea	200	100	..	..	..
Adeena nuggur (Hills)	200	..	..	..	..
Kussoor (opposite Ferozepore)	200	..	60	8	..
Azaree (near Umritsir)	200	100	10	2	..
Kupoorthulla (near the Beeas)	2000	1300	120	12	..
Sultanpore (ditto)	200	..	45	2	25
On the Ferries of the Sutlej	500	800	..	..	..
TOTAL	101,020	33,925	5180	552	995

(Signed) J. D. CUNNINGHAM,

Assistant-Agent-Governor-General
N. W. Frontier.

Return of H. M. Regiments with the Army of the Sutlej, showing the effective strength before entering into Action, and the Casualties after each subsequent Engagement.

Head Quarters, Camp Lahore, 2nd March, 1846.

	Effective strength before entering into the first Action in which each Regiment was engaged.		After the Action at MOODKEE.						After the Action of FEROZESHAH.						After the Skirmish at BUDEEWAL.						After the Action at ALIWAL.						After the Action at SOBRAON.						TOTAL CASUALTIES.					
			Killed.		Wounded.		Missing.		Killed.		Wounded.		Missing.		Killed.		Wounded.		Missing.		Killed.		Wounded.		Missing.		Killed.		Wounded.		Missing.		Killed.		Wounded.		Missing.	
	Officers.	Men.	Officers.	Men.	Officers.	Men.	Officers.	Men.	Officers.	Men.	Officers.	Men.	Officers.	Men.	Officers.	Men.	Officers.	Men.	Officers.	Men.	Officers.	Men.	Officers.	Men.	Officers.	Men.	Officers.	Men.	Officers.	Men.	Officers.	Men.	Officers.	Men.	Officers.	Men.	Officers.	Men.
3rd LIGHT DRAGOONS, Before the Action at Moodkee, on the 18th December, 1845	27	518	3	68	3	82	..	..	3	58	7	67	..	..	..	..	..	..	..	..	..	9	..	..	..	..	..	4	5	22	..	..	6	124	15	121	..	..
9th LANCERS, Before the Action at Sobraon, on the 10th February, 1846	33	599	..	..	..	..	..	..	..	..	..	..	..	..	..	..	..	..	..	..	..	..	..	..	..	..	..	1	..	1	..	..	..	1	..	1	..	..
16th LANCERS, Before the Skirmish at Budeewal, on the 21st January, 1846	28	539	..	..	..	..	..	..	..	..	..	..	..	..	..	2	..	1	..	..	2	57	6	77	..	..	..	..	..	..	..	..	2	59	6	78	..	..
9th FOOT, Before the Action at Moodkee, on the 18th December, 1845	30	874	1	2	1	49	..	..	3	67	6	197	..	18	..	..	..	..	..	..	..	..	..	..	..	..	..	5	1	28	..	..	4	74	8	274	..	18
10th FOOT, Before the Action at Sobraon, on the 10th February, 1846	30	742	..	..	..	..	..	..	..	..	..	..	..	..	..	..	..	..	..	..	..	..	..	..	..	..	1	29	2	101	..	..	1	29	2	101	..	..
29th FOOT, Before the Action at Ferozeshah, on the 21st December, 1845	28	765	..	..	..	..	..	..	3	52	8	185	..	..	..	..	..	..	..	..	..	..	..	..	..	..	1	35	13	139	..	..	4	87	16	344	..	..
31st FOOT, Before the Action at Moodkee, on the 18th December, 1845	31	844	1	24	8	126	..	6	2	59	5	97	..	19	..	12	..	9	..	19	..	1	1	14	..	..	..	38	8	112	..	2	3	129	22	358	..	46
50th FOOT, Before the Action at Moodkee, on the 18th December, 1845	31	675	1	21	6	94	..	4	..	24	3	89	..	2	..	4	..	13	..	8	1	8	9	59	..	..	1	37	11	184	..	..	3	94	29	439	..	14
53rd FOOT, Before the Skirmish at Budeewal, on the 21st January, 1846	47	861	..	..	..	..	..	..	..	..	..	..	..	..	..	26	2	15	..	20	..	8	..	7	..	1	1	4	8	105	..	8	1	83	10	127	..	24
62nd FOOT, Before the Action at Ferozeshah, on the 21st December, 1845	24	768	..	..	..	..	..	..	7	88	10	161	..	..	..	..	..	..	..	..	..	..	..	..	..	..	1	8	1	43	..	..	8	91	11	204	..	..
80th FOOT, Before the Action at Moodkee, on the 18th December, 1845	26	735	..	5	1	20	..	..	5	35	1	73	..	..	..	..	..	..	..	..	..	..	..	..	..	..	..	13	5	74	..	..	5	53	7	167	..	..
TOTAL	386	7880	6	110	19	821	..	10	23	378	35	869	..	39	..	44	2	38	..	47	3	78	16	157	..	1	5	164	54	809	..	5	37	774	126	2214	..	102

EDWARD LUGARD, *Captain,*

Acting-Assistant-Adjutant-General of H. M. Forces in India.